MW01504506

CHEERS

CHEERS

A History of Trojan High School Sports

Traverse City Central High School
Sports Publishing Class

A BETWEEN THE FENCES PROJECT

Published by Between the Fences, Thirlby/Running Community Recreation Fund
P.O. Box 1447, Traverse City, MI 49685

Publisher's Cataloging-in-Publication Data
Traverse City Central High School Sports Publishing Class.
Cheers: A History of Traverse City High School Sports
Between the Fences / Traverse City, Michigan, c1998.
p. ill. cm.
Includes appendices.
ISBN: 1-890587-02-8
1. Sports. 2. History. 3. Traverse City.
I. Title. 1998

PROJECT COORDINATION BY JENKINS GROUP, INC.

02 01 00 99 ❖ 5 4 3 2 1

Printed in the United States of America

CHEERS is dedicated to all athletes, coaches, families and fans, who in giving their enthusiastic support to Traverse City Trojan athletics, have demonstrated their school and community pride. We represent this spirit through the winter sport season of 1997.

Contents

FOREWORD

Volunteer Effort Provides Facilities Between Many Fences

Realizing that Traverse City Area Public Schools' outdoor athletic facilities were in disrepair, outdated or non-existent, Between the Fences was established in 1993 as a non-profit organization to provide and renovate these facilities. In order to avoid using tax dollars, a $4 million community fundraising effort was held so the private sector could provide these facilities that would be owned by TCAPS and used by the community.

The concept for Between the Fences began with Harry Running's generous bequest to TCAPS in 1992 to be used toward the renovation of Thirlby Field. Upon closer evaluation of the condition of the stadium, it was obvious that these funds fell well short of completing the vast extent of renovation required. Not only were the stands and grounds deteriorating, but the condition of the playing field was also of concern due to its overuse.

In 1993, a group of local citizens was inspired to revive this nostalgic landmark and to find a home for soccer. In 1995, Rotary Charities of Traverse City responded to a funding request with a $500,000 grant to Between the Fences. This contribution and Harry Running's gift served as catalysts for the remaining fundraising.

The Coast Guard's gift of 27 acres to TCAPS ensured a site for a soccer complex with regulation fields. As the Between the Fences project developed, it grew to also include resurfacing Central High's track and tennis courts and making softball improvements. Walking paths and open fields were added to the Thirlby Field and Coast Guard plans for public use.

In 1995, the track was resurfaced, three regulation soccer fields were installed and the Thirlby stadium reconstruction began. In 1996, that stadium was dedicated as the Harry T. Running Stadium at Thirlby Field. Also that fall, seating and lighting were added to the soccer playing field and tennis courts were resurfaced.

As summer 1997 approaches, work will continue at these sites as funds are available. The stadium understructure needs to be finished, unused buildings razed, the softball area improved, grass put in and the parking lot and walking path paved. At the soccer complex, remaining projects include developing the additional fields, renovation of the restroom/concession/locker room building, and adding an entrance off Airport Access Road and a paved walking path. At Central High, a restroom/concession building is slated to be built. These improvements are targeted to be completed by 1998, ending Between the Fences' five years of active fundraising. An Endowment Fund to help provide for maintenance of these facilities will then become on ongoing project.

Proceeds from *Cheers* could be an instrumental part of completing the Between the Fences plan.

BETWEEN THE FENCES, 1997

Board of Directors

Diane Portenga, President
Chris Buday, Secretary
Robert Thompson, Treasurer
Tim Burden
Paul Jacobs
Barbara Kausler
Gary Moss
Jim Ooley
Vince Prusick
Mark Spencer
Rick Steckley
Sally Stilwill
Peter Wharton

Ex Officio Board Members

Mike Comstock
John Lober
Larry Sellers
Tom Sloan
John Sonnemann
Larry Truelove
Dave Whiteford
Roger Wood

PREFACE

The 1996 spring schedule saw the addition of a new class offering at Traverse City Central High School called sports publishing. This class evolved when Jerry Jenkins of the publishing company The Jenkins Group approached Between the Fences with the fundraising idea for a retrospective book about the last 100 years of Trojan high school sports.

But who could take on this task? Between the Fences had its hands full with many irons in the fire. However, Joe Tibaldi, high school principal at the time, thought that students would certainly benefit from tackling such a project. Between the Fences funded the class with proceeds of the finished book dedicated to finishing athletic facilities. Sports publishing became a reality when Pat Weber, communication arts teacher at the high school and former *Record-Eagle* employee, agreed to take on this unusual class.

Matt Nordjford, Nate Wildman, Marissa Taylor, Lucas Johnson, Aaron Dennis, Paul Caviston and Nick Anslow came into the class with a variety of skills. Aaron Dennis contributed his artistic talent by drawing the shoes seen at the beginning of each chapter. Several others were computer whiz kids. Several had had some journalism in their schooling. A couple were motivated by their love of sports. Since there was no precedent to follow, the students organized themselves and their teacher by assigning particular sports to each participant, including Mrs. Weber. The sports historic timeline began to emerge and an overview of each sport and its coaches were top priorities.

Guest speakers were frequent visitors in the classroom. Athletic Director John Sonnemann began by giving a comprehensive look at the sports seasons at the high school as well as key contact people in each sport. Students practiced their interviewing skills with tips from Denny Chase of the *Record-Eagle*, who came in to discuss interviews and story angles. Each student was responsible for consulting with someone connected to his/her sport(s).

Most of the historic research has been conducted using yearbooks, old issues of *The Black and Gold* and the *Record-Eagle*, and interviewing past and present coaches. *The Booster News*, although relatively new, was also most helpful. The tedious task of identifying athletes in each sport was the focus as June came around.

In fall of 1997, the sports publishing class continued for the second and final semester. New students joining the class were Tony Allen, Ted Bailey, Joe Cullen, Misty McKenzie, Jordan Solowiej, Kyle Sonnemann, Greg Stroh, Dennis Caviston, Jennifer Stratton and Sarah Wahl. The tasks for these students were to wrap up the research, conduct additional interviews and write the chapters. The stories of each sport reflect achievements through winter sports, 1997. As *Cheers* goes to press, spring sports are still in progress and are, unfortunately, not included.

While the students decided that they would like to write their own chapters covering their sports, only a few pages of anecdotal information is possible in a book this size. Between the Fences hopes that each sport has been represented accurately. In the magnitude of research done by students and reviewed by coaches, hopefully there have been no mistakes. If any are noticed, please contact Between the Fences. In the event there might be a second printing, these would certainly be corrected.

INTRODUCTION

CHEERS

By Pat Weber

"Making your way in the world today takes everything you've got..." So begins the theme song of that memorable TV show CHEERS. What does this stroll down memory lane have to do with sports? In a way: EVERYTHING.

When the students and I began working on this book, we discussed how we would tie it all together. What common thread could we discover about sports for both the players and the fans? For many months we had been mulling over a "theme" which would not be trite or cliche-like. In one yearbook we found clever cartoon-like drawings of feet throughout the pages. We thought that this would work for sports and that each chapter should be introduced by the footwear indicative to the sport. But we still endlessly discussed both what to name this book and how to "glue" it together.

The idea of feet and shoe wear reminded me of that famous last episode of CHEERS. I had recalled that Cliff had waxed poetic about the meaning of life and tying it to good footwear. Several students in class had the tape, so we spent a class period watching it. Cliff's speech was priceless and filled with historic inaccuracies, but it went like this:

Sam says that he just isn't getting the same kick out of life and wondered aloud, "What is the point of life?"

Cliff responds, "Comfortable shoes! Life is just chaos without comfortable shoes." He then points to Aristotle and claims he was the smartest man alive because he wore sandals – the most comfortable shoes in the world.

Woody says, as he is leaving, that whoever replaces Sam has big shoes to fill. But perhaps the most poignant conversation comes after this when Sam and Norm have this exchange. Norm advises, "It doesn't matter who or what you love, as long as you love something totally."

And so several ideas have surfaced. We want to celebrate and honor those coaches, parents, players, teachers and community members WHOSE shoes are big to fill. They have made, and continue to make, significant contributions to the games and competitions our students LOVE to participate in either as players or as fans.

CHEERS is a perfect title for this book. Cheers to those whose footprints we are following – those who've paved the way. Cheers to those athletes whether they have won or lost; they have found their passion and have gone after what they love to do. Cheers to those parents and fans for their enthusiasm and loyalty. And Cheers to Between the Fences for their foresight in recognizing our community's need for good sports facilities for all citizens. Finally, Cheers to us – the sports publishing class – for sticking with this sometimes trying investigative process.

Finally, going back to that familiar song, "making your way in the world today takes everything you've got..."; we've decided that in many ways sports are a life lesson for the real world: friendships formed, the competition developed, heritage and traditions handed down, that connected magic spirit we all feel. CHEERS!

Acknowledgements

First and foremost, Between the Fences would like to thank the Jenkins Group, Village Press and Horizon Books for their contributions of publishing, printing and selling *Cheers* with all profits going to Between the Fences. Without their help, this project would not have been possible. With their assistance, time and ideas, this book should prove to be a chronicle of Trojan sports for the first 100 years as well as help provide funds for the construction of Traverse City athletic and recreation facilities.

Our sincere thanks to:

Jim Anderson
Vicki Asmus
Greg Barner
Ken Bell
Ivanka Berkshire
Black & Gold writers & editors
Ron Bohn
Booster News writers & editors
Sylvia Burns
Terry Burton Photography
Denny Chase
Jon Constant
Don Dunsmore
Lynn Ebinger
Nick Edson
Bruce Falberg
Mark Fries
John Gerhardt
Chris Givens
Horizon Books
Jenkins Group
Waldo Keating
Wayne Kladder
Chuck Lendrum
Bob Lober
John Lober
Russ Luttinen
Jeff Mosher
Dick Murphy
Kelly Neu
Larry Nykerk
Kathleen O'Connell
Record-Eagle photographers
Lyn Salathiel
Chet Salisbury
Mandy Samuelson
Jerry Stanek
Lisa Taylor
Traverse City Senior High Pines writers, editors & photographers
Doug Tornga
Village Press
Polly Walker

Footwear Artwork by Aaron Dennis, Traverse City Central High School, Class of 1997
Copy Edited by Julie MacIntosh, Traverse City Central High School Class of 1996
Editorial Supervision by Pat Weber
Manuscript and Project Supervision by Diane Portenga
Text Design and Layout by Barbara Hodge
Pre-press Planning by Alex Moore
Jacket Design by Village Press

RESEARCH SOURCES

The Black & Gold
The Booster News
Con Foster Museum
Grand Traverse Historical Society
Interviews with coaches
Le Grand Traverse, pub. 1940
Pathfinder School
Preview Community Weekly
Record-Eagle
"Thirlby Field" *Record-Eagle* insert, October 13, 1995. Articles by Ken Bell, Denny Chase and Nick Edson
Traverse City Senior High *Pines*

LESSONS LEARNED FROM A SPORTS FILLED CHILDHOOD

By Jon Burian

"Growing up in this small northern Michigan town, my life has been molded by many different factors. Whether it be my guiding parents, the school system, or even the media, my personality has been shaped by countless numbers of things. Thrown into this huge orgy of happenings is the enormous impact of sports.

At this, I am sure many will scoff. There are people whom I have encountered in my short life who feel that sports are petty and unimportant. They believe that they are a waste of time and money. I believe that this is as far from the truth as anything can be. Sports, whether it be watching or participating in them, have made a deep and lasting impression on who I am.

As I peer deeper, I start to pick up a portion of the huge impact swimming, and every other sport, has had on me. Things like respect, patience, determination and discipline have been pounded into me for as long as I can remember. The importance of these virtues would most likely have been overlooked had I not played sports. Coaches, teammates and my parents have taught me these valuable lessons using sports as a powerful tool."

Taken from "Lessons learned from a sports filled childhood," The Black and Gold, *March 5, 1997, by Jon Burian, Traverse City Central High School Class of '98.*

Thirlby's Lure

By Nick Edson

They come by the thousands, even in the rain and cold....

Most come to watch football, but there are many who attend simply to watch the band, sit with their friends and enjoy Traverse City's biggest social event of the week.

That's the lure of Traverse City Trojan football....

But there is much more at work here than meets the eye.

"It's like a town gathering," said former Trojan star Mark Brammer, who went on to play for Michigan State University and the Buffalo Bills of the National Football League.

"I've been to high school games around East Lansing and here in the Buffalo area and there is nothing that even comes close to Thirlby Field on Friday nights."....

It was a happening, a meeting place for the people of Traverse City to unwind after a hectic week.

In the years since I've moved from the Thirlby neighborhood, I've been to NBA playoff games, a Super Bowl and several World Series games.

The things I remember about those events aren't the games, but the people. The air of excitement outside the stadium, the teenagers congregating to talk, the fans exchanging inside information and the enthusiasm filling the scene with electricity.

That's the same feeling, on a smaller scale, you get at Thirlby Field on Friday nights.

It's a special place to be...a place filled with memories that are renewed every time you step between the fences once again.

Taken from Record-Eagle *insert on Thirlby Field, October 13, 1995, by Nick Edson,* Record-Eagle *sports editor.*

1

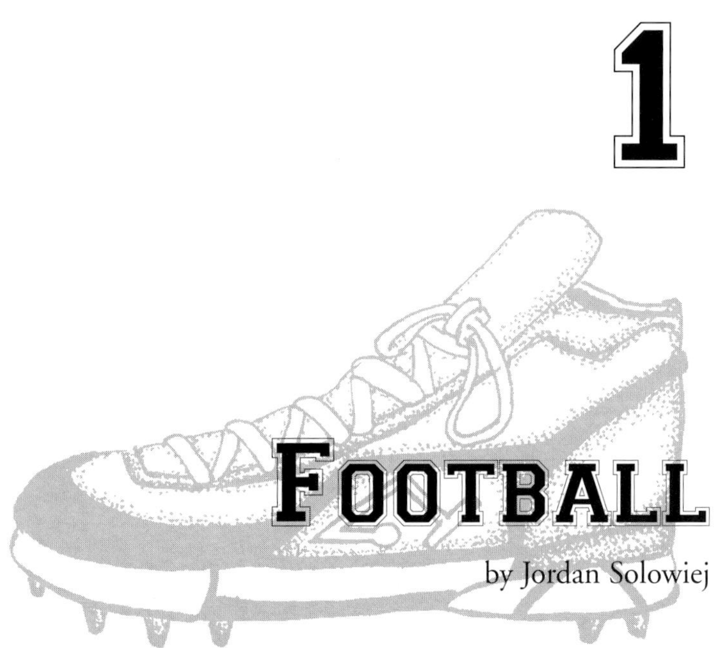

FOOTBALL

by Jordan Solowiej

"Gonna take a little trip to Pontiac. Gonna be State champs when we get back. Big "D" gonna stick em', Big "O" is gonna roll. Gonna be #1 in everybody's poll. When the game is over and the stickin's done, T.C. Trojans gonna be #1!"

– TRAVERSE CITY TROJAN FOOTBALL TEAM

From 30 guys on a side playing a variation of European soccer in the mid 1800s, to the eleven-man teams found on college and high school fields playing football in the 1990s, football has had a colorful history. In Traverse City, football history began in 1896.

That year, Traverse City's first season consisted of two games, both against Cadillac. When Traverse City played Cadillac, they had to take a train to get to the game. They took the Grand Rapids and Indiana Railroad, commonly called the G. R. & I. The first Trojan football team included: ends Nerlinger and Garner; tackles Pennington and Northrup; guards Leighton and Gray; center Gane; halfbacks Hardie and Johnson; fullback, Erde and quarterback Thomas (at that time, only last names were listed). There were also three substitutes filling the roster. The team's average weight was 145 pounds. Mr. Ike Fless, a local business college instructor, was the coach and Mr. Beeman, the faculty manager, was director of athletics.

The Trojans played two games in the first year, losing at Cadillac 12-8, before winning their first game at home also against Cadillac, 16-10. When the Trojans played their first home game, they played in an open field south of the high school on Pine Street. That field ran north and south next to the current football stadium.

Uniforms that first season were purchased by local merchants who supported high school athletics. They consisted of sleeveless jackets and leather helmets. Many players created their own cleats out of leather scraps to give better traction when running. When football first began, players had to buy their own equipment. Instead of football helmets they wore head hardnesses which cost $1.75. They also had to buy their own shin guards at $.50 each. Note the interesting outfits in the accompanying photo – including nose protectors hanging around some of their necks.

ONE OF THE TROJANS' MOST SUCCESSFUL FOOTBALL teams ever was the 1910 team. The Trojans posted a 7-0 record that year, scoring 152 points to their opponents' zero points. The starting eleven players played the entire game, since there were no substitutes. When a clip in a Grand Rapids paper said that Charlevoix claimed the football championship of Northern Michigan, Traverse City disagreed with that claim. Toward the end of the Trojans' season the two teams met, and the Trojans made fools of Charlevoix, spanking them 32-0, and with that sound trouncing the Trojans became the champions of the north.

In 1917, the Trojans once again had a spectacular year. Under coach "Cub" Spruit, the Trojans won the Northern Michigan championship. Traverse City had three key players that year who received state recognition: Loren Bensley, Gerald Tyler and Lawrence Bain.

The 1899 "Traverse High" football team. Back Row: Bill Vogelsong, Archie Novotny, Bob Walters, Tom Wilhelm, Cliff Maynard. Center Row: Butch Hurley, Jack Slater, Ed Boyer. Front Row: Vern Reynolds, Harry Des Press, Bill Snushall, George Raff. Not pictured: Don Margan, Joe Ehrenberger, Harold MacIntosh, Curtis Leighton and Coach Levi Pennington.

One of the most notable games of football's early years was between Traverse City and Pontiac for the 1920 state championship. With the Trojans undefeated, rival Cadillac remained on the schedule. However, that game never materialized. When Traverse City wanted a say in who the referee would be, Cadillac responded with charges about some ineligible Trojan players. Because of this conflict, Traverse City instead scheduled a game with Pontiac for the state championship, which made Cadillac fans furious.

Traverse City offered to host the Pontiac game and hired Chief Nevitt, an impartial referee from Bay City. In order to get to Traverse City, Nevitt had to take the train which stopped in Cadillac. However, angry fans got him off the train at the Cadillac stop and detained him until the train had left. Determined to make it to the game, Nevitt hired a taxi (Model T Ford) which got him to Traverse City, but not until after halftime when he found the score 7-7 with a local official filling in for him. The Trojans had scored when Chet Wheelock passed to Rollie Pierce and quarterback Harold Yunker carried it in from the one-yard line. A second Wheelock to Pierce touchdown pass didn't count on a technicality over when the official had blown his whistle. Nevitt showed up just after that happened and was of the opinion that the score should have counted. The decision stood, however, and with no scoring in the second half, the gamed finished at a 7-7 tie.

After this game, serious consideration was given to building a fence which would give school officials the chance to charge admission to help cover costs of the football program. After a Thanksgiving Day game at Mt. Pleasant which the Trojans won, 42-0, the 1920 season ended with an 8-0-1 record in which Traverse City outscored its opponents 371-7.

Traverse City football teams of the 1920s posted an impressive ten-year record of 61-20-9. Besides focusing on team performances at that time, there was also a concerted effort to build a new football field. In 1921, Traverse City Light and Power built what is now known as the Brown Bridge Dam. When the land was cleared, Brown Lumber trucks carried the logs to town and Hannah and Lay cut the boards. Traverse City students and football players then helped with a city work bee to put a fence up around the field. The Rotary Club offered to paint the fence by assigning sections to each of its members. After painting, the field was seeded, and it was thought to be the best in the north.

In 1924, Traverse City had another awesome football year. Probably the main reason that the fans were so hyped up throughout the year was because the only loss came in the last game of the season against Detroit Northeast who shut out the Trojans 14-0. However, Traverse City once again won the Northern Michigan championship for the second consecutive year.

Again in 1925, Traverse City only lost one game, to Manistee who shut out the Trojans 6-0. Although they lost, the Trojans were still able to win the Northern Michigan championship for the third consecutive year. In their last game of the season, Traverse City pulled out a 17-15 win over a strong undefeated Petoskey team whose star was Irv Menzel, a future Traverse City coach and athletic director. Ages on that team ranged from a 20-year-old to two who were 15. During Coach Spruit's 1923-1925 seasons, he had an impressive 22-3-2 record.

Traverse City won its first Class B state championship in 1928, under coach Gordon MacDonald and assistant L.K. Wallace. Captain Bill Unger paced the Trojans to a 6-0-4 season in which they won the Northern Michigan championship by beating Petoskey 26-0 in a hazardous snow storm which brought three inches of snow and rain. However, Traverse City wanted more than the Northern Michigan championship, so they challenged Dearborn, the Southern Michigan champions, to an unofficial play-off game. Traverse City came out victorious, beating Dearborn 36-6 on Thanksgiving Day. It's interesting to note that

1928 Class B state champions, including (not in order): Captain Bill Unger, Bill Core, Ben Wright, Ben Barnes, Mike Guiffre, Ross Weaver, Bryant Bain, Jack DeWitt Nelson, Roy Ostlund, James Knauf, Morrell Cole, Harry Barnes and Don Ross.

the official MHSAA playoffs which started in 1975 are held on Thanksgiving weekend.

THE 1930S STARTED SLOWLY, with Traverse City 3-3-3 in 1931. Stars of that team were Erich Sleder, in his fourth year on the varsity team, Julius Sleder in his third year, Arnie Bohn and Ted Sebright.

In 1934, the Athletic Board of Control decided that a new athletic park and field house at 13th and Pine Streets were going to be built. The Trojan team was presented with a new and improved football field as well as a field house, one of the finest in northern Michigan. Also included were bleachers, a pressbox, a scoreboard and a running track at this site west of the original north-south field. The day was set for the dedication. In recognition of Dr. E. L. Thirlby's dedication and loyal support to the school's athletics, the field was named Thirlby Field after him. To make the dedication complete, the Trojans played their archrivals, Cadillac, and gave them a "good woopin'," with the final score 33-0. The only loss the Trojans had that year was against Ludington. In that game, Traverse City was actually leading 12-6, but late in the game Ludington completed a huge pass for a touchdown. They made the extra point, and the Trojans lost. From 1936-1939, under the coaching of Les Orr with former Petoskey player Irv Menzel as assistant, the Trojans posted a towering record of 21 victories and six defeats.

In 1937, lighting became an issue for Thirlby Field. Local merchants were supportive since they were unable to attend the Saturday afternoon games. The decision was finally made to erect lights before the Alpena game, but getting them in place was a race against time. The poles and 40 large reflector lights arrived three days before the game. Traverse City Light and Power director Bill Love and his staff managed the task, although the Trojans didn't get a chance to practice under the lights before the game. Traverse City added to the celebration with a 38-0 defeat over Alpena, with Jim Hendryx, Bill Hemming, Earl Glasemer and Tom Bovee starring. The

Thirlby Field in 1937, under new lights.

1937 team was the only team in the 1930s with a perfect 7-0 season, which brought them their first Big Seven Conference title.

THE 1940 TEAM WAS COACHED BY FRED JANKE with Irv Menzel assisting. Quarterbacked by Jack Bensley, the team's running backs were George Perry and Dale Wares and top linemen that year were Jim Woodrow and Jack Hilliker. During the season, the three losses were all by one touchdown to Grand Rapids Union, Grand Rapids South and Alpena. In the 1940 and 1941 seasons, the Trojans posted the same records, going 5-3 both years.

Traverse City's 1942 and 1943 seasons were mind-boggling as the Trojans showed how Traverse City football was played. The Trojans went undefeated those two years under the coaching of Tharel "Dutch" Kanitz and Bill Diekman. The Trojans had a total of 13 wins, no defeats and one tie which helped them in winning the Big Seven championship both years. Led by co-captains Hank Perry and Bud Savage in 1942, they posted a perfect 7-0 record. Other 1942 starters were Cecil Foote, Bud Newton, Dean Wilson, Bud Weede, Bob Hoxie, Bill Van Epps, Norm Wangen, Jack Rokos and Jack Cox. The 1943 team, with Dean Wilson and Jack Solomonson as co-captains, also remained undefeated.

The football teams of 1944, 1945 and 1946 won

ten games, lost thirteen and tied one, against Cadillac 0-0. In the fall season of 1944, the Trojans had a spectacular back named Johnny Ott. Johnny, at 6'1" and 185 pounds, was a pass-snatching and open-field running specialist. He was strong on pass defense and hard to stop, scoring 85 points in eight games. He was the first All-State player in Traverse City history, with teammate and co-captain Bud Weede receiving Honorable Mention from the *Associated Press* and *The Detroit Free Press.* Ott was also named All-Big Eight Conference and All-Northern, as was Weede. In the backfield were co-captain Dick Hoag, Walt Anderson, Jud Hemming and Ott. Because of World War II when some 18-year-olds chose to enlist, Coach Kanitz ended his four-year stint as coach with a 23-11-2 record.

THE SEASONS OF 1947 AND 1948 were nothing special to talk about. Under coach Harold Andreas, the Trojans won only two games, lost 22, and tied three. The two wins came against Big Rapids, and the two ties were with Cadillac and Petoskey.

The 1949 season was an improvement over those last few years, although their record wasn't the best ever at 4-3-1. Jack Emerson scored 18 points against the Mt. Pleasant Oilers to help the Trojans win the Class B North Central Conference championship.

The 1950s had a succession of four Trojan head coaches and included play in three different leagues: the North Central, Arrowhead and Lake Michigan Athletic Conferences. In 1950, Alpena was the northern powerhouse and defeated

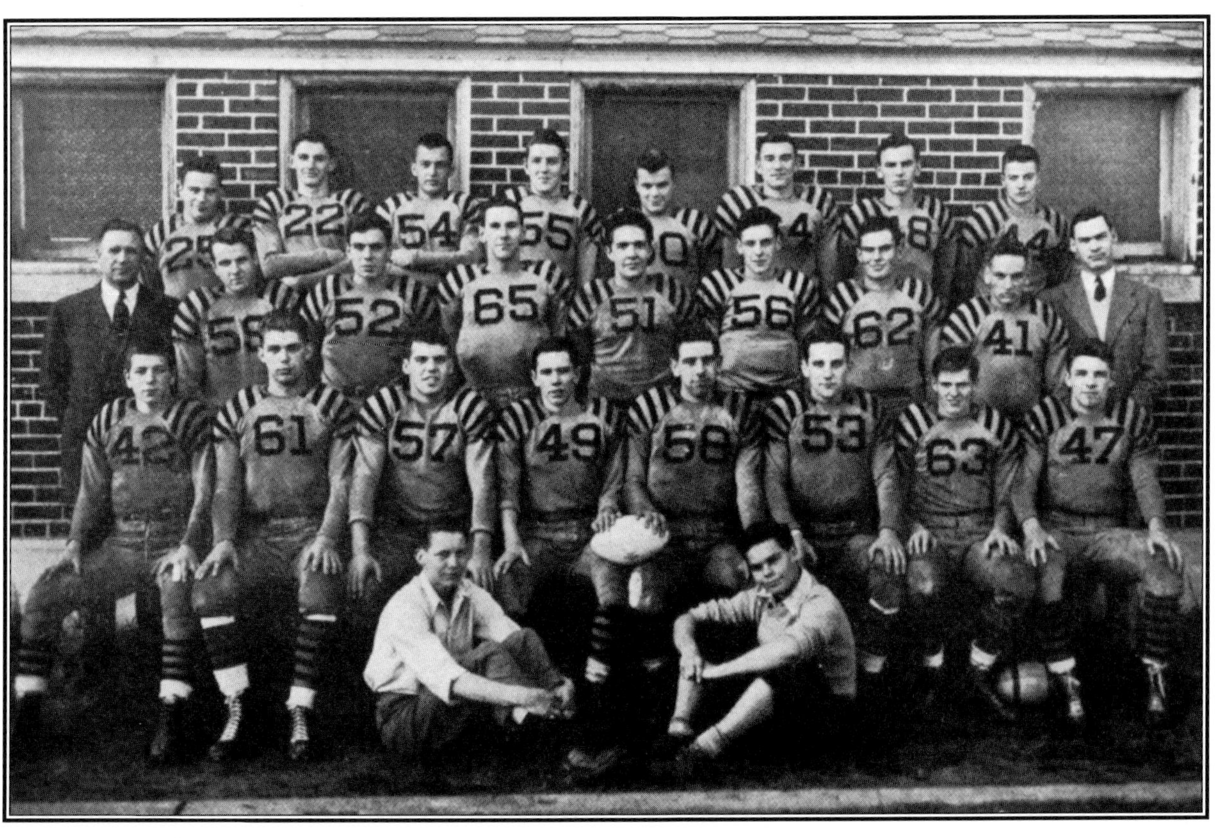

Members of the 1944 Trojan football team which included the first Trojan All-Stater, Johnny Ott. Front Row: Managers Donald Haggard, Dave Derrick. Second Row: Bob Sivek, Clyde Downer, John Ott, Dick Hoag, Bud Weede, Bill Crawford, Peter Krohn, Walt Anderson. Third Row: Coach Kanitz, Jack Hemming, William Straub, Arthur Meereis, Frank Snyder, Dale Christopher, Ward Wehr, Coach Deikman. Back Row: Tug Bursaw, Richard Zimmerman, Larry Babel, John Heiges, Ken Larcom, Kenny Hicks, Howard Wilhelm, George Lawrence.

Traverse City 53-2. However, the Trojans won their last game against Ludington as Jack Emerson scored on a 65-yard run and Don Fraser on a 57-yard run. Also in the backfield was Jack Franke.

In 1951, the Trojans won all of their games at home, but lost all of the ones on the road against some pretty powerful clubs, ending the year with a final record of 4-4. One very special player that season was guard Budd Tompkins. Tompkins became All-Conference, All-North and was named to the All-State team.

Playing their last game in the North Central Conference in 1952, Traverse City enjoyed their best year since 1943. They won all five of their conference games to win the championship. Their overall record was 6-2, with the two losses each by only a couple of points. Outstanding players from the 1952 team were Bill Gregory, Ned Kramer, Dugald Munro, Tom Hall, Dave Bowers, Ben Kreps, Dave Allen, Hank Johnson, Bert Reimer and Jim Hartley.

When Traverse City left the Class B North Central Conference with a championship in 1952, they acclimated themselves well into the Class A Arrowhead Conference starting in 1953, under head coach Irv Menzel. This new conference included Midland, Alpena and Bay City Handy, a new school. Traverse City had an all-star line-up throughout the season with three honorable mentions for the All-State team: fullback Larry Bensley, center James Donoho and guard Jerry Naperalski. Traverse City also had an All-Conference quarterback, Jerry Benton, who passed to All-State end Dave Bowers. Other key players were Don Gordon, Harry Banks, Dick Carmien, Pat Nerbonne and Pete Pritchard.

Also in 1953, Dave Bowers was named All-American, a tremendous feat. What was especially amazing was that he played in a shoulder harness to keep his shoulder from popping out of place. That year he caught 30 passes for 654 yards, scored

1952 North Central Conference Champions. Back row: Coach Irv Menzel, John Heiss, Donn Lindquist, Gordon Timmins, McCarthy, Ed Carpenter, Coach Graybiel. Fourth row: Bernard Kreps, John Perry, George Sarris, John Molleman, John Ohrenberger, Hubert Reimer, Bryce Boursaw, John Marsh, Charles Anspaugh, Tom Harris. Third row: Jon Moore, Jerry Naperalski, Doug Steiger, Pete Rumanes, Don Gordon, Carlton Brazee, Jerry Boursaw, Elmer Jamieson, Royal Bisel, Robert DeYoung. Second row: James Donoho, Larry Bensley, Richard Podleski, Dave Bowers, Ned Kramer, Tom Hall, Robert Wilson, Tom Zimmerman. Front row: Bud Forton, David Allen, Roy Knoll, Bill Gregory, Dugald Munro, Arnold Johnson, James Hartley. Not pictured were Richard Richter and Roberton Pemberton.

five touchdowns, and was also an outstanding defensive end. "He's the best football player I've ever seen in high school," said former teammate Harry Banks. "On defense he smothered everything that came his way. On offense, he was an excellent receiver and a devastating blocker." Bowers made one of Traverse City's best pass combinations along with flanker Don Gordon and quarterback Jerry Benton.

Under head coach Ed Schuknecht in 1955, Dick Bezile was named to the All-Conference team, while the Most Valuable Player award was given to Tom Stephan. Considering all of the games played, the Trojans came out on the short end of a 5-3 record, tying for first place with Bay City in the Arrowhead Conference. In 1956, Traverse City had their highs and lows. The highs were all the players who were named All-Conference: Dick Bezile, Roy Youker, Dick Brovont, George Olman and Gary Keene; their lows were the disappointing record of 3-3-1 and the loss of all the seniors who were graduating from the team.

THE TROJANS, BETTER KNOWN AS THE "RAGGEDY CADETS", (as new coach Bob Bacon called them), ended the 1957 season with a 5-3 record, beating some very impressive Class A and B football teams, with Jim Ooley as assistant coach. Though Traverse City lost three games to some pretty strong teams, they still came out on the winning side with a hard-fought 5-3 record. One highlight was their 13-12 victory over Alpena to end Traverse City's eleven-year losing streak to the Wildcats. MVP that year was Terry Garn.

After the Trojans' long grueling practices and hard-fought games, they ended up with a 6-2 record in 1958. Many picked the Trojans to be a top contender for the number one spot in the Arrowhead Conference that year because of the 20 returning lettermen, but they had a challenge to overcome – they had Midland in their way of a championship.

1956 football coaches, left to right: John Geist, Head Coach Ed Schuknecht, Jim Ooley, Bob Bacon, Walter Thompson, Edmund Howard.

Traverse City played Midland half-way through the season and came up on the short end of a 14-12 loss, a game that was a preview of the two best teams in the Arrowhead Conference. The Trojans had a long list of players with All-Conference honors that year: Ford Carter, Bob Longcore, Bob Stehouwer, Doug Bickle, Bob Moyer, Doug Linder, Dan Exo, Bill King, Ken Bannen, Steve Howard, Bob Anderson, Jerry Springer, Jim Lynch and John Carroll.

Traverse City's 1959 team has been described by many as one of the greatest teams ever to play on Thirlby Field. The reason for that comment is because of their 7-1 record, the great come-from-behind victory over the number three team in the state, Midland, and the Arrowhead grid title trophy. Just as everything was going the Trojans' way, archrival Muskegon blew them out 21-0 at Muskegon on a wet, muddy day. Traverse City had only one loss that year which seemed to have no effect on the rest of the season since the Trojans were ranked fifth in Class A and Doug Bickle was named All-State. He took over all the kicking jobs, averaging 40 yards per punt, 26 yards per pass, and sending many of his kick-offs into the end zone. Players who received All-Conference awards besides Bickle were Bob Longcore, George Boehm and Bob Stehouwer. MVP was Bickle.

IN 1959, THE TROJAN BOOSTER CLUB was organized as an offshoot of football parents' initiatives. Parents Bud King, Bob Anderson and Frank Purvis arranged for players to view movies of the previous week's football games with the coaches. The following year Purvis became official president

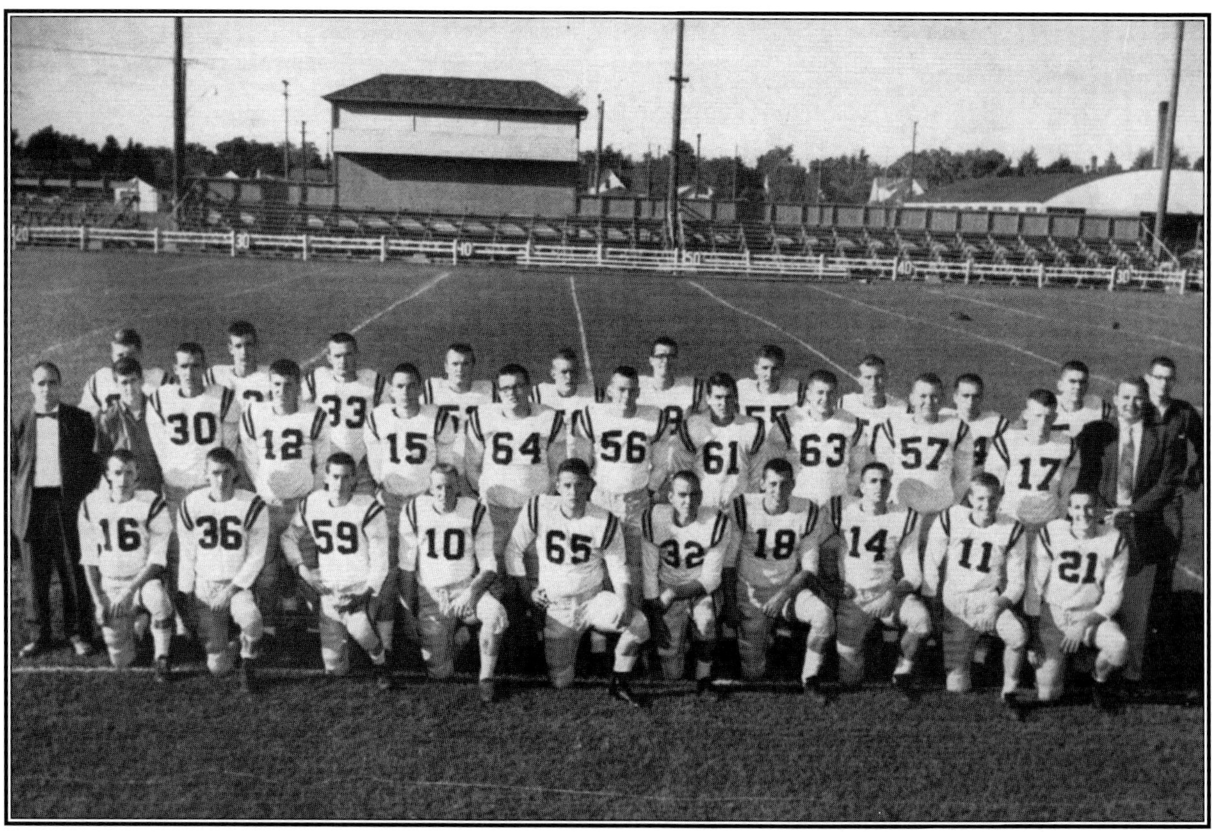

1959 Arrowhead Conference champions at Thirlby Field. Front row: Terry Sanborn, Bob Merchant, Bob Watson, Mike Merrill, Darryl Milarch, Bill King, Bob Stehouwer, Bob Longcore, John Olson, Tom Menzel. Row 2: Coach Bob Bacon, Manager Joe DuPries, Jim Carter, Larry Ealy, Jim Anderson, George Boehm, Jim Lynch, Bill Howard, Dave Pind, Chuck Moorman, Dick Merchant, Coach Jim Ooley. Row 3: John Sommervillle, Doug Bickle, Terry Jenks, Jim Griner, Ron Benson, John Beall, Gary Gee, Dick Bohn, Bob Neuman, Marc Bendickson, Manager Bob Beall.

of the club which started working closely with the athletic department to help provide equipment not otherwise in the athletic budget.

The 1960s were a prosperous time for football, with the Trojans taking five Lake Michigan Athletic Conference titles in that decade. In 1960, the final season in the Arrowhead Conference, the very first Black and Gold game was played with the Black team edging the Gold 14-13. That was also the first year that Traverse City participated in the Lake Michigan Athletic Conference. Traverse City ended the season with a 5-3 record, taking second place in the Conference. George Boehm, one of the best linemen in the state, earned All-State and All-Conference honors with John Bowers also All-Conference.

Big teams aren't always the best teams. Take the 1961 Trojan football team whose average lineman's weight was 162 pounds, with the average back at 152 pounds. Traverse City went an amazing 8-0, beating anyone who stepped in their path of being number one. Finishing second in the state, the Trojans also won the LMAC title in their first year in the new conference. Overall, Traverse City had a perfect season, except for placing second in the state. Named All-State were John Bowers and Ken Schmidt, Trojans who were both two-way players. All-Conference honors went to Bowers, Schmidt, Glenn Merchant, Pedro Rodriguez, Tom Moorman, Chuck Daniels and Jack Howard. Merchant and Rodriguez tied for MVP.

On November 2, 1962, Traverse City's unconquerable 17-game winning streak came to a crashing halt. That day will never be forgotten on the campus of Traverse City Senior High, for Benton Harbor beat the almighty Trojans 20-0. Many people said that the Trojans lost all their spirit, and were totally pooped after their previous 13-13 tie with Grand Haven, but they still had their last game against Benton Harbor to prove everyone wrong. However, the scoreboard said the rest. The Trojans ended their heart-breaking season with a record of 6-1-1. On the up side, it was a banner year for John Bowers. He was a repeat selection to the All-State team and was also named Player of the Year by UPI. In his three-year varsity career, he scored 54 touchdowns and had 3,699 total yards in offense before going on to play four years of football at Princeton. Bowers shared MVP honors that year with Jack Howard. Other outstanding players were Glenn Merchant, Bud Wilson, Joe Niehardt, Jack Murchie and John Sebright.

Even though the Trojans had a record of 5-3 in 1963, they showed how powerful their offense really was. They scored more points than any other Trojan team had scored in the past five years, which was 176 points by the end of the year.

The Trojans' goal: beat Benton Harbor! Playing Benton Harbor on the last game of the 1964 season, they paid back the previous year's shutout. Traverse City won 14-0, as quarterback Len Hawley and John Swanson both scored. The Trojans brought back what was rightfully theirs, the LMAC trophy. Traverse City's season came out on the bright side with a 7-1 record as Bob Diller was placed on the All-State team, named All-Conference and honored as MVP. Guard Diller "was one of the finest linemen ever to come out of Traverse City," praised Coach Bacon. Also earning All-Conference honors were Steve Lockman and Bill Myers.

In 1965, the Trojans had their first losing season under the coaching of Jim Ooley and Bob Bacon. They had been unbeatable for seven straight seasons, but with a 2-6 record, they lost their winning touch for a brief time. Larry Yankee earned All-State honors and MVP recognition. All-Conference awards went to Yankee, Jerry Stanek, Bill Stokes, Jim VanStratt and Bruce Cozzens.

After getting off to a rough start with a tie in their first game and losing their next two, the Trojans were heading for another losing season. Yet, fans have never doubted the Trojans! Winning all the rest of their games, they bounced back from a losing record in 1965, to a winning 1966 season of 6-2-1, led by quarterbacks Scotty Bacon and Paul Jacobs. Also contributing to this successful turnaround were a large number of All-Conference players: Bill Fisher, also named MVP, Greg Shugart, Gary Yankee, Ray Collins, Bill Leismer, Bill Stokes, Rick Kuemin, Jim VanStratt, John Naymick, Tom Kamradt and Loren Hoxsie. This was Coach Bacon's last season with the Trojans, leaving with a ten-year record of 57-22-2.

With Coach Bacon no longer the head coach, Coach Ooley took over the head spot in 1967, and came out on top with a winning team. At the end of a hard-fought 7-1-2 season, Traverse City won its third LMAC title (out of seven years in the league). The 1967 season was a great beginning for a new star head coach, with All-State honors going to Joe Thibedeau.

The Trojan defense was the talk of the state in 1968, for Traverse City only gave up 34 points all year and totally shut out Benton Harbor with no total yards or points in their 44-0 win. With a 7-1-1 record, the Trojans received their fourth LMAC trophy and were ranked tenth in the state. All-State honors went to Vic Cole, with All-Conference to Cole, Steve Wehr, Marty Easling, Bernie Lautner, Dean Mack, Gary Klingelsmith, Rob Manigold, Steve Rollo and Ty Thompson. Most Valuable Player was Wehr.

When Traverse City lost its opening game 34-0 to the hands of Bay City Central, many people doubted the rest of the 1969 season, for there were tough teams just ahead. However, the Trojans made believers out of everyone for they beat the rest of their opponents, except for a 29-20 loss to Grand Rapids Catholic. They ended the season with yet another LMAC trophy and a 7-2 record. Winning All-State honors was Steve Rollo, who was also MVP and All-Conference, along with Bob Donick, Doug Denison, Karl Koivisto, Dean Mack, John Batsakis, Larry Selkirk, Tom Meyers, Jim Demin and Chuck Strait.

Traverse City teams in the 1970s equalled the sixties' winning records. The Trojans' 1960s wins matched the combined totals of Muskegon, Muskegon Catholic and Benton Harbor. They exceeded all previous decades with a Class A state championship in 1978.

After their horrendous loss in 1969 to Bay City Central, the following season the Trojans were hoping for a different ending than that year's 34-0 whopping. This time it was different. In 1970, the Trojans could picture a sweet victory, but they fell short. They suffered a heartbreaking defeat to the number one ranked team with a final score of Bay City Central 2, Traverse City 0. With a 6-3 record that season, they lost the LMAC trophy after three consecutive years of winning the prize. Helping in the 1970 effort were All-Conference players Ken Core, Jeff Thompson, Jim Demin, Phil Jacobs, Mark Cox, Craig Peterson, Dave Whiteford and Paul McQuade.

The season of 1971 was a record-breaking year for the Trojans and the conference: the Trojans had 1,688 total offensive yards; they averaged 337.6 yards per game; they posted a record of 165 total

Leading the 1971 Trojans was All-American Dave Whiteford who went on to play for the University of Michigan.

points; and they averaged 35 points per game. Traverse City set a new single game passing record against the Big Reds of Muskegon with 193 yards, but with all these new records, the Trojans finished their season with an 8-1 record to rank second in the LMAC.

THE MOST MEMORABLE GAME THAT YEAR, which has been called one of the greatest games in LMAC history, was against Muskegon, before the playoff system was in place. No. 1 ranked Traverse City played No. 2 Muskegon in front of 10,000 fans, Hackley Field's largest crowd ever. After an 18-0 lead, a strange bounce on a Trojan punt led to a Muskegon touchdown. From there it was downhill for the Trojans as the Big Reds won, 20-18. Since the Trojans had previously been winning by such large margins, 30-40 points all year, the starters hadn't been playing an entire game. Said Coach Ooley, "Our players got tired in that one and it may have cost us." In spite of that loss, Dave Whiteford had an outstanding year, being named All-American as a defensive linebacker. Like Dave Bowers, the first Trojan football All-American, Whiteford played both ways and received the rare honor of being selected as All-State on both offense and defense. All-Conference honorees were Whiteford, Bob Chase, Chuck Wehr, Bill Allgaier, Bill Babel, Mike McPhilamy and Paul McQuade.

Mark Brammer, a Trojan star of the 1970s who went on to play for Michigan State and the Buffalo Bills.

In 1972, the Trojans regained the honor of being LMAC champs. They had a rough start, however, in the 1973 season, losing their first three games and ending the season 4-5. Making All-Conference for their effort were Tom Chase, John Simone, Dave Halachukas, John Plough and Jason Johnston.

After Traverse City's 3-0 start in 1974, they had a tough task ahead – they had to play a tough Muskegon Catholic Central team. The whole game was like a contest of "king of the mountain," and at the end of this match, the scoreboard read 24-20 with the victory going to Muskegon. The rest of the Trojans' season went picture-perfect, beating the Muskegon Big Reds 40-12, and shutting out Grand Rapids Union 60-12. They ended their season with an 8-1 record for a near perfect season. Dave Halachukas received All-State honors while Mark Brammer was MVP.

WHAT MORE CAN BE SAID ABOUT THE 1975 TROJAN FOOTBALL TEAM? They ended their regular season undefeated with a 9-0 record, and entered the first year of the playoffs a heavy favorite. Their first challenge for the number one spot came against the Kalamazoo Giants in the semifinals, but they had no problems, winning 48-6. Then the top-ranked Trojans were matched with Muskegon Catholic Central, No. 1 in Class B, in a battle now simply referred to as "The Drive." Said Mark Brammer, who went on to play for Michigan

Coach Jim Ooley celebrates a Trojan score.

State and the Buffalo Bills, "'The Drive' was one of the highlights of my football career." Brammer, quarterback Kim Tezak and halfback Rick Waters starred in the Trojans' amazing 92-yard drive in the final three minutes of the game in which Traverse City nosed out Muskegon, 21-20. With no time-outs left, the Trojans were down 20-14, as Brammer caught five passes, Waters three and Dave Beagle had two carries. When Brammer caught the game-winning touchdown pass from Kim Tezak, Thirlby Field went wild.

Then the heart breaker. Traverse City played a tough Livonia Franklin team in the finals and lost a long grueling game 21-7. Even though they lost the big game, The UPI poll and the *Detroit Free Press* both rated Traverse City number one. After all, the 1975 Trojans finished second in the state and number one in the LMAC. All-State honors that year went to Mark Brammer and Rick Waters. Others earning All-Conference were John Fifarek, Greg Hamilton, Jim Hardy, Chris Buday, Kim Tezak and Chuck Fitzgerald. Brammer, named UPI's Michigan Prep Player of the Year, was further honored as Traverse City's third football All-American.

In 1976, Traverse City took off with a 3-0 start, then lost a close game to Alpena 14-7. That was a rebuilding season, due to the fact that the team had lost many of their starters to graduation. Traverse City ended the season with a 7-2 record, and came in second place in the LMAC behind the team that beat them 33-0, the Muskegon Big Reds. Recognized as All-State was Chuck Fitzgerald, a 230 pound, 6'5" tackle whom Coach Ooley recently called, "one of the most aggressive players I've had in my 24 years of coaching." All-Conference players in addition to Fitzgerald were Larry Kinney, Dave Mahn, and Gary Provins.

The Trojan football team had yet another great season in 1977. The mighty Trojans finished their season number one in the north and clinched first place in the LMAC with another 7-2 record. Two-year starter Mark Candey has been called one of the best backs in Trojan history who consistently broke up or intercepted passes and stopped running plays. Earning All-State recognition were Candey and Dan Leppek. Making All-Conference were co-captains Candey and Mark Spencer, Leppek, Mark Korson, Randy Cook, Mark Gabrick, Jon Buday and Jeff Whiting.

"Unbelievable" and "a team of destiny" were words used by Coach Ooley to describe the 1978 Trojan team. The Trojans dominated all season until the Muskegon Catholic game rolled in, a hard-

The Trojan Marching Band heads onto Thirlby Field to inspire fans with yet another outstanding performance.

fought battle the Trojans lost 15-12. That was the only game that the Trojans gave up that year, making their regular season record 8-1, but they weren't done yet. The Trojans were headed to the Silverdome to try to be state champions for the first time. They were ranked as underdogs in each of their three play-off games, but they never gave up and beat all three of their opponents, and with those wins it brought them to the final game against North Farmington.

THE TROJANS DOMINATED THE FIRST HALF of the championship game, scoring 14 points to the Raiders' 0, but in the second half the Raiders tied the game. With 6,000 Trojan fans making the Dome as loud as could be, the Trojans turned that noise into motivation and earned the winning points with Bill Rossetti's touchdown run. That made the final score 20-14 as the Trojans went on to win the title game. The Trojans were the Class A champions for the first time in the history of Trojan football. Traverse City continued to reap honors that year as coach Jim Ooley was voted the 1978 Class A Coach of the Year and Doug Parshall was named All-State after setting a school record of 149 tackles with 48 assists, 4 sacks, 4 fumble recoveries and two pass interceptions. A number of Trojans also were All-Conference picks: Parshall, Bob Brammer, Jeff Whiting, Dennie Weber, Troy Mariage, Al Weber, Frank Vandervort and Brian Blevins.

AFTER TRAVERSE CITY'S STORYBOOK SEASON OF 1978, they were looking to repeat it in 1979. However, Traverse City ended their season 4-5, with very close and disappointing losses to some hard teams. After the Trojans beat the Eskymos 29-14, that game stood out from the rest since Escanaba went on to be number two in the state. A 4-5 record left the Trojans third in the LMAC. However, Traverse City was a well-respected team that year with Rob Wolff, Doug Parshall, Tim Squires, Mark Aldritch, Dan Stricker, Tom Kelly,

The 1978 Trojan team, Traverse City's first Class A football state champions. Front row: Rob Wolff, Steve Bell, Bill Rossetti, Bob Brammer, Tim Slack, Jeff Whiting, Dennis Provins, Brian Blevins. Second row: Kurt Monson, Bill Shaw, Terry Loveland, Tim Squires, Mike Heika, Dan Hague, Rick Scussel, Mike Johnston. Third row: Steve Dohm, Jerry Alexander, Mark Aldrich, Tom Kelly, Lonny Penney, Greg Forton, Dan Strait, Dan Stricker. Fourth row: Brian Riggs, Frank Vandervort, Bryan Keene, Dennis Weber, Al Weber, Grant Fitz, Vince Pugliese, Dennis Schichtel, Bill Pennington. Back row: Dan Lehouiller, Tom Cizek, Dana Bartone, Keith Frankfurth, Troy Mariage, Bob Egeler, Doug Parshall, Jack Brautigam. Not pictured were Ken Griffin, Jon Hilborn, Bill Core, Brent Kelly, Mark Music, Brian McPherson, Larry Czubak, Mike Howard, Steve Don.

Terry Goodell, Brian McPherson and Doug Tompkins named to the All-Conference team. The fall of 1979 was only Traverse City's second losing season in ten years and the fourth in 20 years. The Trojans were 35-11 in the LMAC, having earned eight titles in 20 years. Overall, in 20 years the Trojans were 130-41, quite an impressive record.

The biggest comeback in Trojan football was played in 1980, against Mona Shores. With only three minutes left in the third quarter, the Trojans were down 28-0, but from then on the Trojans never looked back. They showed their best offense of the season, scoring 29 points in 15 minutes to beat Mona Shores in a come-from-behind victory, 29-28. "Even though we were down 27-0, I told the guys we could still come back and beat them," Coach Ooley recalls. The final touchdown was set up by a flea flicker with 25 seconds left, putting the ball on the Mona Shores six. After two more plays, Don Wolf ran in for the tying touchdown and the game was won with Bruce Braden's extra point. To cap off a 5-4 record, the Trojans beat the tenth-rated Flint Northern team 16-0.

EVEN THOUGH THE TROJANS HAD A 3-6 RECORD IN 1982, All-Conference players Scott Ehrenberger and Greg Bohn led the team in some good contests against some very hard teams. In 1983, Traverse City improved to a 9-2 record but had to overcome several injuries and illnesses all year, which went against them in the playoffs. The Trojans won the LMAC championship and ended their almost perfect season by losing to East Lansing in the semifinals. Earning All-State were Greg Bohn and Rob McGuffin.

The Trojans got off to a 5-0 start in 1984, beating everyone in their path. The two games the team lost caused the season to end early, dashing their chances of winning the state title or being conference champions. "We never had a bad game," stated coach Jim Ooley. The Trojans had a very strong offense as well as the backbone of the team: the defense. Every time the offense was inside the 10-yard line, it scored, showing its strength. The Trojans ended their season with a 7-2 record, losing to two very strong football teams. Making All-State was Mike Hayes.

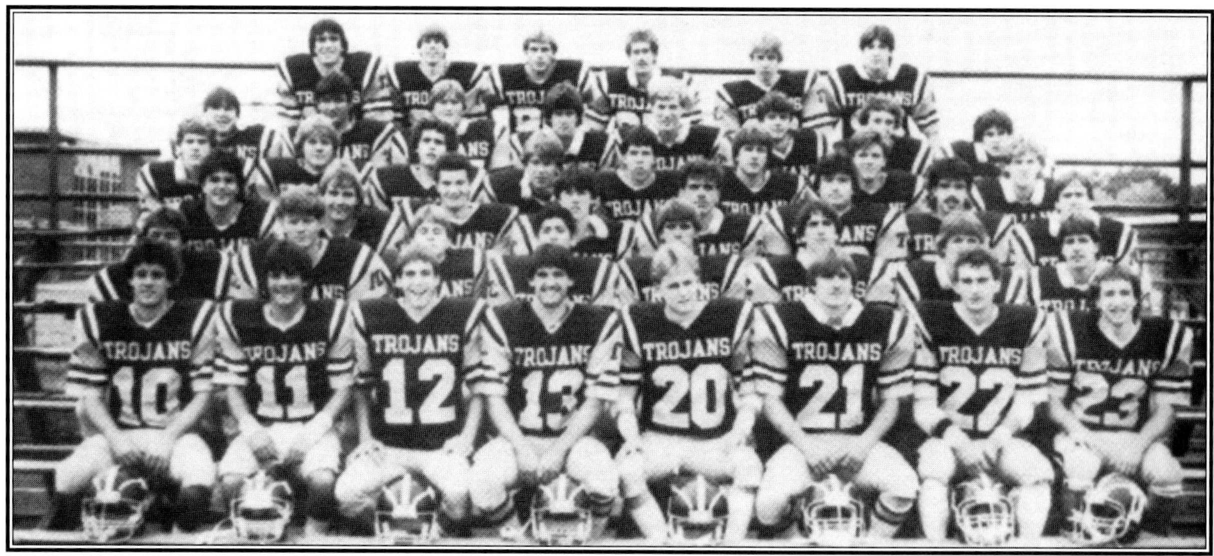

Class A state champions, the 1985 Trojans. Top row: Lance Morgan, Jeff Durocher, Mark DeMeester, Todd Miner, Jon Merchant, Chris Bohn. Row 5: G.F. Stacey, Jack Challender, R. MacPherson, Scott Zimmerman, Ken Kloosterman, C. Leider, Patrick Wright, Chris Valerio. Row 4: David Heller, Steve Nadlicki, Clark Cole, Scott Chupp, Craig Coulter, Otto Socha, Mark Phillips, Michael Round. Row 3: Scott Henry, Tony Olson, Matt Howe, Dan Chapman, J. Gagnon, Jeff Cleland, Robert Butryn, Jeff Campbell. Row 2: Tim Richards, Mark Arnold, Tobin Decker, Charles Flores, Jim Noland, Ed Thaxton, Gary Rakin, Todd Nienhouse. Row 1: Josh Fiebing, Doug Lautner, John Pampu, Chris Hathaway, Marty Lobdell, Tim Lamie, John Heckroth, Charles Hastings.

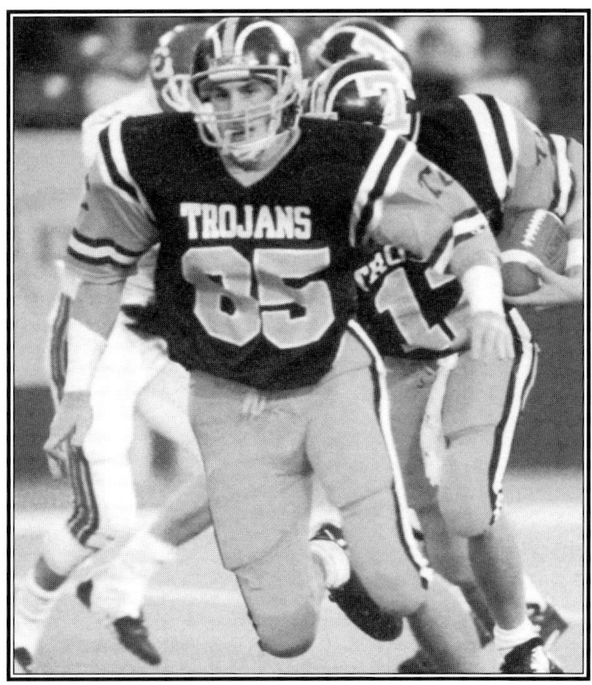

Marc Burkholder goes for a block, a skill that earned him All-State honors and a spot on the University of Michigan team.

In a 1985 game between old rivals, Traverse City pulled off a dramatic win over the Big Reds. With the score tied at 14-14, the Trojans appeared to be on a touchdown drive when Muskegon intercepted a pass and raced toward its goal, scoring with under a minute to play. The Muskegon homecoming crowd went wild until Traverse City used the flea flicker with a pass from Chris Hathaway to Jeff Durocher who lateralled to Doug Lautner, covering almost 50 yards for a touchdown. With the score now 21-20, the Trojans chose to go for two. Durocher caught Hathaway's pass to win the game 22-21.

Later in 1985, the dream of every high school football player, especially a Trojan, came true. The Trojans had a perfect 9-0 record going into the playoffs and were heavy favorites to win the Class A title. In the first playoff game against the Muskegon Big Reds, Traverse City won a snowy battle 28-14 after they had to first clear the snow from the field. Then came Grand Blanc, but the Trojans were too powerful and defeated them 36-20. The Trojans weren't done yet. Ann Arbor Pioneer stood in their way of the championship, but they were no match for the Trojans, who ended up beating them 19-10. Now, the game everyone was talking about, Traverse City vs. Troy for the Class A title. After making it this far, it was felt that the Trojans could win it all! On November 30, the Trojans never let up and whipped Troy 29-3. The Trojans were Class A champions for only the second time, and they deserved it with a final record of 13-0. The season concluded with Gary Rakin earning All-State honors for his part in the year's successes.

THE TROJANS HAD A BETTER SEASON STATISTICALLY, but not record-wise, in 1986. Although they finished the season 5-4, they had gained 724 more yards on the ground, had 118 more yards in the air, and picked up 37 more first downs than their opponents. Traverse City had a good and tough playing season in which Chris Bohn made the All-State team.

"Positive," Coach Ooley said in describing his 1987 team. Each player on the team had the dedication that all successful teams need to be successful. For example, each player put in 25-30 hours a week, and with that type of dedication, the Trojans finished their season with a 7-2 record and Jon

Trojan football coaching staff before Jim Ooley's retirement in 1991. Back Row: Konrad Visser, Ralph Bradley, Budd Tompkins, Ken May. Front Row: Waldo Keating, Steve Simmons, Roger Wood, Head Coach Jim Ooley.

Merchant named as All-State.

On November 26, 1988, the Traverse City Trojans finished a fairytale season by beating Redford-Detroit Catholic Central 13-0 in the Class A championship game held at the Pontiac Silverdome. Several aspects contributing to the victory were the fans and the band's thrilling performance. The Trojans deserved to be number one, and with the Class A championship won, the Trojans proved they were. "Pow," "intensity," "unity," "goal-oriented," "strong willed," were words the players used to describe each other, and on that day the Trojans put all those into one performance and won a state championship. Receiving All-State recognition for their performances were Mark Burkholder and Mike Nadlicki.

TRAVERSE CITY FINISHED THE 1990 SEASON 9-2 and captured the Great Lakes Athletic Conference with a win over Alpena 46-7. Traverse City's star running back Jason Dettwiler finished the season with over 1,000 rushing yards, and Ti Decker and Malachi Gallegos received All-State honors. Geoff Moeke planned to remember "the relationship among the players. It got so close it was like a family."

Traverse City had almost a picture perfect 1991 season but two things happened which shattered that, a loss in the playoffs and the retirement of a coach who will never be forgotten as long as Trojan football goes on. Coach Ooley's Trojans went the distance and even beyond in the regular season which finished at 8-1. The season opened with a Class AA No. 1 *Detroit Free Press* ranking and continued with highlights such as beating the Muskegon Big Reds twice, defeating Midland Dow who at the time was ranked No. 1 in Class A, and tying Alpena for the Great Lakes Athletic Conference title.

In the playoffs, Traverse City trounced Muskegon 24-7 before losing the regional title to eventual state champion Saginaw Arthur Hill. The Trojans made a valiant comeback when they were down 21-0 with 17 minutes remaining in the game. Traverse City scored on three of four possessions in those last minutes as a result of Josh

1988 Class A state championship team. Front Row L to R: Pat Blume, Greg Lobdell, Trev Gillow, Scott Harris, Eric Breithaupt, Mike Noland, Bill Cannon, Josh Wuerfel, Chad Dutmers, Kelly Clark. Row 2: Noah Flores, Brad Warren, Tom Tefft, Jason Kreta, Chad Stachnik, Andy Wright, Mark King, Mike Nadlicki, Nathan Alger, Scott Smith. Row 3: Brad Kanicki, Dan Sarya, Ben Ferris, Dave Drake, Tom Cannon, Jim Deir, Troy Sutherland, Andy Baillie, Sean Knapp, Trey Brooke. Row 4: Scott Carter, Matt Collins, Chad McPherson, Chris Oosse, Joe Soffredine, Jeff Heimforth, Darin Ehrenberger, Travis Fetters, Doug Hulett, Andy Squires. Row 5: Coach Ken May, Coach Roger Wood, Eric Jensen, Marc Burkholder, Jason Warner, Kyle Zenner, Ti Decker, Mike Waller, Derek Hanson, Terry Hansen. Back Row: Gramps Smith, Coach Budd Tompkins, Coach Kit Simmons, Head Coach Jim Ooley, Paul Tompkins, Aaron Simmons, Tammy Breadon (student trainer). Not pictured: Lloyd O'Brien, Mike Dalrymple, Jonathon Keenan, Brad DePew, Derek Morton.

Howie's recovered fumble, a Matt Bourdo to Jeff Gregory 46-yard pass, two touchdowns by Jason Dettwiler and one from Craig Kashazta. However, the final score was 21-18, dashing the Trojans' dream of winning another state championship. At the same time, coach Jim Ooley announced his retirement after 25 years as head Trojan football coach. Appropriately, his final season was a 9-2 winning one, in which Shawn Alpers and Jason Sleder were named All-State and 13 Trojans were placed on the All-League first team.

Coach Jim Ooley brought three state titles to Traverse City in his 25 years of coaching the Trojans and led them into the state playoffs seven times. When he left coaching with a 179-60-4 record, Trojan fans knew he would be deeply missed. "Jim Ooley is the man most responsible for what we know today as Traverse City football," praised friend and fellow coach Waldo Keating.

With Coach Ooley retired, new head coach Roger Wood took over control of the Trojans. In Coach Wood's first year, the Trojans went 5-4 in 1992 and repeated the same record the following year. The pivotal game of the 1993 year came against the Big Reds of Muskegon which the Trojans lost in a close 14-7 contest. All-State picks were Jeremy Hogue and Karl Schultz in 1992 and Carson Rose in 1993.

In early 1994, plans began to be made to replace the Thirlby Field stadium which had been built in 1934. The stadium was outdated and in need of repair as the years had taken their toll. With games now drawing crowds of up to 6,000 fans, the bleachers and other facilities were inadequate. Realizing this need, local attorney Harry T. Running left a bequest to the school system for the purpose of renovating Thirlby Field. However, this

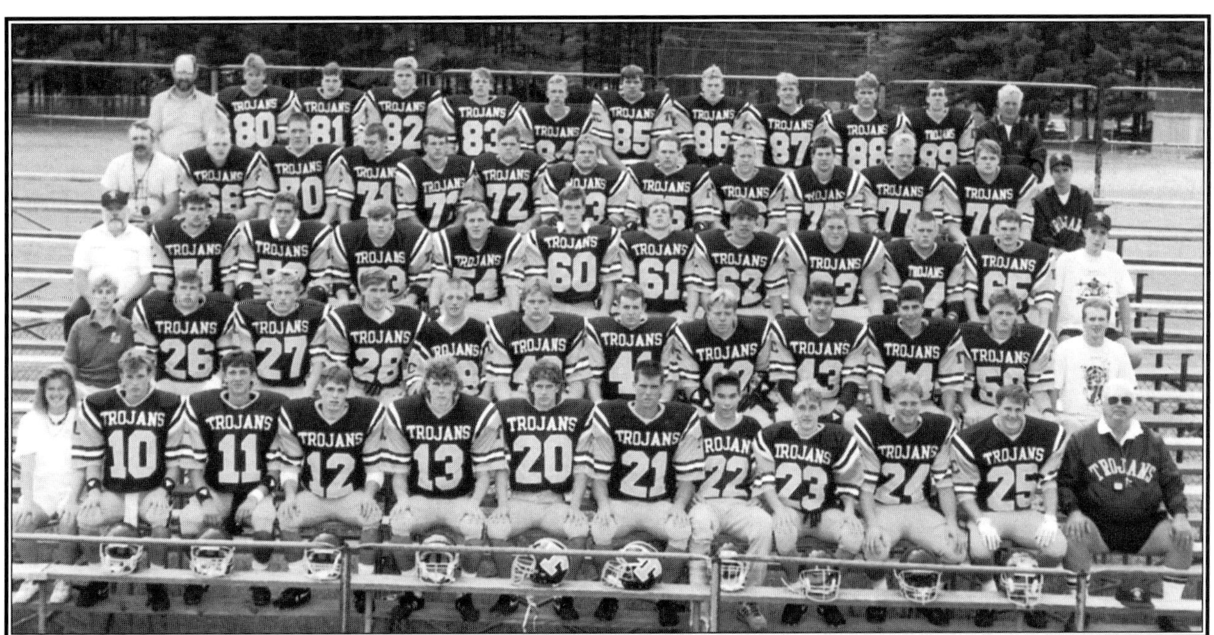

The 1991 Trojans, Coach Jim Ooley's last team before his retirement. Back Row: Coach Ken May, Karl Schultz, Brian Esman, Jeff Gregory, Joe Thomas, Justin Leuenberger, Mike Schmidt, Kain Simmerman, Dave Baumann, Carson Rose, Cody Klingelsmith, Coach Budd Tompkins. Fourth Row: Coach Roger Wood, Tom Meier, Justin Melton, Dan Erfourth, Dave Sivits, Gary Francisco, Jeff Cozzens, Jason Fromholz, Tim Smith, Ryan Rompola, Josh Walter, Jeremy Hogue, Scott Harnick. Third Row: Coach Steve Simmons, Chris Burns, Jason Steed, Josh Howie, Eric Liggett, Justin Erickson, Josh Ruttkofsky, Eric Burtt, Jason Sleder, Travis Horn, Brian Kipke, Josh Kratky. Second Row: Trainer Amy Machata, Shawn Alpers, Maurie Dennis, Trent Fetters, Aaron Peoples, Greg Bright, John Lenzini, Bob Balderach, Craig Kashazta, Zac Gallegos, Matt Howell, Marlin Starkey. Front Row: Nicole Puffer, Jim Nagy, Matt Bourdo, Jeff Hall, Knute Zehner, Jason Piedmonte, Jason Dettwiler, Rob Sharp, A.J. Smith, Mike Pilon, Chris Knight, Head Coach Jim Ooley.

generous gift was not enough to complete all the construction now necessary on this old structure. A group of former players had the idea to form a non-profit organization called Between the Fences to raise private funds, in addition to Harry Running's gift, for the renovation of this school facility. After approaching Traverse City Area Public Schools (TCAPS), both groups felt that the alternative of trying for a bond issue would likely not pass since that would raise everyone's taxes. Soccer boosters soon joined this effort as soccer games were also played on Thirlby Field at that time. Since this overuse of the field often made the ground a muddy mess and soccer needed their own regulation-sized playing fields, the plan grew to include finding a home for soccer. Soccer parent Diane Portenga became president, former Trojan star Dave Whiteford began drawing up architectural plans and fundraising went into full gear.

Traverse City got off to a great start in 1994, winning its first three football games against Marquette, Escanaba and Detroit Cooley and outscoring their opponents, 107 to 7. After their awesome start at 3-0, the Trojans took a deep dive into the losing pool. The Trojans lost three straight games to Jackson Lumen Christi, Ann Arbor Pioneer, and their rivals the Big Reds of Muskegon. After the Trojans' 3-3 start they got back on the winning side by beating Alpena 26-6, yet the winning side exchanged hands against Okemos. Okemos shut out the Trojans 17-0, and Traverse City was once again even at 4-4. The final game of the season came against Benton Harbor at home where the Trojans put on a show. The Trojans kept Benton Harbor from scoring the whole game and defeated them 45-0. You could say that the game was "in the hands of the Trojans."

In the summer of 1995, Between the Fences tore down the south bleachers and old lights and replaced them with a pre-cast concrete bleacher system plus new, more effective lighting. That fall, the Trojans closed out Coach Wood's last season with another 5-4 record after beating some very impressive teams. As a tribute to Roger Wood's impact on his players, parent Cam Howie stated, "My son Josh [1991 team member] said following his college football career that Coach Wood taught him everything he needed to know about high school and college football. No coach in his experience taught him more."

Much activity occurred in 1996. The north side of the old Thirlby stadium, as well as the press box, came down to make way for concrete seating on that side with a new press box above. Sections were also added to the previous year's bleachers on the south side which now increased the stadium's seating capacity from 4,500 to 6,000.

At the first home game, the new stadium was dedicated as the Harry T. Running Stadium at Thirlby Field in recognition of the gift that began the renovation project. In addition, that fall marked the 100th anniversary of Traverse City football, which was celebrated at the first home game as well as at a centennial banquet the preceding night that saw the return of many Trojan football personalities. Ken May made his debut as head coach amidst these festivities.

In his first year as head coach in 1996, Ken May broke the seemingly endless 5-4 record with an improvement to a 6-3 season. He led the Trojans to beat Bay City 33-28, the first time they had been beaten at home in over two years. Bay City, who was ranked No. 1 in the state, scored right off the bat, but the almighty Trojans answered immediately with a kick-off return for a touchdown, with both scores coming within the first minute of the game. It was the most memorable game of the season, because it was a true battle all the way to the end. They also faced an out-of-state team, Naperville North, the previous year's Illinois state champs, but lost by a score of 21-20.

In terms of football, Traverse City must be considered the undisputed champion of the Lake Michigan Athletic Conference. With an overall LMAC record of 81-29-2, the Trojans had nine outright conference titles and two ties. Muskegon and Muskegon Catholic were second with four titles and one tie, while Grand Haven and Mona

Shores tied for a title. This strength in one of Traverse City's conferences illustrates the success of the Trojan football program as it has been recognized as a state power over the past 100 years.

CLASS A FOOTBALL ALL-STATE

First Team

1944	John Ott	
1951	Budd Tompkins	
1953	Dave Bowers	
1959	Doug Bickle	
1960	George Boehm	
1961	John Bowers	Ken Schmidt
1962	John Bowers	
1964	Bob Diller	
1965	Larry Yankee	
1667	Joe Thibedeau	
1968	Vic Cole	
1969	Steve Rollo	
1971	Dave Whiteford	
1974	Dave Halachukas	
1975	Mark Brammer	Rick Waters
1976	Chuck Fitzgerald	
1977	Mark Candey	Dan Leppek
1978	Doug Parshall	Tim Squires
1983	Rob McGuffin	Greg Bohn
1984	Mike Hayes	
1985	Gary Rakin	Tim Lamie
1986	Chris Bohn	
1987	Jon Merchant	
1988	Mark Burkholder	Mike Nadlicki
1990	Malachi Gallegos	Tias Decker
1991	Shawn Alpers	Jason Sleder
1992	Jeremy Hogue	Karl Schultz
1993	Carson Rose	
1996	Matt Brayton	Matt Kropf

FOOTBALL ALL-AMERICAN

1953	Dave Bowers
1971	Dave Whiteford
1975	Mark Brammer

TROJAN FOOTBALL COACHES

Beeman	1896-1897	Waldo Spruit	1921-1927
Elmer Brown	1898	G. MacDonald	1928-1935
Robert Walter	1899	Les Orr	1936-1939
No Record	1900	Fred Janke	1940-1941
Walton Gray	1901	Tharel Kanitz	1942-1946
No Record	1902-1909	Harold Andreas	1947-1948
Pat Thacker	1910-1912	Ed Graybiel	1949-1952
Dowden	1913	Irv Menzel	1953
Exerby 1914	Ed Schuknecht	1954-1956	
Sam Upton	1915-1916	Bob Bacon	1957-1966
Waldo Spruit	1917-1918	Jim Ooley	1967-1991
Anderson	1919	Roger Wood	1992-1995
A.J. Duncanson	1920	Ken May	1996-present

A portion of this football information was taken from excerpts of Record-Eagle *articles written by Ken Bell.*

2

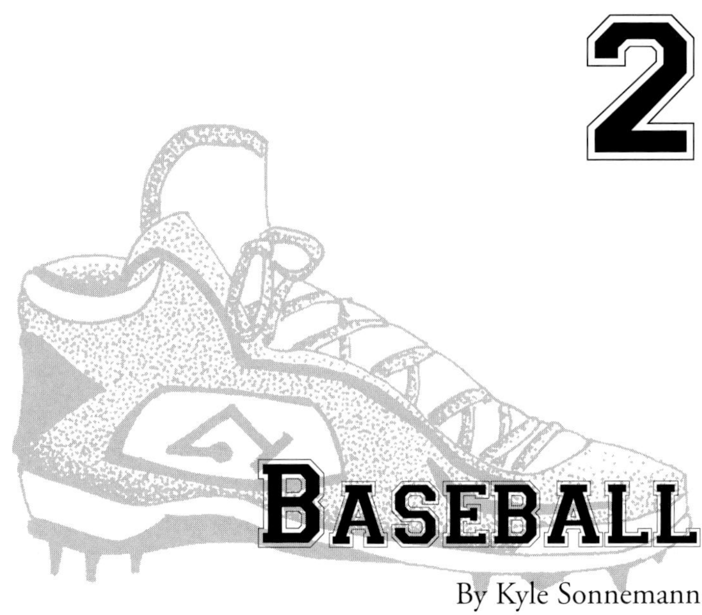

Baseball

By Kyle Sonnemann

"It was the last inning in a game between Traverse City and Cadillac. Cadillac had two outs, Traverse City was up by one run. Then the Cadillac head coach switched the batting order and sent up to the plate a different player than was in the batter's box. I was scoring and when I saw what happened, I checked the rule book and Cadillac was breaking the rules. The game was appealed by Traverse City to the umpire who after checking the books, which I kept, called the game in Traverse City's favor. Traverse City won seven to six."

– Peter Joe Garthe

Baseball has been America's pastime since the mid 1800s, and Traverse City is no exception. From being called "rounders" to what we call it today, baseball has been played all over the world. For 98 years this sport has been one of the leading ones in Traverse City sports history.

Traverse City began playing baseball interscholastically in May of 1898. Coaches were called "coachers" and often played when the team was having trouble or short on players. The first game was played at the 12th Street Park on May 1st. In that game Traverse City played Manistee, but lost 12-7.

In 1900, the most interesting game was played in the spring season. This game was played between Traverse City and Benda's Twirlers, another Traverse City team. Traverse City was at bat in the suspenseful last inning with two men out. All of a sudden, the third base coach made a mad dash for home, pretending to be a base runner. The ball was thrown wildly to the catcher, who missed the ball, and the runner scored. The catcher got the ball and tried to pick off the runner coming from second to third, but again the ball was thrown wildly, and the winning run scored. Benda's Twirlers vehemently protested the two runs because they were scored on a play that would have retired the side, had it not been for coacher's fake move. Traverse City's captain, with a demonstration of sportsmanship, gave the game to the other team.

Nine years later, there was enough passion for baseball to organize a nine-player team. The best athletes, however, gradually gave up their places on baseball teams to play football. But in 1909, the athletics department made a call for candidates and a good number of fans responded. After the men went into training under the guidance of Coach Wiley, the team realized that it had some expert players. Although the team did not have the deserved aid of the school, it nevertheless finished a very triumphant season.

The team of 1916 was one of the best at that time. Traverse City's first season game was played on the home diamond against Cadillac. Despite a hard fight to win by Cadillac, Traverse City was crowned the winner of this game. On to play Honor, and again the Trojans had the home diamond advantage. The "good-old" Black and Gold reigned supreme once more with a score of 9-1. Cadillac was the next opponent after Elk Rapids. Once before they had been defeated on Traverse City grounds, but they had a sneaky suspicion that they could turn the tables on their own field. Traverse City, of course, had something else in mind and with a final score of 10-6, totally wiped the thought of winning out of Cadillac's mind. In this game, Higgins pitched an outstanding game and struck out a total of 23 men with his machine gun-like arm. Higgins, with this game, broke the

The first Traverse City baseball team in 1898: (not in order) captain Frank Novotny, Steve Lardie, Alfred Ayers, Upsal Hobbs, Will Leighton, Bert Montague, Tom Wilhelm, Charles Walsh, Joe Ehrenberger and manager Ed Thirlby.

record for all games played on the Cadillac diamond and came within one strike-out away from the world's high school strike-out record.

In 1939, Traverse City had another great year in baseball. Garland House, business manager for the team, broached something different and new in the way that spring sports were played in Traverse City. He organized a baseball schedule and operation that really worked. Prior to this time, the baseball season had been hit or miss and interest was not always high. House had games booked with other schools in the whole northern Michigan area. New uniforms and other equipment or supplies were acquired and bought for this season. The team had to find a home diamond where they could play their games, which they found at the State Hospital where the state generously granted them the use of a diamond on their grounds.

It finally came time to get ready for the season opener, so coach Archie McLean announced the first practice. When the teenage boys heard about this, they decided to go to the practice. They were a grand bunch of young athletes. This season was a successful one, even though a short one. The team had restored hope that baseball was to be a stable part of the school's athletic curricula. It was the philosophy then, as it is today, that the more competitive sports available for the students, the better their high school experience.

What did the school do to keep baseball alive in Traverse? That is a good question. The high school founded a Baseball Club in 1940 in which the players, or any boys who enjoyed the "American Pasttime," could get together after school and talk

The 1916 Trojan baseball team.

about ways to keep baseball alive in the world's Cherry Capital. It was successful; baseball never was threatened again.

GAINING FAME THROUGH THE YEARS, baseball scaled to bizarre recruiting heights in spring of 1941. A whopping thirty-seven players reported to Irving Menzel who had become manager for that year. However, only 27 made the team for the entire season. They traveled to Benzonia for the opening contest, but lost 2-1. The Trojans came back with a good game of sportsmanship and a win against Elk Rapids 6-5. The team of 1941 walloped the rest of their opponents, except for the hard-hitting Leland team. The Black and Gold lost on the home diamond 6-1, only the second loss of that season.

Traverse City's 1943 team went undefeated for the whole season, out-batting, out-pitching, and out-fielding everyone in their path of wrath. Williamburg was to be the team's first victim, being shut out 6-0; the Trojans then went on to Leelanau to clean them out 3-1. Traverse City blasted Elk Rapids right out of the water with a 25-0 skunking. Williamsburg, the best all-around team, held Traverse City until the end when the Black and Gold defenders pulled it off with ease, 26-6. In a return engagement with Leelanau, the Trojans washed them out 15-5. Traverse City won the rest of the games in the season by a nice range of points.

In 1951, "Dutch" Kanitz, the new coach who had been around three years before, produced another great season. Winning 10 out of 11 games, this unstoppable team went down in Trojan sports history as one of the best teams with the one of the best seasons. The only loss of the season was against Northport which Traverse City avenged 9-6 when they met again a couple weeks later.

The last year of coaching for "Dutch" Kanitz, 1959, was yet another notable season. The Traverse nine pulled off a 7-3 winning record and finished

The 1940 Trojans, after baseball's revival as a high school sport: (not in order) Jim Stoll, Jim Sbonek, Charley Frye, Bill Howard, Garth Dean, Gene Stoll, Darwin Hopkins, Wey Wenzel, Dick Loomis, Leonard Brief, Gilford Brief, Dick Nelson, Lars Halverson, Jim Palmer, Ken Nelson, Eric Halverson, Dale Slocum, Ed Broomhead, Dick Stowe, Mort Bruyette, R.D. Langs.

as one of the runners-up in the Arrowhead Conference. Al Lockman took the coaching position after this year.

New coaches Ed Merchant and Ron Gray began the 1966 season with 20 very healthy athletes since the two coaches emphasized an important but usually overlooked aspect of baseball, that of physical conditioning. It paid off for them. The Trojans defeated Muskegon Catholic in the LMAC championships although they went on to be crushed by Muskegon. However, Muskegon was defeated in the finals by Benton Harbor to place the Trojans third in the conference.

Under head coach Dick Murphy, the Trojans proved to be an LMAC knockout in 1976. Traverse City finished second with a 7-2 record, only to be beaten out of first place by Muskegon Catholic Central. Craig Bush proved to be very valuable as he led the team in pitching and batting, allowing only five earned runs throughout the season. The overall season record was 14-8.

The 1981 season was one of rebuilding and gaining experience. Led by seniors Craig Elzinga and Bill Core, three sophomores, Dan Majerle, Scott Brautigam and Darren Hinsenkamp moved up during the season and learned a valuable lesson. Elzinga had the top batting average of .345, while pitcher Steve Majerle had the most RBI's with 10 and also topped the home run count with two. When it came to speed, Elzinga won in this category by ripping off 11 bases. Who did the team depend upon for pitching power? That was tacked on the shoulders of Mike Harger, Steve Robbins, Ray Sweeny and Steve Majerle, who together were a powerful combination. Sweeny commented on the season saying, "I think our offense had more

The undefeated 1943 Trojans: (not in order) Captain John Fouch, William Moore, Ken Manigold, VanDerMolen, Bud Savage, George Hay, Cecil Foote, Richard Bauman, William Sampson, John Ott, Donald Berg, Harold Guy, John Smedley.

Coach Al Elzinga is presented a gift by Phil Thiel as Coach Dick Murphy receives one from Bob Quick.

potential than we showed."

For the first time ever, the 1984 Trojan varsity baseball team won the league championship outright after tying for the LMAC championship the year before. They went 7-3 in the league which added up to an overall season record of 22-14. Coach John Gerhardt, who had been head coach since 1982, was very pleased with his team, particularly because in this season all the top athletes were juniors. "We had a tough season with having such a young team. Our goal was to break even for the first half, and just to do better in the second half of the season, which we succeeded in doing.

Seniors Todd Marone, John Marshall and Jeff Johnson wait for their turns at bat in 1984.

The baseball team which inaugurated the Thirlby Field diamond in 1951. Back Row: Coach Kanitz, Howard Hockstad, Calvin Kroupa, Thomas Gilpin, Albert Carlisle, Jack Emerson, Carroll Harger, Louis Rumanes, Topping, Fred Fuller. Front Row: Charles Johnson, Jack Franke, Ballentine, Jack Bush, Enger, James Wood, Thor Noteware, Ralph Smith, Alex Pitylak, Royal Bisel.

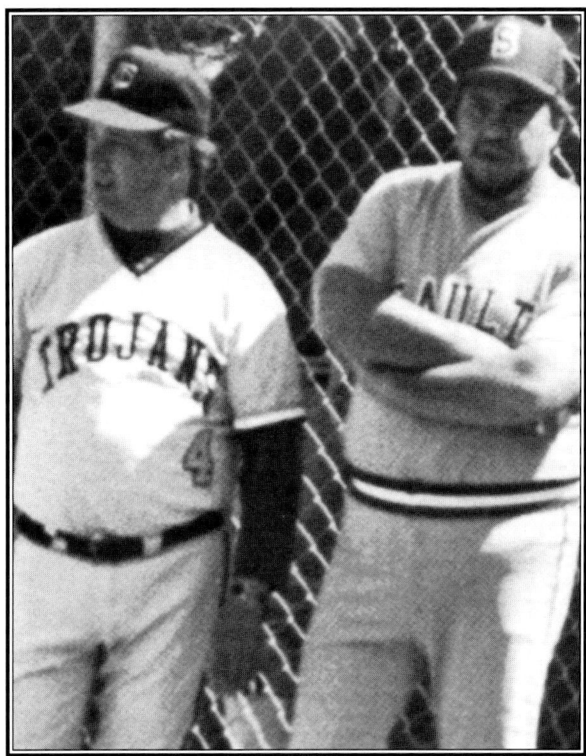

Coach John Gerhardt observes a 1988 game with the opposing coach.

All the talent came together at the end."

In 1985, the Trojans won their third straight championship in the last year of the LMAC. These were the Trojans' only championships in the history of the league and Tony Mallwitz was the starting and winning pitcher in all three games.

Malachi Gallegos slides safely into base.

Frank Rokos, the Trojans' only All-Stater in baseball, with a 12-0 record in 1992.

The Trojan baseball team was again a record-setting one in 1988. The most important record was 30 wins and seven losses. Traverse City had seven players who earned their third varsity letter. Jon Merchant was voted Most Valuable Player and Bruce Burdick received the Coaches' Award. Despite their riveting performance through the season, the team missed their chance to play districts with a 3-1 loss to archrival Alpena.

Since Alpena was the leader in many high school sports in 1993, they became the prey of all Trojan sports teams. "Everyone wants to beat Alpena; they're the biggest rival to Traverse City," said Brent Straitiff '95. Midland Dow was yet another rival to the Trojans. The varsity team met their match with this team and their flawless pitcher, too. Yet despite the loss, the team was still able to keep its sense of humor. "We're a bunch of jokesters. We joke around a lot...," said Andy Low '95.

But on the serious side, baseball has had an excellent run in the last 98 years. In recent years, several Trojans have won distinctive recognition. In 1993, Frank Rokos pitched his team to 12 wins and no losses to become, to coach John Gerhardt's knowledge, the Trojans' only first team All-State baseball player. Also in 1993, John Lenzini received a Michigan High School Baseball Coaches Scholarship to Indiana University. In 1996, Kevin Sonnemann was awarded the MHSAA Scholar-Athlete Award in baseball.

TRAVERSE CITY HAS NEVER WON A DISTRICT BASEBALL TITLE, but has come heart-breakingly close four times in the last 14 years. They lost the championship game in 1983, 5-2 to Midland Dow; in 1992, 1-0 to Bay City Western; 5-4 to Mount Pleasant in 1993; and in 1996, 5-1 to eventual state champion Mount Pleasant.

Traverse City has recovered from almost losing the pastime to having it become one of the most popular sports for its students to play and enjoy. James Grey '92, said it all when he said, "I don't do drugs, I do baseball." So, cheers to the baseball athletes and cheers to the supporters and coaches. Take me out to the ball game!

CLASS A BASEBALL ALL-STATE

1993	Frank Rokos

TROJAN BASEBALL COACHES

1909	Coach Wiley
1939	Archie McLean
1941	Irv Menzel
1951	"Dutch" Kanitz
1960	Al Lockman
1966	Ed Merchant & Ron Gray
1976	Dick Murphy
1982 - present	John Gerhardt

TROJAN BASEBALL RECORDS

Most career home runs	13	John Ansted Dan Majerle
Most home runs in a season	4	Dean Galla Vic Breithaupt Ed Thaxton
Most RBI's in a season	46	Ed Thaxton
Season high batting average	.486	Tom Haney
Career high batting average	.417	Brad Ballentine
Most career victories by a pitcher	16	Andy McCombs
Most season victories by a pitcher	12	Frank Rokos
Best team record	1992	33-7

3

Boys Track and Field

By Aaron Dennis

To reach a goal we must at times run with the wind, other times against it.... But we must certainly run, not walk or stand still.
– Author Unknown

There is no shot clock. No power plays. There will never be a last second touchdown. There are no goals to score. No out of bounds. Track and field is an anomaly amongst high school sports. Only its cousin cross-country is similar.

The Traverse City boys track team has been one of the top programs in the state of Michigan for many years. Since track and field became interscholastic, the Traverse City team has won the regional championship eight times and in 1992 won the state championship.

Unlike other sports, there are no tryouts for track and field. There is no limit on the size of the team. However, for track meets only a limited number of athletes can compete. All the members of the team get to participate, but only the top athletes attend the more competitive meets.

Track and field consists of 17 events: high jump, long jump, pole vault, shot put, discus, 100-, 200-, 400-, 1600-, and 3200- meter runs, 110-meter high hurdles, 300-meter intermediate hurdles, and 400-, 800-, 1600-, and 3200- meter relays.

Athletes choose to compete in those events for many different reasons. Former runner Matt Drinkert '91 said, "Track was a great way to get in shape and to prove your physical capabilities to your peers and others." Current coach John Lober thinks students compete in track to find a place to fit in. "Let's face it," he states, "kids want to be a part of a group. Some groups are pretty bad; they involve gangs and drugs. But there are positive gangs, like football, basketball, or track gangs."

Lober believes that playing sports is not easy and therefore builds character. He says that athletes "learn tough lessons about hard work, sticking to things and getting knocked down and getting back up. Nobody said life was a bed of roses. But we can teach them to cope with things better."

SINCE ALL OF THE EVENTS IN TRACK AND FIELD ARE TIMED OR MEASURED, setting records is an extra incentive for the athletes. Most of the current high school records have been set in the last ten years, perhaps because of more effective training methods and better athletes. However, some records have been around for a very long time and may never be broken. For example, in 1982, All-Stater Jim Hensel pole vaulted 16'1/2." Not only is it the best vault ever at Traverse City Senior High, but it is also the best ever by a high school athlete in Michigan. Even more impressive, in terms of longevity, was the record set for the 110-meter intermediate hurdles by Bill Mann in 1955. His record of 14.0 seconds was challenged in 1982 by Scott Krupilski (with a time of 14.1 seconds) and more recently, in 1994, by Sam Sheffer (with a time of 14.29 seconds). But Mann's record still stands today.

Finally, there's John Lober. Lober has been coach of the boys track team since 1977. In 19 years he has led the team to five regional titles, two more than in the 48 years before he was named coach. Lober has been inducted into the Michigan High School Coaches Hall of Fame, has twice been named both M.I.T.C.A. and the M.H.S.C.A. Coach of the Year, and was selected the Region 4 National Coach of the Year in 1991.

Coach Lober's record speaks for itself. Since he took over as coach in 1977, the boys varsity and junior varsity teams have combined for a record 210 wins, 28 losses, and 2 ties. No other track and field coach in Traverse City history has achieved such success.

TRACK HISTORY

By Pat Weber with John Lober

From the text of the book, *The Grand Traverse,*

The 1992 boys team which won the first Trojan track state championship.

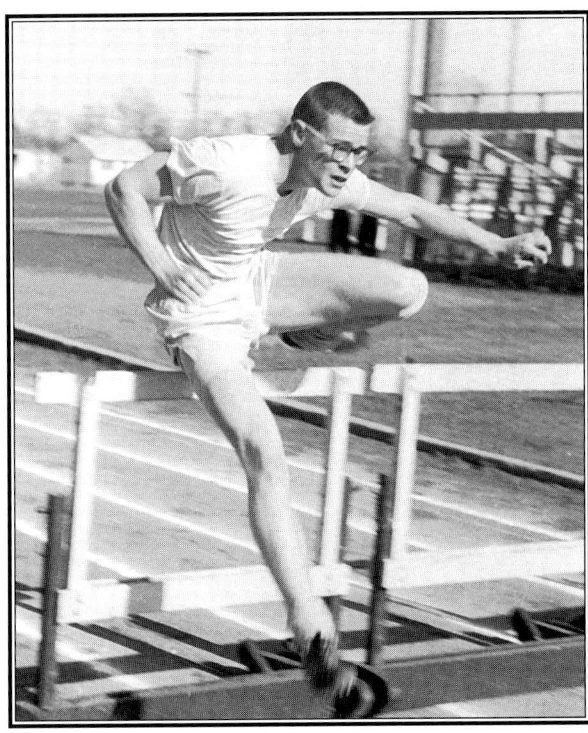

Bill Mann '59 with 14.0 in high hurdles, a record which stands today.

written by students in 1940 about the history of the area, we confirmed information regarding track in the first decade of the twentieth century. In fact, Traverse City's track team won the Northern Michigan championship in 1910 and took fourth place in the state interscholastic meet.

However, track and field predates even this 1910 account. The second high school annual from 1901 records a field day (they had them sometimes both in the fall and spring) where Ed Boyer seemed to be a one-man team. He won the 20 yard dash, the broad jump, the running high jump and the 100 yard dash. Herb Somers won the pole vault at 7 ft. and James Milliken won the running broad jump at 17 ft. A woman named Barbara Corbett won the lone girls race. Of course, Title IX was some 71 years into the future then.

The track team of 1906 won their first meet with Manistee, but placed second at the large five-school meet they were expected to win in Charlevoix. Oscar Amsbuechler was the team captain and at over 200 lbs., nobody crossed him. He went on to compete in the United States Interscholastic Meet in Chicago in the discus and hammer throw, but came home with no ribbons. Team members in 1906 included Charles Hodge, Harold Titus, Ed Fellers, Ernest Miller, Robert Walker, George Whiting, Ralph Hunter, Willard Getchell, Roy McGarry and Leon Slater. The team of 1907 was captained by Charles Hodge. Coach Davis issued diet restrictions that ordered the team to not eat any cake, cookies, candy, pork, peanuts, doughnuts nor pie.

THE MOST SUCCESSFUL HOME TRACK MEET (and probably the first multi-school meet) took place in 1908. Having Manistee and Petsokey unable to attend meant that Traverse City would easily come out on top against Charlevoix, Pellston, Frankfort and East Jordan. Pellston and East Jordan each sent only one representative. Pierson was the guy with all the ribbons at the end of the day and a hero for his Traverse City Central High School crowd. Winning the high jump, broad jump, pole vault, high hurdles and low hurdles put this track star on the map. Pierson's long jump mark of 19'9 1/2" made him a state champion. The 1909 4 X 200 relay team made up of Harry Wait, Walter Hanson, Fred Pierson and Lester Simpson set a mark of 1:46.6 and earned them the grade as state champions.

The 1906 half-mile relay team: Ed Feller, Charles Hodge, Ralph Hunter, Ernest Miller.

Lloyd Cleveland was elected team captain in 1911 with sights on another great year in track. However, the most successful 1910 team had featured mostly seniors so perhaps this was a rebuilding year. Late in May the senior class ran their annual excursion to Petsokey on the steamship Missouri, taking the track team along to hopefully once again secure the Northern Michigan championship. For the first time in some five to six years, the boys placed second rather than first, losing to Petoskey.

Hugh Desmond captained the 1912 team while Mr. Voelker, a member of the faculty and former Olivet track star, was coach. Track then seemed to disappear for about 18 years and we are left to wonder why.

Fast forward to 1931, when Erich Sleder set records in the 100 yd. dash at 10.1 and the 200 yd. dash at 22.6 which held for 30 years. Then in 1933, state recognition came to the relay team of Julius Sleder, Bill McGarry, Willard Harris and Roy Lannin. This group was ranked third in the state. Trackmen were called "Thinclads" back then, and the toughest competition seemed to be with Cadillac. The 1939 team featured state champion Curt Alward with a mark of 23.7 in the low hurdles. Other standouts included Bob Loomis in pole vault, Bill Milliken in the high jump and Bob Drake, Mac Cox and Jack Renehan in the 440, 880 and mile respectively.

Coach Irv Menzel guided the 1940 track team to the first "modern" regional championship (the boys basketball team won the Class B state championship that year too). Russ Canute made All-State in the 220 low hurdles. Runners-up in 1943, then once again champs in 1946, coach Lee

1982 boys track team members. Row 1: Scott Krupilski, Jim Paffi, Phil McKiernan, Brandon Morgan, Charlie Loesel; Row 2- Blaine Bendickson, Chris Miller; Row 3: Karl Ensfield, Tim Mason, Keith Peters, Craig Wells, Jim Hensel, Kurt Noller, Lisa Boike-Mgr.; Row 4- Ken Orchard, Greg Nienhouse, Joe Neihardt, Don Mastromatteo, Mark Blodgett, Ken Neal, Kevin Nelson; Row 5-Coaches Joe Neihardt, Tim Donahey, Jeff Lasich, John Lober, Mgr. Rick Fuller. Included in this team were 3 high school All-Americans, 2 national champions and 3 state champions.

Brannock had some great teams. Pete Krohn was the hurdle and high jump star. Dan Owen was Traverse City's "dashman" and "Cy" Lemcool was state interscholastic half-mile champ. Ed Vanderley was the state shot put champion in 1940 and 1942.

TRACK MEETS ORIGINALLY TOOK PLACE AT THE FAIRGROUNDS which are now the Civic Center. Today, elementary track programs run their meets each spring in this same location. In about 1929, track moved to Thirlby Field and remained there until 1978 when an all-weather track surface was completed at Traverse City Senior High. This track was recently resurfaced by Between the Fences.

The long tradition of excellence over the years has been guided by approximately 15 track coaches. From those early 5-8 man teams, high school track has evolved to where some 150 students participate each season. Long train trips have been replaced by bus trips in and out of state. A strong elementary feeder program, along with excellent junior high recruitment, is the basis for the successful track and field program at the high school.

Track greats through the years include Bob Pemberton, who in 1954 set the record in the 100 yard dash at 9.95. He was the first sprinter to break 10.0. He also ran the 220 in 22.2 and led that year's team to the regional title. The next year, Fran Wanageshik was the first high jumper to make the 6' mark; he made All-State in 1955. Then Bill Mann set a 14.0 record in the high hurdles in 1955 to be the # 2 all-time record holder in Michigan. In 1957, Dick Bezile was named All-State after becoming the state champion in low hurdles with a record time of 20.10. In 1966, Jim Anderson was the first long jumper to go over 22'. Bill Oberling ran a 9:57.7 two-mile in 1967, while Dale Root was the first 50' shot putter in 1970. In 1972, Stan Robbins was the first runner under 2:00 in the 880 and under 4:30 in the mile. Kurt Friese was the first 400m runner to break under 50.0 in 1978 and Mark Herman was the first sophomore to break 2:00 in the 880. Terry Goodell made the All-State team in both 1979 and 1980 in the discus.

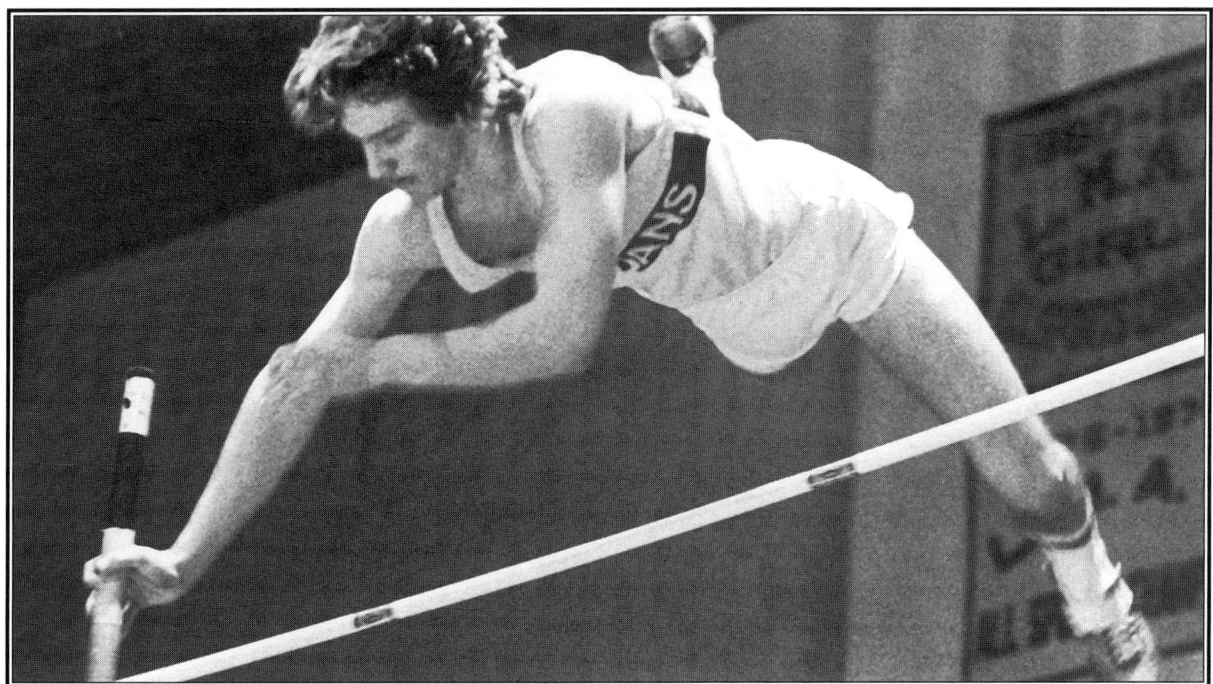

All-American Jim Hensel, Michigan's first pole vaulter to clear 16'.

Then came the 1982 team to beat all teams, containing several All-Americans and numerous record-breakers. John Lober adds, "One of the greatest teams ever at Traverse City Senior High was in 1982, when the team won the regional meet and ended up in fifth place in the state." At meets throughout the season were individual performances that are still in the record books. Team members Scott Krupilski and Jim Hensel led the way. Krupilski, Traverse City's best hurdler, placed in four events in the state meet with: a state record pole vault at 15'8"; 14.4 in the high hurdles; 1:29.6 in 800 relay; and 37.1 in the 300 hurdles. In addition, he was a national champion in decathalon. The Trojans' top pole vaulter, Jim Hensel, set five school records: 16'1/2" pole vault; 10.9 100m; 22.2 200m; 43.7 400 relay, 1.29.6 800 relay. Krupilski and Hensel made All-American in 1982, while Mark Blodgett was named All-State and All-American in 1983.

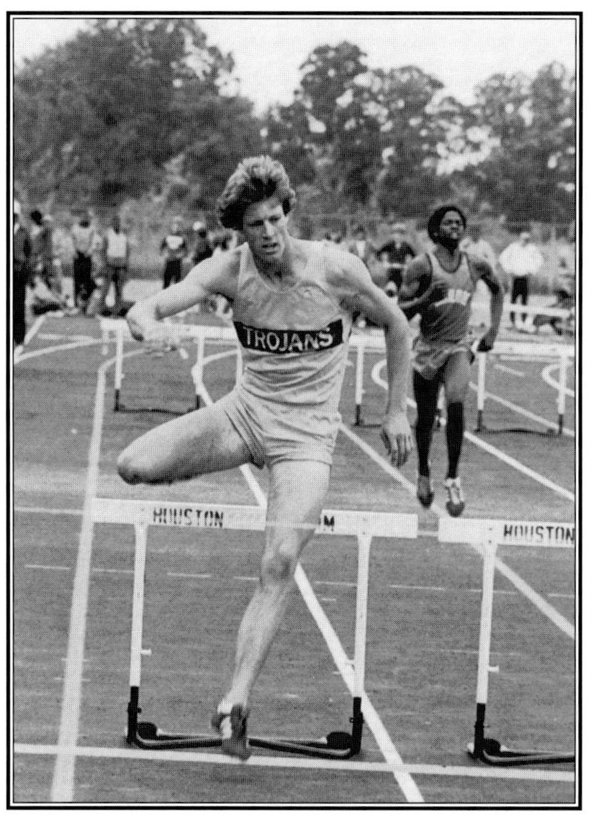

All-American and state champion Scott Krupilski running hurdles, one of the events in which he starred.

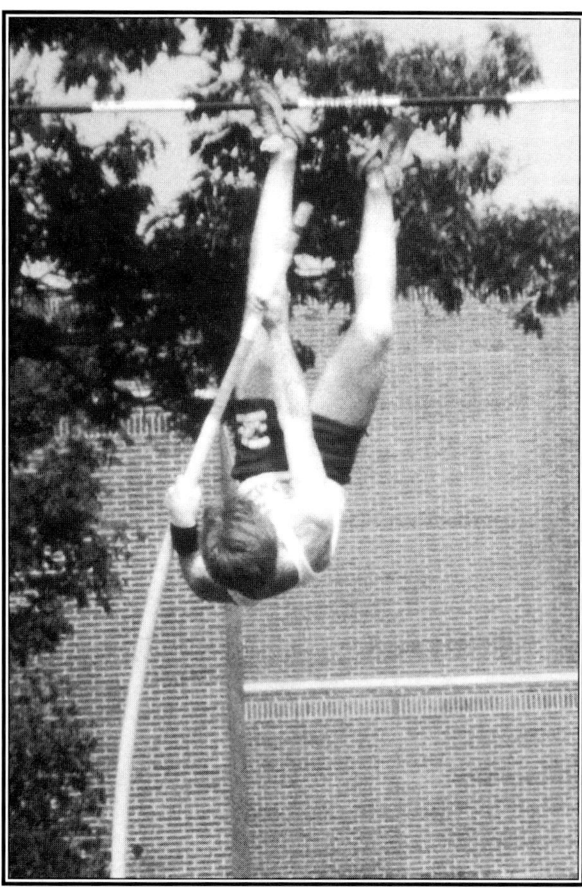

A state champion and All-American in the pole vault, Mark Blodgett exhibits the strength of the early 1980s boys track team.

POLE VAULTING HAS HAD A FINE TRADITION at Traverse City Senior High beginning with Jack Bensley in 1941. He cleared 11' with a bamboo pole. Loren "Scrub" Bensley in 1954 vaulted with a steel pole to 11'21 1/2". Once fiberglass came onto the track scene, vaulters had to adjust. Joe Neihardt moved from steel to fiberglass in 1963 and set a school record vault of 13'2". He went on to coach from 1967 to 1976 and saw his vaulters go 14', 15', and 16' in those years. David McGlothlin '76 was the first to hit the 14' mark. Then Jim Lotan '77 made the 15' mark and became an All-Stater when he went 15'1". Hensel cleared 16' in 1982, but it was Krupilski who won the state meet then with a 15'8" vault. Traverse City has had five different state champions in pole vaulting. Each March a pole vault clinic is held here which attracts track personnel state-wide.

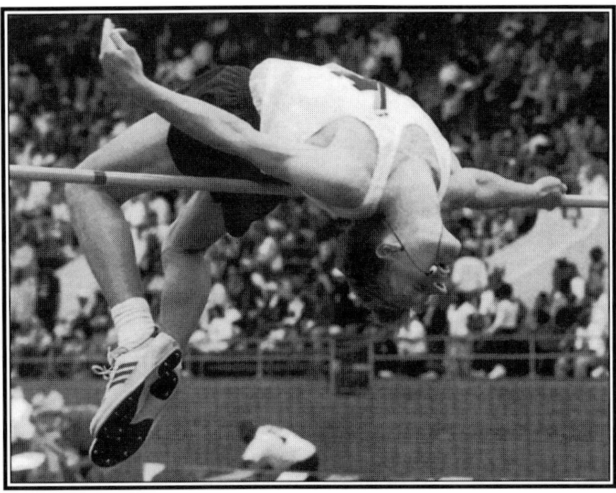

In 1990, Ben Ludka became Traverse City's fourth All-American with a state record high jump of 7' 1/4".

All-Staters in the next few years included Greg Nienhouse in pole vault; Dan Sievers in discus; Bim Scala in pole vault in 1985 and 1986 (set a state record in 1986 at 15'9"); Tom Guy in pole vault; Ben Ludka in high jump - he was also named All-American with a state record of 7'1/4 ". John Lober was named Coach of the Year in 1982 and writer Ken Bell was honored in 1991 as a track official and sportswriter for his 30 years of service. The Ken Bell Track Meet was inaugurated in his honor.

Track has had a long and honorable position on the sports scene at Traverse City Central Senior High. Kids who run track become life-long fitness experts and carry the memories of representing their school in a sport that creates winners of anyone participating. Cheers to all of them.

John Lober, who has been the highly successful head boys coach since 1977.

BOYS TRACK & FIELD ALL-AMERICAN

1982	Scott Krupilski	1983	Mark Blodgett
1982	Jim Hensel	1990	Ben Ludka

TROJAN BOYS TRACK HEAD COACHES

1929-1930	Gordon MacDonald	1952-1953	Dean Wilson
1931-1933	Art Richter	1954-1955	John Picard
1934-1936	Gordon MacDonald	1956-1962	Richard Frank
1937-1939	Les Orr	1963-1965	Jim Ooley
1940	Irv Menzel	1966-1968	Dan Young
1941-1942	Phil Balyeat	1969-1976	Joe Neihardt
1943-1947	Lee Brannuchs	1977-present	John Lober
1948-1951	Frank Russell		

TRAVERSE CITY TRACK & FIELD HALL OF FAME

1940	Russ Canute	220 Low Hurdles	All-State
1940	Ralph Vanderley	Shot Put	All-State
1942	Ralph Vanderley	Shot Put	State Champion
1955	Fran Wanageshik	High Jump	All-State
1955	Bill Mann	High Hurdles	
1957	Dick Bezile	180 Low Hurdles	All-State
1963	Joe Neihardt	Pole Vault	All-State, TC's first 13'er
1977	Dave McGlothlin	Pole Vault	TC's first 14'er
1977	Jim Lotan	Pole Vault	All-State, TC's first 15'er
1979	Terry Goodell	Discus	All-State
1980	Terry Goodell	Discus	All-State
1980	Jim Hensel	Pole Vault	All-State
1981	Scott Krupilski	Pole Vault	State Champion
1982	Scott Krupilski	Pole Vault	All-State, All-American, National Champion Decathalon, #6 all-time
1982	Jim Hensel	Pole Vault	All-State, All-American, Michigan's first vaulter to clear 16'
1982	Mark Blodgett	Pole Vault	All-State
1982	John Lober	Coach	Mich. H.S. Coach of the Year
1983	Mark Blodgett	Pole Vault	State Champion, All-American
1984	Greg Nienhouse	Pole Vault	State Champion
1984	Dan Sievers	Discus	All-State
1985	Bim Scala	Pole Vault	All-State
1986	Bim Scala	Pole Vault	State Champion
1987	Tom Guy	Pole Vault	State Champion
1990	Ben Ludka	High Jump	All-State, All-American
1991	Ken Bell	Sportswriter/Official	30+ years as sportswriter & official at TCHS track meets

OTHER GREATS

1931	Erich Sleder	100 yd. dash - 10.1; 220 yd. dash - 22.6 (dash records that held for 30 years)
1954	Bob Pemberton	100 yd. dash - 9.95; first sprinter to break 10.0 in dash; ran 220 in 22.2; led team to regional title
1955	Fran Wanageshik	First 6' high jumper
1959	Bill Mann	14.0 in high hurdles, the #2 all-time record in Michigan
1961	Jim Anderson	First long jumper over 22'
1963	Joe Neihardt	TC's first great vaulter; coached TC championship vaulters & track teams 1968-1976
1967	Bill Oberling	First 2-miler under 10.00 (9:57.7)
1970	Dale Root	First 50' shot put
1972	Stan Robbins	First runner under 2:00 in 880 and under 4:30 in mile
1978	Kurt Friese	First 400m runner under 50.0 (49.5)
1980	Mark Herman	First sophomore to break 2:00 in 880 91:59.6)
1982	Scott Krupilski	Placed in 4 events in state meet: 1st in pole vault -state record 15'8"; 4th in HH 14.1; 5th in 880m relay 1:29.6; 5th in 300 LH 37.1; national champion in decathalon
1982	Jim Hensel	5 school records: 16' 1/2" pole vault; 10.9 100m; 22.2 200m; 43.7 400 relay; 1:29.6 800 relay
1986	Bim Scala	State meet pole vault record 15'9"
1987	Mike Poehlman	First long jumper over 23'
1990	Ben Ludka	State Class A high jump record 7' 1/4"; school record 300m IM hurdles 38.6
1992	Shawn Alpers	All-State in shot put & discus; school records
1995	Kevin Brokaw	First under 9:30 in 3200m (9:25.1)

TRAVERSE CITY HIGH SCHOOL TRACK STATE CHAMPIONS

Year	Event	Class	Name	Mark
1908	Long Jump	A	Fred Pierson	19'9 1/2"
1909	4 x 200	B	Harry Wait Walter Hanson Fred Pierson Lester Simpson	1:42.6
1939	Low Hurdles	B	Curt Alward	23.7
1942	Shot Put	B	Ed Vanderley	47'4"
1946	800	B	Carl Lemcool	2:06.3
1957	Low Hurdles	A	Dick Bezile	20.10
1981	Pole Vault	A	Scott Krupilski	14'10 1/4"
1982	Pole Vault	A	Scott Krupilski	15'8"
1983	Pole Vault	A	Mark Blodgett	14'5"
1984	Pole Vault	A	Greg Nienhouse	14'5"
1986	Pole Vault	A	Bim Scala	15'9"
1987	Pole Vault	A	Tom Guy	13'11"

SCHOOL RECORDS

Event	Mark	Name	Year	Honor
Shot Put	57'11"	Shawn Alpers	1992	All-State
Discus	170'3"	Shawn Alpers	1992	All-State
High Jump	7' 1/4"	Ben Ludka	1990	All-American
Pole Vault	16' 1/2"	Jim Hensel	1982	All-American
Long Jump	23'5 1/2"	Mike Poehlman	1987	
110m High Hurdles	14.0	Bill Mann	1955	
100m Dash	10.9	Jim Hensel	1982	
200m Dash	22.2	Jim Hensel	1982	
400m Dash	49.5	Kurt Friese	1978	
800m Run	1:55.4	Jeff Linger	1988	
1600m Run	4:21.7	Jeff Linger	1988	
3200m Run	9:25.1	Kevin Brokaw	1995	
300m Int. Hurdles	38.6	Ben Ludka	1990	
400m Relay	43.7	Hensel, Bendickson, Ensfield, McKiernan	1982	
800m Relay	1:29.6	Hensel, Krupilski, Morgan, Paffi	1982	
1600m Relay	3:24.8	Smith, Doty, Wetter, Cook	1994	
3200m Relay	7:56.65	Smith, Namboothiri, Wadkins, Hayes	1991	

SCHOOL RECORDS (Continued)

6400m Relay	18:09.4	Wheeler, Decker, Wolf, Brokaw	1995
Sprint Med. Relay 400-200-200-400	2:31.2	Collins, Lobdell, Harris, Flores	1988
Sprint Med. Relay 800-200-200-400	3:43.5	Cook, Smith, Schulz, Rose	1993
Middle Dist. Relay	5:48.8	Montie, Smith, Schulz, Franko	1993
Dist. Med. Relay (set indoors)	10:43.3	Smith, Wetter, Cook, Wheeler	1994
High Hurdle Shuttles	62.2	McComb, Sheffer, Howie, Sharp	1992
Low Hurdles Shuttles	58.54	McComb, Sheffer, Howie, Sharp	1992

ACADEMIC ALL-STATE

1991	Jay Namboothiri
1992	Jeff Gregory
	Andy Hayes
	Josh Howie
	Ken Neal
1993	Sam Sheffer
1994	John Cook
1995	Kevin Brokaw
	Adam Wheeler
1996	Mike Cell
	Charlie Wolf
1997	Joe Agostinelli
	Joel Gaff
	Kevin Hall
	Robert Haveman
	Eric Houghton
	Matt Kropf
	Brent Sheffer

ALL-TIME TOP TEN

HIGH JUMP

Ben Ludka	7'1/4" *#$	1990
Jeff Gregory	6'9" $ *	1992
Charlie Loesel	6'8"	1984
Rob Sharp	6'8" $	1991
Keith Peters	6'7"	1982
KenNeal	6'6"	1982
Scott Krupilski	6'5"	1982
Sam Sheffer	6'5"$	1993
Marty Stevenson	6'3"	1993
Jay Gainforth	6' 2.5"	1994

LONG JUMP

Mike Poehlman	23'51/2"	1987
Scott Krupilski	22'71/2"	1982
Jim McGlothlin	22'41/2"	1973
Scott Zager	22'31/2"	1978
Ken Neal	22'31/2"	1982
John Loesel	22'3"	1983
Dave Whiteford	22'21/2"	1971
Jim Anderson	22'11/2"	1961
Charlie Loesel	21'10"	1984
Joe Neihardt	21'91/2"	1983

POLE VAULT

Jim Hensel	16'1/2" *#$	1982
Bim Scala	15'9" *^	1986
Scott Krupilski	15'8" *^	1982
Mark Blodgett	15'6" *^$	1983
Jim Lotan	15'1" *	1977
Joe Thomas	15'0" *	1991
Steve Kent	15'0"	1986
Tom Guy	15'0" *^	1987
Josh Howie	15'0" @	1992
Dave McGlothlin	14'7"	1977
Greg Nienhouse	14'6" *^	1984

SHOT PUT

Shawn Alpers	57'11" *	1992
Terry Goodell	55'8"	1980
Greg Bright	55'6"	1993
Dan Sievers	54'7"	1985
Don Mastromatteo	54'61/2"	1982
Dave Sanford	54'5"'	1993
Jim Johns	54'31/2"	1988
John Johnson	53'61/2"	1971
Tim Richards	53'41/2"	1987
Matt Averill	53'2"	1995

DISCUS

Shawn Alpers	170'3" *	1992
Terry Goodell	169'8" *	1980
Tim Lamie	163'3"	1986
Don Mastromatteo	162'8"	1982
Dan Sievers	161'6" *	1985
Matt Kropf	159'4"	1996
Kevin Nelson	152'4"	1983
Joe Neihardt	149'2"	1983
Arne Sarya	146'11"	1979
Charlie Brammer	143'8"	1982

100 METERS

Jim Hensel	10. 9	1982
A.J. Smith	11.03	1992
Fred Kundrata	11.1	1979
Mark Krupilski	11.1	1983
Greg Nienhouse	11.1	1984
Scott Harris	11.1	1988
Eric Murphy	11.17	1995
Carl Ensfield	11.2	1982
Tim Mason	11.2	1982
Sean Flory	11.2	1990
Blaine Bendickson	11.2	1982

200 METERS

Jim Hensel	22.2	1982
Bob Pemberton	22.2	1954
Bill Myers	22.3	1964
Jim Wakefield	22.5	1970
Scott Krupilski	22.6	1982
Brandyon Morgan	22.6	1982
Kurt Friese	22.7	1978
Fred Kundrata	22.7	1981
Scott Rowe	22.8	1981
Scott Harris	22.8	1988
Rob Sharp	22.8	1991

400 METERS

Kurt Friese	49.5	1978
Ben Lautner	50.2	1969
Scott Krupilski	50.4	1982
Brandom Morgan	50.4	1982
Jeff Lasich	50.6	1980
Jason Smith	50.6	1991
Bill Myers	50.6	1964
A.J. Smith	50.6	1994
Nathan Unkefer	50.9	1996
Scott Rowe	51.1	1981

$ M.I.T.C.A. Indoor State Champion ^ State Champion * All - State
#1 All-Time in State @ Academic All-State

ALL-TIME TOP TEN

800 METERS

Jeff Linger	1:55.4	1988
John Elsenheimer	1:56.2	1978
Jason Smith	1:56.4	1991#
Stan Robbins	1:57.0	1973
Jon Cook	1:57.5	1994
Mike Franko	1:57.6	1993#
Maecus Montie	1:57:7	1993
Kevin Clarke	1:57.7	1985
Ken Neal	1:58.5	1982
Mark Herman	1:58.8	1982
Brian Schaub	1:58.8	1988

1600 METERS

Mike Cell	4:19.8	1996
Jeff Linger	4:21.7	1986
Kevin Brokaw	4:22.0	1995
Mike Franko	4:23.2	1993
John Elsenheimer	4:23.2	1978
Adam Wheeler	4:24.4	1995
Ken Orchard	4:24.4	1985
Stan Robbins	4:26.6	1973
Andy Hayes	4:26.8	1992
Craig Malmstrom	4:27.8	1984
Tom McKaye	4:28.3	1983
Charlie Wolf	4:28.4	1996

3200 METERS

Kevin Brokaw	9:25.1	1995
Charliw Wolf	9:29.8*	1996
Mike Decker	9:36.0	1995
Jeff Linger	9:36.6	1988
Adam Wheeler	9:41.0	1995
Kurt Johnson	9:43.0	1983
Eric Houghton	9:43.0	1996
Ken Orchard	9:43.5	1983
Andy Hayes	9:46.0	1991
Jim Wise	9:48.0	1977

110 METER HIGH HURDLES

Bill Mann	14.0	1959*
Scott Krupilski	14.1	1982
Rob Sharp	14.25*	1992
Sam Sheffer	14.29	1994#
John Benedict	14.4	1977
Ben Ludka	14.5	1990
Scott Hariis	14.5	1989
Tom VanAlstine	14.67	1987
Ken Neal	14.8	1982
Joe Tanis	14.9	1973

300 METER INTERMEDIATE HURDLES

Ben Ludka	38.6	1990^
Rob Sharp	40.5	1992
Steve Oosse	40.5	1992
Scott Harris	40.7	1989
Marc McComb	40.7	1992
Matt Kropf	40.76	1996
Sam Sheffer	41.1	1992
Joel Gaff	41.57	1996
Mike Ascione	41.6	1994
Jason Whittaker	42.0	1996

* #4 All-time in State ^ #8 All-time in State

ALL-TIME TOP TEN
-RELAYS-

400 METER RELAY

HENSEL, BENDICKSON, ENSFIELD MCKIERNAN	43.7	1982
HENSEL, ROWE, MASON, ENSFIELD	44.1	1981
SHARP, PEOPLES, DETTWILER, SCHULTZ	44.1	1996
PLUMMER, SMITH, WHITTAKER, HITE	44.4	1996
BENEDICT, MCGLOTHLIN, UNDERWOOD, WYCKOFF	44.4	1977
NEIHARDT, MASON, ENSFIELD, KRUPILSKI	44.5	1983
ARNOLD,BARTONE, LOESEL, SCALA	44.6	1985
PARK, KNOWLES, GILMORE, STASINSKI	44.7	1973
HARRIS, LOBDELL, CANNON, CARTER	44.7	1989
SCHULTZ, DETTWILER, PEOPLES, SMITH	44.7	1992

800 METER RELAY

KRUPILSKI, HENSEL, MORGAN PAFFI	1:29.6	1982 *
ROWE, HENSEL, KRUPILSKI, MORGAN	1:30.6	1981
KAMRADT, GEIGER, CANDEY, LAUTNER	1:32.0	1969
MYERS, KORTOKRAX, ALLISON, HAMMER	1:32.2	1964
GILMORE, CHASE, KNOWLES, MCGLOTHLIN	1:32.3	1972
FRIESE, SLACK, WHITING, WYCKOFF	1:32.4	1977
KUNDRATA, WHITING, WHITING, CODDINGTON	1:32.4	1978
ARNOLD, PEAVLER, LOESEL, SCHWENTER	1:33.0	1985
DETTWILER, SCHULTZ, KASHAZTA, SMITH	1:33.08	1992

* 5th place in STATE

1600 METER RELAY

WETTER, DOTY, WHEELER, COOK	3:24.8	1994
FREISE, SLACK, WHITING ELSENHEIMER	3:25.6	1978
FRIESE, SLACK, ANDERSON, ROGERS	3:25.9	1977
HAYES, WADKINS, NAMBOOTHIRI, KASHAZTA	3:26.5	1992
KAMRADT, GEIGER, CANDEY, LAUTNER	3:27.0	1968
SMITH, MAREK, OOSSE, LUDKA	3:27.0	1990
ROWE, MCKIERNAN, MORGAN, REED	3:27.7	1981
SMITH, KASHAZTA, DETTWILER, NAMBOOTHIRI	3:27.7	1991
LANE, CHRISTOPHER, OGDEN, ROBBINS	3:28.4	1973
SEBRIGHT, SMITH, JONES, MYERS	3:28.4	1963

3200 METER RELAY

SMITH, NAMBOOTHIRI, WADKINS, HAYES	7:56.64	1991 *
FRANKO, COOK, WHEELER, MONTIE	7:57.4	1993 % All-State
WADKINS, FRANKO, HAYES, NAMBOOTHIRI	7:59.1	1992 @ All-State
COOK, DOTY, SMITH, WHEELER	8:00.1	1994 ^
CLARKE, PAUPORE, HENGESBACH, FIEGEL	8:00.9	1984
STONE, CELL, AGOSTINELLI, UNKEFER	8:02.0	1996
SMITH, MAREK, MANTHEI, VANWINGERDEN	8:09.0	1990 #
SCHAUB, COLLINS, MATA, LINGER	8:09.0	1988
CLARKE, CUNNINGHAM, CRAIN, SNELL	8:14.0	1985
WHEELER, FISHMAN, DECKER, BROKAW	8:14.0	1995
FLORES, TANONA, COLLINS, BROWN	8:21.5	1987

* 5th place in STATE
* 8th place in STATE

@ 2nd place in STATE
^ 6th place in STATE
%3rd place in STATE

ALL PERFORMANCES THRU 1996 SEASON

4

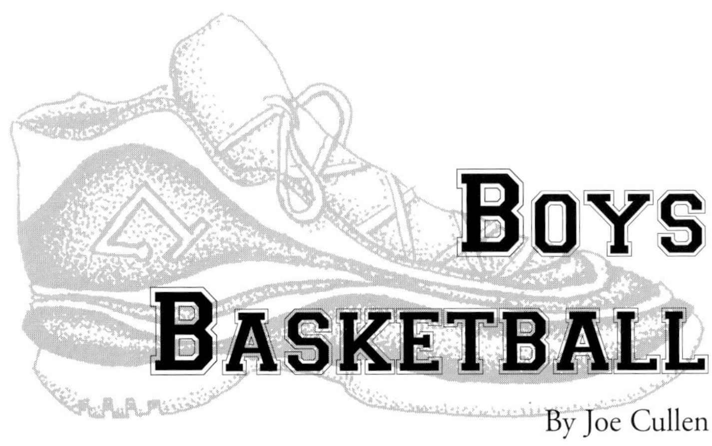

Boys Basketball

By Joe Cullen

"Basketball is like a family. You have to blend individual skills for the benefit of the team."

– Coach Jon Constant

Basketball has become very popular over the years. It has been in town for 90 years and like everywhere else, the Trojans have had their up and down seasons. The bumpy road to the 1940 state championship was a long one, and Traverse City still hopes to repeat that season.

In Traverse City, basketball began in 1907 and was coached by Mr. Ruggles. For these first few years the basketball team played at Campbells' Hall which later became the Wilson Furniture Company on Union Street. In 1917, they started playing home games in the Methodist Church gym and the City Opera House. The basketball team of 1924 was the first team to use the high school's new gym in a game against Grand Rapids. Traverse City has won more basketball championships than any other school in this area, with an all-time record of 268 wins and 115 losses.

The uniforms certainly have changed throughout the years. From 1907 until 1935 the uniforms did not have numbers on the front of them. Lettering said "Traverse City" on the front and the numbers were only on the back. In 1935, numbers were placed on the front of the jerseys. In the early 1900s, knee tights and long sleeve shirts were the uniforms. The shorts that were worn were so small and up so high that it looked liked the players were wearing underwear. Now the shorts come almost all the way down to the knees and below.

Organized in December, 1907, the first Trojan basketball team. Top Row: Whiting, Hall, McGarry. Middle Row: Hanson, Coach Ruggles. Front Row: Cleveland, Hanson.

THE 1929 BASKETBALL SEASON was the most promising one in several years. The team posted a 12-2 record and accumulated three wins and one loss during the tournament. Traverse City won the district and regional championships, but lost to Stambaugh in the state finals by a score of 16-13.

Winning 10 out of 12 games during the regular season, the 1930-1931 Trojan basketball team showed a great deal of heart and determination since all of the players were inexperienced. Playing the Cadillac Vikings in the first game of the tournament, Traverse City dominated for an 18-9 victory. The next game against Alpena ended with another commanding performance by the Trojans with a score of 26-13. This victory qualified the Trojans to play Petoskey in the finals, where Traverse City battled to an 18-18 tie. However, the Petoskey Northmen won the game by means of the state point system which provided that in case of a tie, the victor was determined based on a team's schedule (a Class B team playing an A team would earn more points) and game scores.

With the high school gym destroyed by fire and the new one not yet completed, the Trojans had a rough season in 1937. Playing all their games away except for the Petoskey game, the Trojans had to play with determination. Playing with all their effort, the team won eight games and lost three. In the first two games against Charlevoix and Ludington, the Trojans suffered brutal defeats. The next three games were victories, then another loss to Ludington, and the last five games were wins for the Trojans. Finishing second place in the Big Seven Conference league, Traverse City barrelled through the Class B tournament at Petoskey and went down fighting at the state championship quarterfinals.

The Trojans had another successful year in 1939, but came up short in the finals. Traverse City lost to Cheboygan which ruined the hopes of winning the title. A big win over the Chippewas secured a third place in the Big Seven Conference. Playing Petoskey in the regional tournament, the Trojans came out victorious once again and slipped into the finals against Rogers City. In a nail-biting game to the end, Traverse City lost 15-13. This was the year before the boys won their first championship.

Traverse City has won only one state championship in basketball and that was in 1940. Amazingly, the Trojans posted a 9-5 record that year. In the regional tourney, however, Traverse City beat Petoskey, Rogers City, and Manistee. In the state tournament Traverse City beat Sandusky and South Haven. The last team that the Trojans had to beat to win the state championship was Detroit St. Theresa. The Trojans came from behind to beat St. Theresa 26-23 and become the Class B state champions. The team returned home the next day to be honored by the whole city.

THE YEAR OF 1941 WAS ONE OF ONE- AND TWO-POINT UPSETS, which turned out to be a great season for the Trojans. In the season's opener against Class A Grand Rapids Central, the Black and Gold pulled out a 26-25 victory. With the momentum from last year's championship, the Trojans traveled to Ludington and squeezed out a 25-23 victory. Not only was this game a big win, but it also was the first time that Ludington lost on its home court in 10 years. Through the season the

Trojans had won 15 straight victories. The chain of victories was snapped by Manistee's 28-16 win over the Trojans.

The Trojans fought hard but lost the first two games of the 1943 season by a total of two points. Playing even harder, Traverse City won 13 games in a row to finish out the season by beating Petoskey and Rogers City three times each. Ending the season strong, led by center and captain Jack Cox, Traverse City won the Big Eight Conference championship.

On December 3, 1949, the Trojans were victorious over Mount Pleasant, the 1948 conference champions, and this win gave Coach Menzel his 100th victory in eight years as the Trojans' head coach. Menzel was the Trojans' longest running basketball coach, with 20 years experience.

In 1954, Traverse City became a Class A conference member. Not since the 1940 Trojan champions had Traverse City had a team to be so proud of. The Trojans won the Arrowhead Conference without a loss. The team went to the regional tournament finals, but lost to Lansing Sexton.

The Trojans of 1962 had one of their worst sea-

The 1919 Traverse City basketball team. Front Row: Larry Bain, Harold Sherman, "Red" Higgins, Jerry Tylor, Phelps Foster. Back Row: Coach Mark Worth, Dick Round.

sons ever, posting a 1-16 record for the season. The only win came against Holland with a score of 57-45. In the district tournament, the Trojans lost to Grand Rapids Union. The next year the Trojans went 2-14 for the season and 0-10 in the conference. They lost to Grand Rapids Creston in the district tournament. For 1962 and 1963, the Traverse City Trojans had a combined record of 3-30. The year of 1965 is the Trojans' worst season to date. They went through a lot of hard times in a losing season. Posting a 0-16 record, they finished last in the conference. However, despite these records in the 1960s, two very skilled Trojan players emerged to take All-State honors. John Naymick earned a spot on the first team in 1968, with Tom Kozelko named to the second team. Also that year, Naymick was named LMAC All-Conference after leading the league in scoring. The next year, Kozelko was honored as first team All-State.

During his time as a Trojan from 1967-1969, center Tom Kozelko broke the Trojans' all-time scoring record with over a thousand career points. He later went on to play for the Capital Bullets (Washington Bullets) for three years. After he played with the Bullets for a while, he came back to Traverse City and became an assistant coach for the Trojan basketball team.

In the late 1960s and early 1970s most of the seasons were mediocre. However, an outstanding player from that era was Dave Whiteford, the 1972 leading scorer. The Trojans were on the losing side until 1976 when they finished first in the LMAC.

1940 Class B state championship team. Back Row: Coach Les Orr, Jack Bensley, Dale Wares, Jack Heimforth, Mac Cox, Richard Fitzmaurice, Charles Frye. Front Row: George Umlor, Bill Milliken, Jack Morgan, Bob Hemming, Francis Rollo, Jack Hensel.

Seven games of that season were decided by one or two points. A heartbreaking loss to Midland Dow stopped the Trojans' bid for the state championship. In 1978, Tom Aja averaged 19 points per game and made the All-Conference and All-State teams.

Due to injuries in 1982, many of the key players were out most of the season. The substitutes who had to fill in took the team to a third place finish in the LMAC. After key players returned to the team at the end of the season, the team finished with a record of 14-9. The Trojans then won the district championship, but lost in the regionals to Manistee by one point in overtime. "They developed into the best Traverse City team in 30 years," boasted Coach Malmstrom. Dan Majerle and his brother Steve were selected as first team All-Conference.

THE ERA OF THE MAJERLE BROTHERS HAD BEGUN. When people hear the name Majerle they think of Dan Majerle. However, Dan was not the only basketball player in his family; he had two other brothers who played the game as well. Steve was the first Majerle son to play for the Trojans. He played on the junior varsity team in 1980 and on the varsity team in 1981 and 1982. Dan played on the varsity team all three years from 1981 to 1983. He not only made the 1983 All-State team, but he also scored 826 points that year, averaging 36 points per game that season. During his time on the high school basketball team, he scored over 3000 points! He was one of the greats in Traverse City Trojan basketball history.

Dan's last year at the senior high was an exciting season which was saddened when team member Tom Clark died in a car accident during the season. That obviously left a mark on the team although it brought them even closer together. In the conference championship against Benton Harbor, Dan Majerle scored 48 points. He was a one man wrecking machine and a spectacular sight to watch. The Trojans ended up winning the conference. The 1983 team was the first Class A Trojan team to get to the state quarterfinals. In that game, Flint

1954 Arrowhead Champions. Players Pat Nerbonne, Bob Pemberton, Ron Witt, John Price, Fran Wanageshik, Jean Curtiss, Don Gordon, Robert Drulard, Dave Bowers, Jerry Benton, Ralph Green, Bill Estes, Bill Jerome, Harold Banks and James Donoho with Mgr. Gordon Snyder and Coach Irv Menzel.

Former Trojan Tom Kozelko as a Capital Bullet.

Central ended Traverse City's playoff run.

Dan later went on to play college basketball for Central Michigan University. After college Dan went into the NBA and was drafted by the Pheonix Suns in 1988. He played there for six years and then was traded to the Cleveland Cavaliers in 1995. He became a free agent and is now playing for the Miami Heat. The last Majerle son to play basketball was Jeff Majerle. He played during the late 1980s, being named All-State in 1987, and he also went on to play for Central Michigan University.

IN 1988, COACH JON CONSTANT'S THIRD YEAR AS COACH, he was named state Coach of the Year. The year was a success as Montay Merriman averaged 15.5 points per game and helped lead the team to a 19-4 record. In the district finals against Midland Dow, the Trojans suffered an upset for the fourth year in a row. The score was 83-72, with the Trojans on the small end of the score.

The 1989-1990 Traverse City Trojans were one of the best teams in school history. This team had it

1983 Trojans. Front Row: Dan Majerle, Tony Thorpe. Second Row: Coach Dave Malmstrom, Ross Bissell, Chip Jerome, Tom Clark, Steve Rife, Mike Core, Trainer Greg Meredith. Back Row: Ass't Coach Tom Kozelko, Tim Elzinga, John Wilson, Gordon Chappell, Trevor Dyksterhouse, Dave Smidt, Ron Schuler, Ass't Coach Larry Burns.

Trojan Dan Majerle shows the skill that led him to a career in the NBA.

all: depth, talent, three-point shooters and a fast-paced offense which averaged 82 points a game while only giving up 58 points. This team scored over 90 points in nine games on the way to a 17-3 regular season record. Led by seniors Chad Allen (23.4 points per game), Chris Peck, Jason Durocher, Matt Kramer and Ken Thomas, the Trojans won many exciting games including 96-92 over Escanaba, 69-66 over Rockford, and 77-67 over Benton Harbor. Most home games were sold out.

The 1990 Trojans upended Alpena 90-42 and Escanaba 88-58 to win the district trophy. In the regionals, Traverse City beat a tall Rockford team 55-49 and Midland 60-59 to claim the regional championship before losing to Saginaw in the state quarterfinals. This team made 39% of its threes and averaged 12 more rebounds per game than their opponents. It was truly a great team.

In recent years, basketball's poularity has increased even more. In 1992, the Traverse City

Chad Allen leads the 1990 Trojans to a regional title.

Trojans went 13-4 for the season. In the playoffs they beat Alpena and blew out Marquette 92-38, which was followed by a win over Rockford. However, a loss to Grand Haven knocked Traverse City out of the playoffs. Posting a 16-2 record in 1993, the Trojans lost to Escanaba in the second round of the district tournament.

The last two years of basketball have been good. In 1996, the Trojans went 16-4 for the season. On December 27, the Trojans beat Harper Woods Notre Dame in the Traverse City Invitational to start an 11-game winning streak. That streak came to an end on February 16, when Holland Christian defeated the Trojans 87-79. Something peculiar about the basketball team that year was that the starting line up was made up mostly of juniors. Forward Lucas Leete was the only starting senior. The Trojans played Saginaw in the state quarterfinals where they lost, ending their tournament play. "It's always (nice) to win, but we had a lot of fun this year," said Drew Crandall '97. Saginaw went on to become Class A state champions.

The 1997 season started with a win against the prior year's state champ, Saginaw. Then a record-setting season began to evolve. The team ended its run with a 19-1 best-ever record after replacing three starters, their sixth man and another teammate due to suspensions and an injury at the 13-game winning mark. These players had been together since seventh grade and their game was magical. The team was noted for its depth throughout the state. However, the players who stepped up brought the standing-room-only crowds to their feet numerous times. Never had there been such an emotional season as the 1997 one. The playoffs were a short run, however, as Traverse City lost to Alpena, an old foe, in the first round.

Over the past 90 years, the Traverse City Trojans have had many winning seasons. They have made a name for themselves in basketball that will never be forgotten. The coaches and players are looking forward to another exciting season next year with the talent pool split between the two high schools. Keying this transition is the philosophy: "If we're going to win we have to play unselfishly and think

The talented 1988-89 Trojans. Back Row: Trainer Tammy Breadon, Coach Jerry Schreiner, Steve Hondorp, Marc Burkholder, Jason Durocher, Chad Allen, Steve Nykerk, Chris Peck, Coach Jon Constant, Mgr. Jamie Callahan. Front Row: Mike Kurtz, Trev Gillow, Ken Thomas, Chris Thaxton, Cam Kennedy, Ryan T'Kindt. Not pictured: Matt Kramer.

Jon Constant coaching from the sidelines.

as one," concludes Coach Jon Constant, who was once again named Coach of the Year in 1997, a tribute to him and to his staff. Cheers to all of them!

BASKETBALL SCORING

Regulation court size for basketball is 94 feet long and 50 feet wide, but high school courts are mainly 84 feet long and 50 feet wide. The ball that is used to shoot with weighs 20-22 ounces. High school games last 32 minutes long and play four-minute overtimes if the game is tied after regulation time has expired. Scoring can be done in different ways. A field goal can be scored anywhere on the court and results in two points if it is shot in front of the three-point line. Any shot made behind the three-point line results in three points. A free throw is awarded by a foul or a violation of the rules and is worth one point. Until 1937, a center jump was held after every field goal. Now, this is how the game is started and after every basket, the defense inbounds the ball.

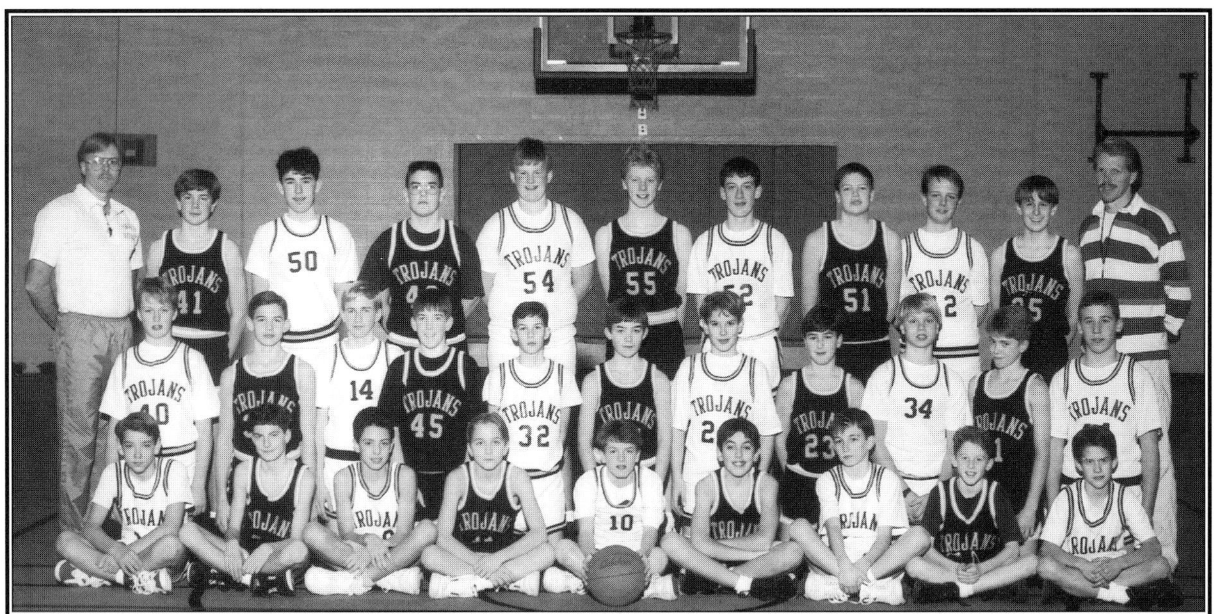

Having a strong feeder program to develop athletic talent creates winning results and lasting friendships. Do you recognize some future Trojan players in this West Junior High seventh grade basketball team? Back Row: Coach Ken Bell, Matt Kropf, Robert Strang, Ryan Gardiner, Matt Brayton, Matt Niblack, Cory Holmes, Doug Baumann, Ben Hogg, Lance Grim, Coach Bob Johnson. Middle Row: Brian Hargraves, Shane Lishawa, Andrew Oster, Jeff Rademacher, Steve Swaney, Mike Tate, Drew Crandall, Ryan Ribel, Dan Thomas, Kyle Kilcherman, Jon Plummer. Front Row: Jason Pryor, Chris Garvin, Doug Crawford, Dave Matthews, Jeff Schmalenberg, Jamie Berry, Alex Messing, Keith Lupiloff, Brent Jarosz. Not pictured: Kalen Robinson.

CLASS A BASKETBALL ALL-STATE

1968	John Naymick
1969	Tom Kozelko
1982	Dan Majerle
1983	Dan Majerle
1987	Jeff Majerle
1990	Chad Allen
1996	Ryan Ribel
1997	Jeff Rademacher

TROJAN BASKETBALL COACHES

1907-1918	Mr. Ruggles
1918-1922	Mark Worth
1922-1926	Waldo Spruit
1932-1936	Gordon MacDonald
1937-1940	Les Orr
1941-1961	Irv Menzel
1961-1963	Dean Davenport
1964-1966	Ike Gillespie
1967-1970	Wayne Hintz
1971-1973	Jim Raymond
1974-1978	Joe LeMieux
1979-1985	Dave Malmstrom
1985-present	Jon Constant

5

Girls Basketball

By Misty MacKenzie

"Try your best, work hard at all the practices, and never slack off."
– Karissa Greiner '93

Over the years, girls basketball has changed dramatically. From the uniforms to how the game is played, girls basketball has had an interesting history here in Traverse City.

Surprisingly, Traverse City's first interscholastic women's team, the first ever competition in girls basketball, took place in 1911. Although compiling an 11-0 record in their first year was impressive enough, the girls won all but two games by more than 9 points; the others were won by at least 4. Traverse City's pioneers for girls basketball were Lucille Holiday (jumping center), Lucy Kelly (side center), Edith Parr (team captain and guard), Lottie Kyselka (guard), and Bertha Miller and Myrtle LaFranier (both guards), with coach Miss Newman, all shown in the picture on the next page. Being undefeated for the very first year was going to be a tough act to follow.

After 1911, Traverse City had hit and miss interscholastic competition. However, they often competed against each other in intramural match-ups, with one class challenging another class. In 1914, the girls team compiled a 3-1 record playing Elk Rapids and Suttons Bay several times. An excerpt from the yearbook states, "Determined to defeat our conquerors, we met Suttons Bay on our own floor, and in spite of a very hard battle and extremely cold floor, Traverse won the game, altho [sic] extra time was needed to play off the tie." The score was 14-12. It seems that hyperbole in sports writing has been in vogue forever.

In 1919, interscholastic competition again kept the girls basketball team busy. Coach Miss Betty Gordon oversaw captain Irene Lather and Ruth Petertyl (both forwards), Germaine Newton and

How did they play with those big bows in their hair?

Geraldine Klaasen at guard, Marian McCool at center, Irene Pfannenschmidt as the side center and Helen Kilbourne as substitute. They lost their first game to Bellaire 22-21.

In 1922, the team presented their case for the state championship. Coach Miss Marjorie Hayes stood unchallenged for the number one spot in northern Michigan having beaten Buckley 25-8, Frankfort 39-13, Charlevoix 81-3, Reed City 19-12 and 2-0, Charlevoix 2-0, and Bellaire 24-14. The season was marred, however, by the ineligibility of two star players. Florabelle Lautner was the captain of this team. Helen Boughey, Maurine Kelly and Katherine Nutten played forwards, while Irene Braun and Lautner were guards. Mary Lawton was the jumping center and Dorothy Novotny was the running center. Marian Coy took over for the ineligible players.

Another undefeated season occurred in 1923, but long train rides affected the 1924 girls basketball team's success. The yearbook explained, " Our first games against Kalkaska, Elk Rapids and Northport were merely getting us into shape for what was to come. Then came one of our biggest games. We went to Muskegon and, arriving nine hours late, we succeeded in outplaying them in the first three quarters, but, by luck, in the last eight minutes Muskegon made three baskets, making the final score Traverse City 17, Muskegon 20. Then we won the Frankfort and Manton games and left for Saginaw... Again hard luck followed us. Our train was eight hours late and we arrived half an hour before it was time to go on the floor. The team worked hard and Mary Lawton's shooting, as usual, was exceptional, but the Saginaw sextet proved, in the last quarter, to be too much for the fatigued Black and Gold team." After beating Bellaire, the team set out to avenge the loss to Muskegon. Eight hundred fans packed the bleachers for " ... one of the scrappiest games of the season... The visitors, amazed at Mary Lawton's shooting, blocked by our guards and completely exhausted in trying to keep track of 'Toppie' Freiberg, went down to defeat 29-7." Beating Boyne City 37-32 and then East Lansing 31-11 (East Lansing had not lost a contest in three years) gave Traverse City the Northern Michigan championship. Coach Margaret A. Gilbert couldn't have been prouder of her team.

1924 girls basketball team (in no order): Gertrude Brown, Emily Urban, Mary Lawton, Allene Nickerson, Mildred Wightman, Marion Monroe, Dorothy Freiberg, Betty Lawton, Mina Bannon, Violet Newstead.

Fifty girls came out for basketball practice in 1925, which shows the popularity of this sport and what a series of winning teams does for developing enthusiasm. The team record that season was equally impressive at 5-1. Only two outside games, both against Boyne City, were on the calendar for the 1926 team. Traverse City prevailed in both contests.

From 1927 through the 1930s, only interclass competition dominated girls basketball. It was in 1935 that girls basketball went from the old three-court method to the more advanced and speedier two-court game. This was where the three guards played on one-half the court and the three forwards played on the offensive side of the court. This style of basketball prevailed until the late 1950s.

WHEN BASKETBALL REAPPEARED IN 1973, it would take years of hard work to bring it back to its 1920s heyday. Vicki Bush was the coach in those early years. With a fairly respectable 9-10 record, the 1973 team placed third in the LMAC at 5-5. In 1975, they were 7-11 overall and 6-4 in the LMAC. "These games could have gone either way; it was the lack of experience and the injuries that hurt the team," stated coach Vicki Bush about her 1975 girls basketball team. In eight of the eleven games, the girls lost within six points.

It wasn't until 1976 that a winning record was posted as Traverse City's "Lady Trojans" turned the game around. Unlike the previous four years, the team came out with a much higher winning percentage and record. The girls pulled off their season with an astounding 12-9 record in the regular season and a second place victory in the LMAC. Even after injuries, the team won six of their last seven games. Judy Sheffer was voted MVP.

Even though the 1977 team had only one senior and two returning varsity players, they still

1973-1974 girls varsity basketball team coached by Vickie Bush (in no order): Paula Sammons, Julie Gabier, Pat Crossley, Linda Heika, Julie Herman, Connie Novak, Jerra Hilaker, Diana Allen, Vickie Pickard, Norma Rabinski, Cindy Ott.

managed to pull off a 4-6 record, placing fourth in the LMAC. "With only two returning players from last year's varsity, one challenge this year was to develop varsity-caliber play and to gain experience at varsity level. We finished strong, winning five of our last seven games," praised coach Vicki Bush. In 1978, Barb Becker was voted MVP as she led in points, steals and assists.

With a 5-5 record in the LMAC, and a 9-11 record in the regular season, the 1978 "Lady Trojans" started a downhill streak that would continue for more than just that season. "Our defense was excellent, but we lacked consistent individual performances," commented Coach Bush. Sue McGeorge was voted MVP.

Sadly enough, the team continued on its downward fall in 1979. It was a disheartening season for Traverse City, compiling only a 3-17 record. Playing under new coach Jim Anderson, a former Trojan basketball standout of the early 1960s, the team had to recreate their whole system of play. Gina Pulcipher was voted MVP for the season.

Picking up their record a little bit, and knowing their coach much better than the previous year, the Trojan girls basketball team pulled off a 9-13 season the next year along with a third place finish in the LMAC. Injuries were a major factor in holding back the girls this season. Kristin Zimmerman made first team All-Conference and All-Area as well as MVP, while Pam Kloosterman made honorable mention All-Area.

The "Lady Trojans" of 1982 pulled together and completed their regular season and the LMAC with a winning record of 14-5. Coach Anderson described the team as having real "chemistry" with each other. The year showed a new and impressive trend beginning with the team. "We've turned the corner, so to speak, of our basketball program."

First girls basketball team to win regionals, the 1983-1984 team. Front Row: Molly Piche', Debbie Anderson, Kristi Oom, Trainer Rhonda Fite. Back Row: Coach Jim Anderson, Amy Hurst, Dawn DeYoung, Sheryl Reed, Chris Nadolski.

This year also marked an increase in student fan support. "Having more peers there gave the girls a little extra confidence in themselves. It makes a tremendous difference having fans there. It goes to improve the play of the game by increasing the player's spirit," explained Coach Anderson. Sheri Kreple and Danielle Daniels made All-Conference; Daniels and Pam Kloosterman made All-Area.

In 1983, the "Lady Trojans" reached a most important goal that had so far eluded them. Never before had they won a regional title. The "Lady Trojans" had the best girls basketball season that Traverse City had ever seen throughout its history. With a record of 17-6, the district title and an LMAC title tie with Benton Harbor, the girls did not let their fans down. When asked what he thought of the season Coach Anderson said, "Fabulous. We have reached goals that have never been reached before in Traverse City girls basketball history." Molly Piche' made All-State honors while Dawn DeYoung received Honorable Mention. All-Area honors went to Dawn DeYoung, Debbie Anderson and Molly Piche', with an honorable mention to Chris Nadolski. All-Conference went to Piche' and De Young. " We felt close, just like a family," stated center DeYoung.

THE 1984 "LADY TROJANS" ENDED THEIR SEASON with an outstanding, and best ever, 18-2 season record. They also placed second in the LMAC and won the district title. They lost the regionals in a thriller against Flint Northwestern 34-25, and the conference title by losing only to Benton Harbor twice. Dawn DeYoung earned repeat All-State honors and went on to play for Michigan State University the following year.

Dawn DeYoung goes up for a shot.

In 1985, the team had only one returning letter winner, Suzy Merchant, six juniors and two sophomores, and they still came out with a 14-8 record. Also, for the first time, there were two freshmen added to the team, Wendy Merriman and Lisa Anderson. For being such an inexperienced team, they didn't show it. "For a team with no seniors, I'm most pleased with the girls," said Anderson. "When you look at the experience we gained, you've got to be optimistic about the next two years, particularly next year." Suzy Merchant earned All-State recognition in both 1985 and 1986.

Suzy Merchant, an All-State choice in both 1985 and 1986.

"Mean fighting machine" was the motto of the 1987 "Lady Trojans." Winning the district title with an impressive 35-1 run, the team was disappointed to lose to Saginaw by one point in the regionals, 45-44. "This year we played with more of a team effort, rather than for our own individual achievements," stated Lisa Anderson `88. Junior Wendy Merriman earned All-State recognition.

The "Lady Trojans" of 1988 set their goals high. Winning the LMAC, district, and regional titles was exciting and very emotional for the girls. The state title was finally within reach. They worked hard but were defeated by Flint Powers in the quarterfinal game, 51-38. The season was summed up by Becky Schafer `89 who said, "We had a great season. Everybody worked really hard."

"The most unique thing about our team is that we stick together as a team. Everyone tried their best," stated Jayna Greiner` 90. With an almost even 10-11 record, Traverse City's "Lady Trojans" learned the meaning of hard work and practice. The girls learned much this year and looked forward to doing better the next year. Autumn Rademacher, who just finished her career at the

1991-1992 Great Lakes Conference champions. Front Row: Libby Hoxsie, Tara Plummer, Brittany Adams, Jenny Pelon, Katie Tavener, Kari Grim, Nicki Biggs. Back Row: Mgr. Tom Kasper, Trainer Eric Niezgoda, Autumn Rademacher, Karissa Greiner, Nicki Ritter, Carolyn Eikey, Shannon Burkholder, Coach Ron Bohn, Coach Jeff Lockman.

Autumn Rademacher tries to set up one of her many baskets.

University of Detroit as they made a run in the early 1990s NCAA women's competition, starred during these rebuilding years.

NEW COACH RON BOHN MADE HIS DEBUT IN 1991 with an impressive 18-3 season. Brenda Adams captained the team as they won the new Great Lakes Conference, but fell short in winning the district. A strong bench nicknamed "the pinesisters" helped the 1992 squad to a 17-4 record and once again the girls captured the conference championship. Autumn Rademacher became the first girl to make 1,000 baskets in one season. She made also made the All-State team.

"The clock ticked away as one final shot was released into the air. One last basket would steal the victory. The crowd gasped. The ball circled the basket and silently dropped through the net as the buzzer blared through the silence. Crowds cheered as excitement filled the room. Victory, once again, was theirs," described a fan. Traverse City's 1993 "Lady Trojans" had another excellent year. With an awesome 18-2 record, the fans really got their money's worth and the team got the satisfaction of knowing that their practicing and hard work really paid off. Like 1993, 1994 boasted great stats with an 18-4 record. Six returning players plus senior transfer Jessica Leete at 6'2" made it happen for the "Lady Trojans."

A disappointing season for the 1995 "Lady

Coach Ron Bohn offers some last-second instructions to the 1993 Trojans as they cling to a four-point lead.

Trojans" at 11-9 didn't dishearten the girls. Christy Mathieu stated, " Even though our record is not good, we have a lot of heart and it's a kind of team that will go far this year and in the future." Lisa Harris commented on team spirit saying," I was just a sophomore, I did not know anyone, but everyone was accepting."

The 1996 season proved to be true to the predictions of the 1995 squad. A 17-3 record ensued with many heart-stopping moments like Sara Dennis' lay-up against Gaylord with three seconds on the clock. The stong elementary and junior high feeder programs paid off this year as most of the girls had had years of playing, thanks to these experiences.

Tallying one more win than the last season, the 1997 team compiled an 18-3 record. Impressive play by the entire team made the season a memorable one as most of the girls again had years of basketball experience to draw on. "I became interested in basketball in third grade when my best friend and teammate Abby Mahan '97 got me into the game," commented Meghan Nachazel. The two Dennises, Sara and Courtney, put up impressive numbers along with Lisa Harris, particularly against Petoskey. Harris received a full-ride scholarship to Hofstra University in New York as a reward for her hard work both in the classroom and on the court. That year's team lost Harris and seven other seniors.

The 1996-1997 season marked the 86th year of girls basketball at Traverse City Central Senior High. Two junior varsity teams forecast an interesting future as more girls will get the opportunity to play in the years to come as the schools split. Next year begins a new era of rebuilding and beginnings. Cheers!

GIRLS BASKETBALL CLASS A ALL-STATE

	First Team	Honorable Mention
1983	Molly Piche'	Dawn DeYoung
1984	Dawn DeYoung	
1985	Suzy Merchant	
1986	Suzy Merchant	
1987	Wendy Merriman	
1992	Autumn Rademacher	

TROJAN GIRLS BASKETBALL COACHES

1919	Miss Betty Gordon
1922	Miss Marjorie Hayes
1924	Margaret Gilbert
1972	Vicki Bush
1980	Jim Anderson
1991	Ron Bohn

Cheerleading

by Pat Weber and Sylvia Burns

"'Fight Loco' from my cheerleading days had rigid arm movements and quick formation changes which inspired the entire student body to cheer along. As a coach in the 1980s, I saw cheerleading become more of a performance which included dance and gymnastic movements."

– Barb White Maitland

The essential connection between Trojan fans and their teams has, for a very long time, been the high school cheerleaders. The cheerleaders were not only known for their performances on the field and floor, but also for organizing pep assemblies and rallying the school to enthusiastically support the athletic program. For girls, it was one of the few opportunities to partake in athletics before Title IX. However, this has not been a female dominated activity.

Early Trojan cheerleaders of 1911 sported sweaters not unlike those of today, with accentuated large hair bows. It's interesting to note that the same six girls also formed the first girls basketball team in 1911.

In 1917, one of the very first cheerleaders was a man named Mark Worth, who was also a teacher at the high school. His official title was "yellmaster." In 1929, Anna May York, Virginia Chapman and Theron Akers were cheerleaders. Through the 1930s, there were a variety of cheering combinations – such as two males and one female, two females with one male, or three females – who wore slacks, sweaters and street shoes (high heels – ouch!).

Over the years the footwear, uniforms, hair styles and male-to-female ratio have changed as much as the hemlines. The four girls on the 1940 squad wore skirts for the first time. However, the two guys on the 1941 squad wore trousers.

In 1944, the cheerleaders were elected by a popular vote of the students. Then in 1947, a cheering section was organized to encourage school spirit. William Gerard was the faculty advisor and essentially this was the beginning of the "Pep Club" which would last for four decades. The squad received new uniforms that year and while the two boys wore pants, the girls wore skirts for basketball and slacks for football.

IN 1950, THE PEP CLUB PURCHASED BLEACHERS, a score board, lights, concession booths, and a neon sign for Thirlby Field. During these years, the cheerleading squad had a reputation of being the best dressed and best trained in the state. These years, as in prior years, the cheerleaders were chosen by an election of the student body and were usually the most popular kids in school. Pep Club oversaw these groups and actually narrowed the field of participants by sponsoring tryouts. Token males now and again graced the cheerleading ranks. These boys came from the Varsity Club and

1911 cheerleaders: Bertha Miller, Lucy Kelly, Lucille Holliday, Dottie Kyselka, Edith Parr and Myrtle LaFranier.

Teacher Mr. Mark Worth, 1917 yellmaster.

were strong enough to do the lifts and coordinated enough to do the splits and the precision choreography necessary to team with the girls.

In the 1950s, 1960s and 1970s, the big events during homecoming to build school spirit were the bonfire and the snake dance through town the night preceding the game. Today that snake dance has been replaced by a parade of floats through the downtown area the night before homecoming, followed by an activites night on Thirlby Field where competition between the classes has become quite fierce. The papier-mache' Trojan head worn by a student first appeared in the late 1950s and became the school mascot that cheered at both basketball and football games.

Uniforms were white wool sweaters and pleated skirts in the 1950s and 1960s. Footwear had been saddle shoes and bobby socks in the 1940s and 1950s; tennis shoes replaced the rigid saddle shoe in the 1960s, but bobby socks were still "in".

Eligibility cards were used for the first time in 1965 and this squad was the first to attend a summer cheerleading camp. At camp they were voted Best Dressed Squad and received a second place for Best All-Around Squad. Nancy Hadley was awarded a trophy for Best Individual Cheerleader. Mounts began to be incorporated into the cheering routines at this same time and remain popular today.

The 1966 varsity squad led the first cheerleading clinic for area cheerleading squads. Then in the late sixties, the cheerleaders began attending national camps and always came home with high marks, ribbons and top place finishes. Five boys from the Varsity Club were added to the 1969 squad and they were all called "the terrific ten". This continued in 1970 when the team won a fifth place trophy for form, routine and variety in cheers at the Camp All-American. Nancy Braden won fourth place individual at this camp.

IN 1971, THE CHEERLEADERS attended the United States Cheerleading Association camp at which time the mini-trampoline was added to some cheers. The squad increased from five to nine girls in 1974 when Debbie Bussa received a first place individual award at the United States Cheerleading Association camp. The squad as a

Virginia Chapman and Anna May York, 1929-1930 Trojan cheerleaders.

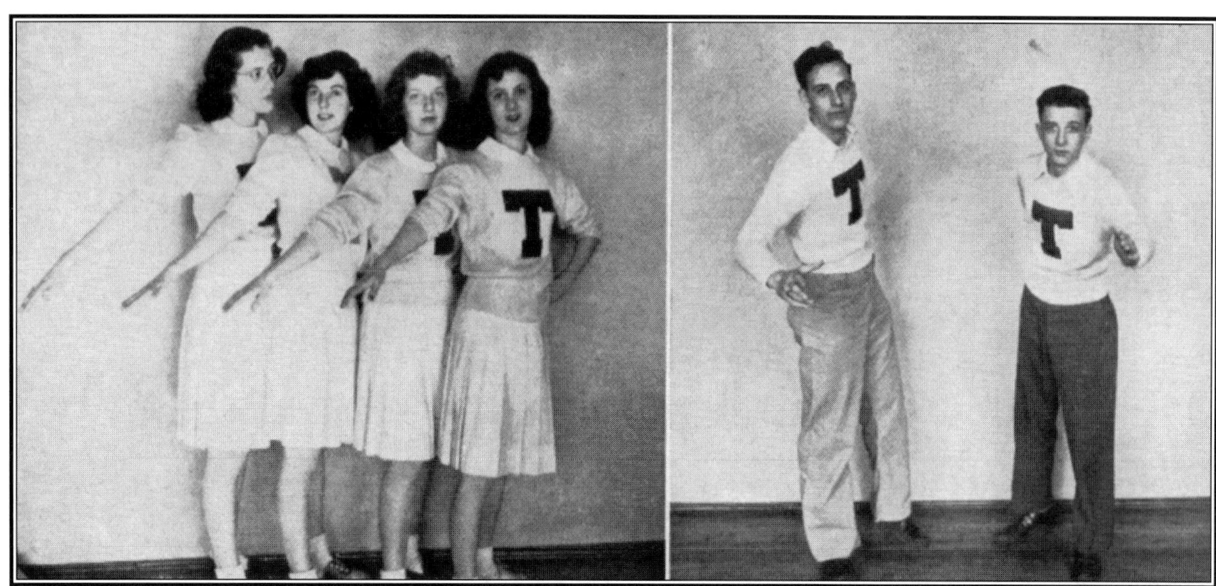

1946 cheerleaders: Jean Sutter, Pat Kalahar, Nancy Dean, Pat McLean, B. Banton, John Gilmore.

whole took the first place trophy and came home with seven ribbons to boot.

Throughout the 1970s and 1980s, making signs and decorating the school to encourage school spirit and enthusiasm became popular, continuing the tradition which had really begun in the early 1960s at the then brand new high school. Known as Pep-O-Rama week, students painted and decorated the gym windows during the basketball season. Today, homecoming tradition has classes competing as they paint the windows in the administrative offices at the north end of campus.

In 1981, a second varsity squad called the "White Squad" was added to cheer at home soccer games. Mike Lyon joined the fall varsity squad. By 1992, the varsity had increased to 11 girls; one squad for fall sports, another for winter.

In 1990, the team took a second place in the United States Cheerleading Association camp. Jenny Williams, Brandi Lorenz and Mickey Schichtel were all invited to become cheer instructors at the USCA camp. In 1994, for the first time, sophomores were allowed on varsity. The 1995 squad achieved the Camp Champs trophy at the University of Michigan Universal Cheerleaders Association camp and as a result were invited to cheer at the Citrus Bowl. Major fundraising ($14,000 worth) paid for the trip to Orlando and an awesome four-day whirl of every attraction the area offers.

However, cheerleaders have been accustomed to fundraising for themselves for decades. Not recognized as a varsity sport until recently, no funding was available for cheerleading through the athletic department and for decades they

1958 varsity cheerleaders: Judy Toerper, Mary Wagaman, Margo Hensel and Jan Lehnhardt.

1962 cheerleaders leading school spirit: Shirley Cavitch, Mary Ellen Pike, Marcia Stehower, June Johnson and Marg Meach.

relied upon themselves and the Pep Club when money was needed.

Cheerleaders even return as advisors. Barb White Maitland, who was a cheerleader in the late 1960s and early 1970s, offered her services as cheerleading advisor for three years in the late 1980s. Sue Mack, did the same thing in 1984; she had been a cheerleader in the mid-1970s. By far, the two women who made it happen and kept the squads together were Maxine MacInnis (1964 to 1971) and Sylvia Burns (1973,1977-1982,1984-1986). Additionally, coach William Gerard had a long run from 1947 to 1957, followed by Mary Jane Draper from 1958 to 1963. Ralph Grueber, Lisa Bluhm and Allison Wadsworth have kept track of the squads through the 1990s.

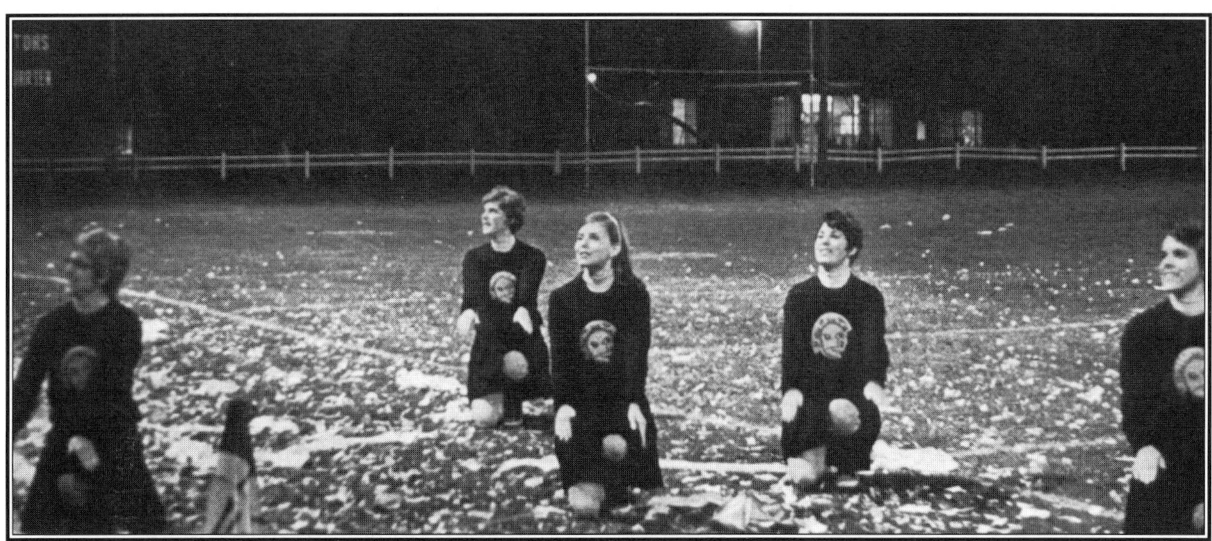

1970 varsity cheerleaders performing at Thirlby Field: Nancy Braden, Barb Bell, Pat Greiage, Barb White and Kay Wilson.

1981-1982 cheerleaders: Front: Nancy Schwenter. Middle: Kyle Hayes, Kathleen Christopher. Top: Lisa Foerster, Diane Zientek, Jill Campbell, Barb Aldrich, Kris Anderson.

Despite Title IX and the many women's sports that eventually evolved throughout the late 1970s, cheerleading remains a mainstay at the high school. Interscholastic competition has now come of age and our cheerleaders remain among the best.

1993 Cheerleaders at Thirlby Field: Back: Susan Riggs, Amber Rushlow, Kristin Fralick, Tammy Shawbitz. Front: Cheryl Donohoe, Jenny Cook, Jessica Kratky, Dawn Bennett.

CHEERLEADING COACHES

1956	William Gerard
1961	Mary Jane Draper
1966-1971	Maxine MacInnis
1972	Lynn Mixer
1973	Sylviz Burns
1974	No coach
1976	Pat Drzweicki
1977	Claudia English
1978-1980	Sylvia Burns
1982-1983	Sandy Harms
1984	Sue Mack
1985-1986	Sylvia Burns
1987-1989	Barb Maitland
1990	Ralph Grueber
1991-1994	Lisa Bluhm
1995	Allison Wadsworth

7

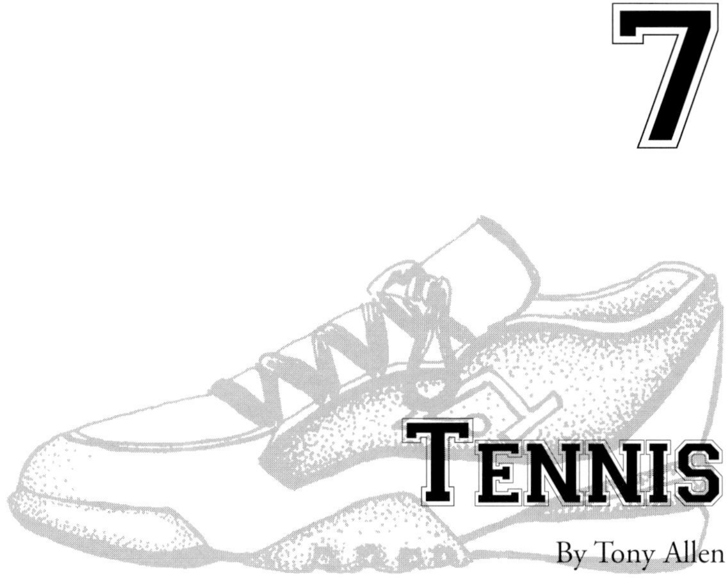

Tennis

By Tony Allen

"The ultimate measure of a man is not where he stands in moments of comfort and convenience but where he stands at times of challenge."
– Martin Luther King

The long and illustrious tradition of Traverse City High School tennis started way back in 1928 when an elimination intramural tournament was held with the winners receiving positions on the boys team. In the team's first season of competition, captain Jim Thirlby was the runner-up for the singles title. The first man to coach the team was coach Gordon MacDonald, but since he was busy with the Trojan golf team, Dale Carter soon took over the job of coaching the 1928 tennis players. In a very short time, he developed a team that won the regional meet held in Traverse City.

1940 Trojan tennis team: Front row: Bob Smith, Dick Loomis, John Collins. Back row: Bruce Wangen, Dale Wares, Jack Bensley, Dick Fitzmaurice, Coach Robert Meggison.

The early success of Traverse City tennis quickly diminished as the team faded out of existence due to a controversy spanning a period of years. Brighter days were ahead for the netters, though, as tennis revived again in 1939. Bob Loomis, who won the regional and Northwestern Michigan Invitational Championships, Bill Helrigle, Laverne Grueber, Bill Milliken, Bob Smith and Jack Bensley were the core of this team. New coach Robert Meggison took the job of coaching this squad of both inexperienced and experienced players after Irving Menzel was forced to turn over his duties due to conflicting programs.

IN 1941, BILL NOVAK became the first full-season coach and is really considered the founder of Traverse City tennis. That year Dick Loomis played his third year of Trojan tennis to complete one of the finest tennis records at Traverse City High School. Wilfred (Bill) Brammer went to the state singles quarterfinals that year. In 1942, Dick Loomis won the regional and Northwestern Michigan Invitational Championships, and made it to the state finals. Novak's squad posted a winning record each year until 1945, when rain and bad weather basically ruined their season. After that, the success of the netters changed for the worse. The only bright spot of the latter half of the decade came in 1947, when they faced their first conference opposition. Traverse City tennis finished the decade with a tough season in 1949 with a record of one win and seven losses. The teams at this time played at two clay courts on old state hospital grounds on the corner of Silver Lake Road and Division, not far from the old Central High School on 7th Street. The team would run between the school and courts for practices.

At the beginning of the fifties, a couple of coach Ed Howard's teams had a difficult time as they went two consecutive seasons without a win. They finished the decade strong though, with their best season coming in 1958, when they finished with a record of 7-2. Playing on the four courts at Thirlby Field, the team won the Arrowhead Conference and finished third in regional play. Coached by Bob Bacon, the Trojan football coach who also ran the city tennis program, the team won conference action with Tom Novak taking all singles contenders and Ross Biederman and Bruce Eckhardt taking all doubles. Unbeaten Novak and once-beaten Biederman won the regional doubles cham-

1958 tennis team: Front row: Dick Keene, Willard Wilcox, Corbin Davis, John Kiblinger, Eric Thoreson, Jerry Rittman, Bob MacEachran, Skip Ball, Ken Wilson. Second row: Terry Sanborn, Terin Wales, Tom Novak, Bruce Eckardt, Ross Biederman, Jim VanBrocklin, Lon Brugh, Jerry Jerome, Coach Bacon. Third row: Jim Martinek, Dennis Kantz, John Nelson, Fred Kirby, Steve Kantz, Larry Anderson, Mgr. Elliott Weitz.

pionship and traveled to Kalamazoo, where they made it to the state semifinals. In 1960, the #1 singles player was Bob Graham.

TENNIS BEGAN THE SIXTIES with some wins, some losses. But that would quickly change. In 1962, four courts were built at the new high school on Eastern Avenue with the entire $3000 needed coming from the Pep Club. In 1964, coach Lyndon Salathiel took over the team with returning lettermen Bob Manthei, Pete Read, Jim Milliken, Jim Weaver and Chris Batdorff. By 1966, he had turned an inexperienced 2-6 team to a vastly improved 7-2 team. Under coach Ron Johnson in the mid-sixties, the netters continued their winning ways and finished league competition in second place each year. In 1968, seniors Tom Alward, Tim Moore, Marty Begley and Rick Nottke, in addition to doubles teams of Steve Batdorff and Bob Smith, Jeff Power and Doug Morrison, Bill Calcutt and Don Thibedeau, placed second in the Lake Michigan Athletic Conference which had become the Trojans' conference in the sixties. The decade ended by bringing in a new coach, Larry Nykerk, in 1969.

The 1970s also began with a fair performance as the team had a third place finish in LMAC league competition, partly the fault of unreliable spring weather. In 1973, the Traverse City tennis team was in the Class A state finals for the first time and placed 12th. By 1975, they had four straight league wins and their best finish yet at regionals: second. Part of the success in the mid-1970s can be attributed to the construction of indoor tennis facilities. With Logan Racquet Club in Traverse City and courts at Sugar Loaf Resort, year-round play was finally possible.

In spring of 1974, Penny Milliken was the first and only girl to play varsity tennis on the boys team. She and #1 doubles partner Bruce Taylor won the LMAC title. That fall brought a milestone to Traverse City High School sports as the tennis scene saw the inaugural season of interscholastic competition for girls. Gail Riley was the first girls

1966 tennis team: Coach Lyn Salathiel, Tim Moore, Bill Hilt, Richard Stulen, B. Swan, Dave Manthei, Al Kniss, Harvey Calcutt, Don Hakala, Adair Correll, Manager Mac Beers, Dave Mikowski. Not pictured: Mike Hains, Bruce Cozzens, Warren Raftshol.

coach and held that position during the team's developmental years of 1974 to 1979. In 1976 came another first to girls tennis as they competed in their first season of conference play, finishing third in the LMAC with eight wins and three losses. By 1978, with Jody Becsey the #1 player, the team placed second at the LMAC championship where the doubles team of Libby Williams and Kelly Kerlin were conference champions.

In the mid 1970s, brothers Steve Preston and Jon Preston were Traverse City's first two state top-ten ranked players, with Jon's impressive 24-2 record in 1975. He and Dave Schmidt were the top players in 1976, winning most of their matches. Traverse City tennis placed between sixth and 13th in the state finals every year in those years. The boys team won its first LMAC conference title in 1975 and continued the streak through 1978, replacing Muskegon (also a state power) which had been the conference power until then. The 1975 team also had the first 20-win season. The 1977 team under captain Bill Bogley had a great season, capturing the LMAC championship. In 1978 and 1979, J.P. Milliken was the #1 player and the first to win the LMAC title at #1 singles, repeated by Doug Enders in 1981.

THE WINNING WAYS OF TRAVERSE CITY tennis continued through the eighties, helped by additional courts and a summer development program. In 1981, four more tennis courts were added at Senior High and the original four resurfaced. This was made possible after the Trojan Athletic Booster Club, led by co-chairs Mary McClure and Larry Nykerk, raised $65,000 in cash and in-kind services for this purpose. Former coach Bill Novak returned to the courts to build a shelter and storage area there. At the same time, Larry Nykerk and Cliff Girard started the Grand Traverse Tennis Camps, attracting over 500 participants a year. Margaret Lilly coached the girls team for one season in 1980, after which Larry Nykerk also began as girls coach in 1981. In the eighties, weekend tournaments began which took the teams around the state. Further travel and tougher schedules resulted in making the Trojans even stronger.

The years from 1983 to 1985 were the era of the Caldwell brothers who played #1 singles those

1978 girls tennis team: Michelle McGuffin, Jenny Tway, Connie Zacks, Amy Dunscombe, Libby Williams, Coach Gail Riley, Sara Skrubb, Caroline Koestner, Kelly Kerlin, Janet Lombard, Patty Cartwright and Jody Becsey. Not pictured: Cathy Rahm.

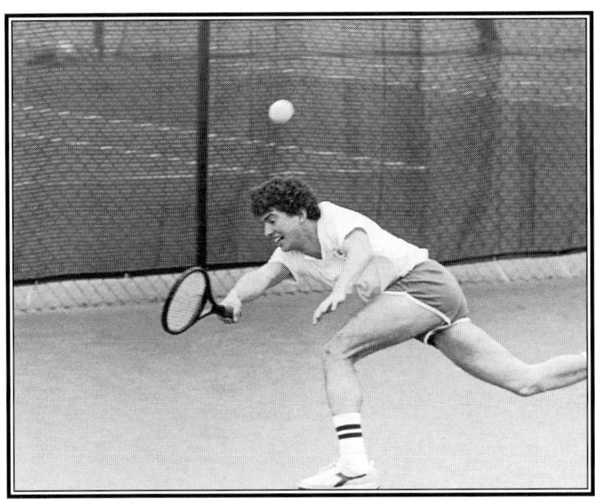

Chris Caldwell, Traverse City's first All-State tennis player, reaches for a shot.

years. Chris Caldwell was Traverse City's first All-State player, earning that honor in both 1983 and 1984. In 1984, Chris also received All-American honors. Rob Caldwell earned All-State recognition in 1985 when he was the #1 player. In 1983, both Rob Caldwell and Blake Ringsmuth made the final round in singles at the state finals. Ringsmuth was a quarterfinalist, semifinalist and finalist in his three years on the team.

The early eighties were led by Shawna Willman, who was #1 singles in both 1981 and 1982, and Julie Beeker, #1 in 1983. In 1983-1984, Sue Kausler and Stacey Kausler, "twins with wins," went two straight undefeated seasons at #1 doubles, compiling a 28-1 record each season. Also helping the 1984 team place sixth in the state were Andrea Brunackey and Jenny Moore who reached the state finals at #2 doubles. This 1984 team was the first girls team to break into the top ten at the state meet. Top singles players from 1984-1986 were Jill VandenBerge in 1985, and Trini Wysong who was #1 in 1984 and 1986.

The years 1985 and 1986 were years of firsts. In 1985, when the school board finally let freshmen

1984 Trojans, the first girls team to earn a record-high sixth place at the state meet. Back row: Stacey Kausler, Biz Ditta, Jenny Columbus, Andrea Brunackey, Jennifer Moore, Sue Kausler, Laurie Smith, Coach Larry Nykerk. Middle Row: Erika Gravlin, Kathy Miller, Holly Wilson, Katherine Johnson, Jill VanderBerge. Front row: Allison Stegenga, Kristin Good, Trini Wysong, Chris Rose, Chris Chirgwin.

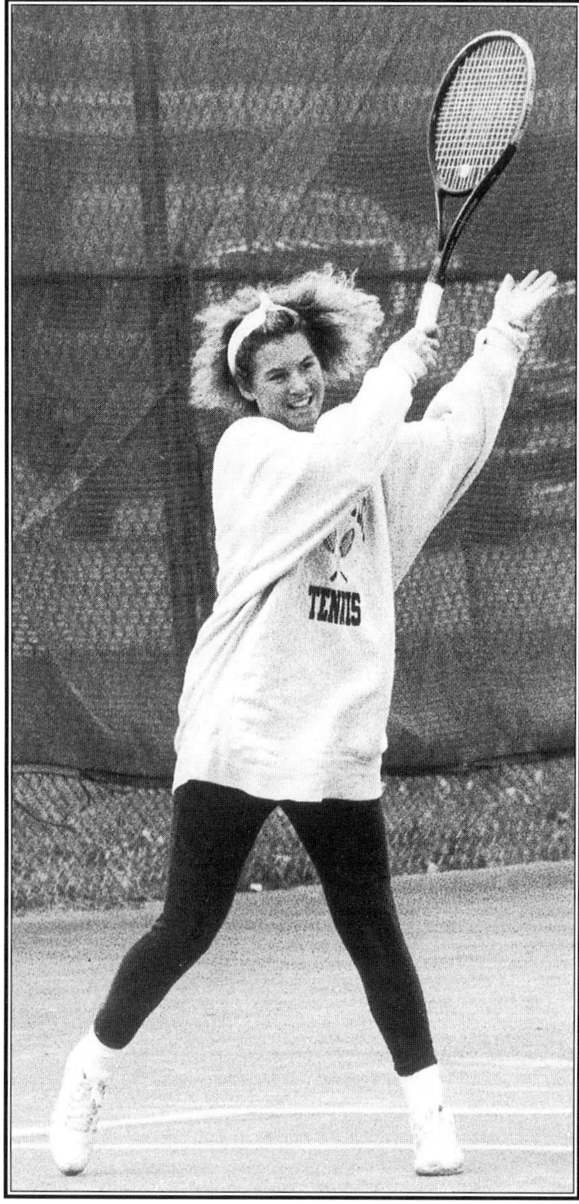

Meg Wilson, the first Trojan girl All-State tennis player.

play in varsity sports even if that sport was offered at the freshman level, Kim Schultz became the first ninth-grader to play varsity tennis. In 1986, Traverse City became independent, ending 17 years of LMAC league play during which Coach Nykerk won 13 LMAC titles, more than any other Trojan coach in any sport. In 1986, a pleasant surprise for the girls team was winning their third straight regional championship, where Shelly Fochtman became the first freshman to claim a regional title, winning at #1 doubles.

The 1987 girls team also put together a very outstanding year. The youngest Trojan team ever showed their opponents a tremendous amount of talent. In the top four spots were sophomores Shelly Fochtman (#1 singles) and Meg Wilson, junior Kim Schultz and freshman Amy Portenga. After the teams' previous successes, thirty girls tried out for the team the next year, the most ever for girls tennis. Because of that surge of tennis players, they started a junior varsity team for the first time in 1988.

AS IF THINGS COULDN'T GET ANY BETTER, 1989 brought yet another milestone to girls tennis. Meg Wilson became the first Traverse City girl to win regionals at #1 singles, was seeded #6 at the state finals in the toughest flight, and then became the first Trojan girl tennis player to be named All-State. Although the team finished eighth at the state finals, Coach Nykerk praised this year's group as one of his "best ever" teams, explaining that "with a couple of breaks we could have finished as high as third." After knocking off second-seeded Okemos, sophomores Kathryn Kendall and Erin Trahan were state semifinalists where they nearly upended #3 Mona Shores. Wilson played two years in the #1 spot, followed by Amy Portenga at #1 singles in 1990.

The year 1988 began a string of nine straight years of All-State boys players, starting with Karl DeVries in 1988 and 1989. This number of especially strong players was instrumental in producing the longest Traverse City win streak, 44 consecutive victories from 1991 to the present. Also helping in these wins was Steve Nykerk, a state quarterfinalist all three years from 1987-1989.

Aaron Murray, the first three-year #1 singles boys player, received All-State honors each of those years, 1990-1992, where he was a state quarterfinalist each year. In 1992, he also earned a fourth seed at the state finals in the tough #1 singles spot. Bryan Nykerk was All-State in 1993. Kyle Gernhofer was the second three-year #1 player, also getting All-State honors each year from 1994-1996. Gernhofer compiled a record 110 career wins at singles and got an exceptionally high second seed at #1 singles in the 1996 state finals. He reached the state quarters or semis three of his four years, quite a feat at singles. Boys teams in the years from 1989-1995 all won regional titles.

IN 1995 AND 1996, A NEW STATE RULING creating doubles All-State recognition allowed Kyle Kilcherman and Kyle Tousain to receive that honor after they reached the state finals at #1 doubles. In 1996, the #2 doubles team of Andrew Hamilton and exchange student Thomas tenHoedt became the first Traverse City state champions, also earning them doubles All-State honors. Both of these doubles teams entered the state meet as #1 seeds. Hamilton and tenHoedt finished their championship season at 40-0, helping the team to a fourth place state finish after being ranked as high as second during the season. Brent Bak was another Trojan to be named All-State on that strong 1996 team. Each year from 1994-1996, the boys team finished in the top five in the state, helped by Kilcherman, Hamilton and Tousain who capped three straight years with showings in the state quarters, semis or finals. In 1996, both Tousain and Kilcherman went over the 100 career win mark; Kilcherman got 102 in doubles and Tousain reached a record 123 wins. Together, they hold the school record for 102 career doubles wins.

The first girl to reach 100 wins was Gretchen Shaw, who accomplished this playing the challenging positions of one year at #2 singles and three years at #1 singles. She was named All-State in both 1992 and 1993. In 1993, the successful doubles team of Alison Hoffman and Sommer Gillow recorded 91 career doubles wins in three years and were the #2 seed at state finals. In 1994, Stacey Portenga was at #1 singles, making the

1989 girls tennis team: Back Row: Coach Nykerk, Dana Steckley, Donyel Carter, Meg Wilson, Amy Portenga, Jill Nykerk, Stephanie Willard. Front Row: Laurie Davison, Niki Taberski, Erin Trahan, Tiffini Gregory, Shelly Fochtman, Kathryn Kendall.

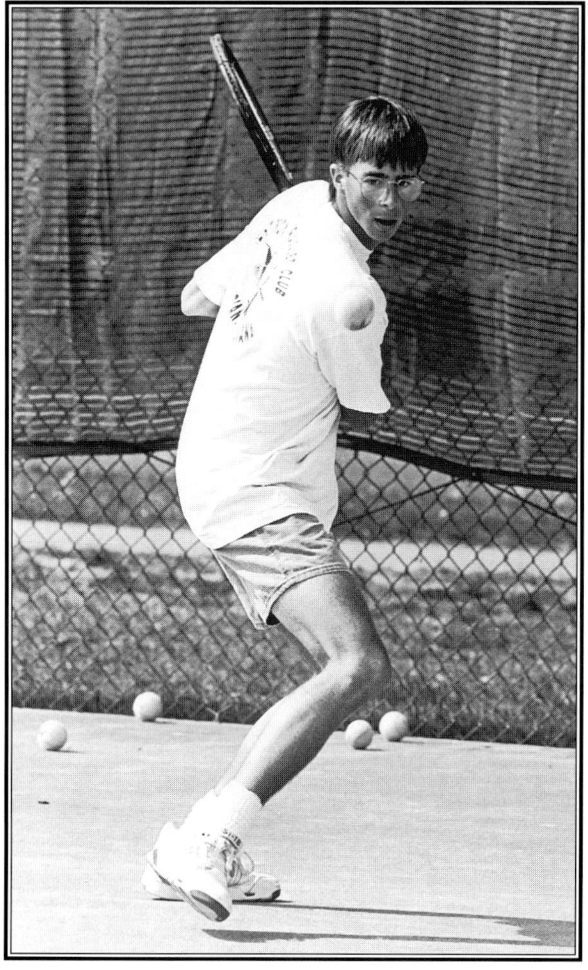

Aaron Murray, the first Trojan to be named All-State three straight years.

Portengas the only sisters to have both played in the #1 spot. Stacey was the third Traverse City girl to be named All-State when she received the honor that year. Stacey set girls records with 116 career victories and four regional titles. Other girls to break 100 wins in 1994 were Julie Eckhold and Jill Gregory. Katie Jacobs racked up an impressive 91 wins in just three seasons of both singles and doubles. Gregory and Eckhold helped the 1992-1994 teams to top ten finishes by advancing well at the state meet, Gregory to the quarterfinals and Eckhold to the semis in each of those three years.

In both 1993 and 1994, the girls team won an unprecedented "golden regionals" with champions at all seven flights; never before had this been done by a Trojan boys or girls tennis team. Players who were responsible for this accomplishment were: Gretchen Shaw, Stacey Portenga, Katie Jacobs, Julie MacIntosh, Jill Gregory, Julie Eckhold, Alison Hoffman, Sommer Gillow, Jenny Brady and Sara Chambers in 1993; Portenga, MacIntosh, Eckhold, Gregory, Jacobs, Christina Stavros, Robin Ford, Lisa Webster, and freshmen Emily MacIntosh and Heather Willson (the youngest doubles team ever) in 1994. The 1993 team placed sixth at the state finals for only the second time in Trojan history.

Julie MacIntosh captured the #1 spot in 1995, followed by Christina Stavros in 1996. In 1996, sisters Caroline and Judith Monte were the first Traverse City girls team to be named doubles All-State after they reached the final round at states at #1 doubles. The #2 doubles team of Sarah Stilwill and Lisa Webster (the #3 seed) and #3 doubles Heather Willson and Sarah Howard (the #1 seed) also reached the finals, helping the 1996 team to become the third girls team to reach sixth place in the state. That year #2 singles player Robin Ford tied Stacey Portenga's record for 116 career victories, while Lisa Webster recorded 98 career doubles wins in just three years on varsity. By winning regionals, this team capped eight years as regional champions, 1989-1996.

These strong team performances in the eighties and nineties were the result of an increasingly rigorous schedule helped by amazingly active parent support. In these years the focus went from dual matches (the boys teams have been undefeated since 1991 and the girls since 1989), to tournament play. Travel became more frequent as Coach Nykerk's Trojans became the most traveled team in the state, going downstate often to play mainly top-ten ranked teams. The addition of more tournaments is seen in the season-final records of both the boys and girls teams, now often reaching 40 matches a season.

According to Coach Nykerk, no one in the state plays as many matches as Traverse City since we are not in a conference and can therefore schedule as many matches as we like. Because of this, there are probably few other schools who have players with 100 wins. Considering the amount of travel Traverse City must do, these become especially impressive records.

Twenty boys teams from 1973-1996 have been ranked in the top ten in the state; 12 girls teams from 1983 to 1996 have also received this ranking. Much of the reason for the success of these teams lands on the shoulders of long-time coach Larry Nykerk, who after 29 seasons, has the longest run of any Traverse City head coach, the third highest total dual meet wins (464) of any Michigan tennis coach and the most tournament wins (139) of any Michigan coach. Traverse City tennis has come a long way in over sixty years of existence. There were highs and lows over the years, but since the 1980s they have been all highs. At this point in 1996, the boys have won five straight regional titles and the girls eight straight regional titles. The sport has grown immensely and hopefully it will continue to grow for years to come. Cheers to the life-long sport of tennis.

Traverse City's first tennis state champions, Thomas TenHoedt and Andrew Hamilton at #2 doubles in 1996.

First Trojan "Golden Regionals" winners, the 1993 girls team. Back Row: Sara Chambers, Alison Hoffman, Casey Cross, Julie MacIntosh, Jill Gregory, Stacey Portenga, Gretchen Shaw, Coach Nykerk. Front Row: Julie Nelson, Julie Eckhold, Jenny Brady, Sommer Gillow, Robin Ford, Katie Jacobs.

CLASS A TENNIS SINGLES ALL-STATE

1974	Steve Preston	
1975	Steve Preston	
	Jon Preston	
1976	Jon Preston	
1983	Chris Caldwell	
1984	Chris Caldwell	
	Blake Ringsmuth	
1988	Karl DeVries	
1989	Karl DeVries	Meg Wilson
1990	Aaron Murray	
1991	Aaron Murray	
1992	Aaron Murray	Gretchen Shaw
1993	Bryan Nykerk	Gretchen Shaw
1994	Kyle Gernhofer	Stacey Portenga
1995	Kyle Gernhofer	
1996	Kyle Gernhofer	
	Brent Bak	

Ranked #2 in the state before finishing 4th, the 1996 boys team set both of these records for Traverse City tennis. Back Row: Matt Jacobs, Matt Cozzens, Kyle Kilcherman, Mike Loesel, Kyle Gernhofer, Kyle Tousain, Coach Larry Nykerk. Front Row: Eric Holden, Mike Behm, Kory Gernhofer, Thomas tenHoedt, Brent Bak, Andrew Hamilton.

CLASS A TENNIS DOUBLES ALL-STATE

1995	Kyle Kilcherman/Kyle Tousain	
1996	Andrew Hamilton/Thomas tenHoedt	Caroline Montie/Jamie Montie

*PRINCE HIGH SCHOOL ALL-AMERICAN

1984 Chris Caldwell

TROJAN TENNIS RECORDS

Girls	Year of Record	Record
Sue Kausler/Stacey Kausler	1984	2 undefeated regular seasons
Gretchen Shaw	1993	3 years at #1 singles
Stacey Portenga	1994	116 career wins 4 regional titles
Emily MacIntosh/Heather Willson	1994	youngest doubles team (both freshmen)
Robin Ford	1996	116 career wins
Lisa Webster	1996	98 career wins in 3 years
1984 girls team		6th place state finish
1993 girls team		6th place state finish
1996 girls team		6th place state finish

Boys		
Aaron Murray	1992	3 years at #1 singles
Kyle Tousain	1996	123 career wins
Kyle Gernhofer	1996	3 years at #1 singles
Andrew Hamilton/Thomas tenHoedt	1996	first state championship (#2 doubles) 40 consecutive wins
Kyle Kilcherman/Kyle Tousain	1996	102 career doubles wins
1996 boys team		4th place state finish #2 state ranking

TROJAN TENNIS COACHES

BOYS

Gordon MacDonald	1928
Dale Carter	1928
Irving Menzel	1939
Robert Meggison	1939-1940
Bill Novak	1941-1943
Harold Andreas	1944-1946
Morris Carpenter	1947
Lee Brannock	1948
Harold Andreas	1949
Ed Howard	1950-1953
Robert Bacon	1954-1961
Tom Fennel	1962
Lyndon Salathiel	1963-1966
Ron Johnson	1967-1968
Larry Nykerk	1969-present

GIRLS

Gail Riley	1974
Margaret Lilly	1980
Larry Nykerk	1981-present

* *It should be noted that in tennis, the All-American honor is based upon a commercial sponsor and is not consistently underwritten by a sponsor year to year.*

8

BOYS GOLF

By Jennie Stratton

"Golf is a game whose aim is to hit a very small ball into an even smaller hole, with weapons singularily ill-designed for the purpose."
– WINSTON CHURCHILL.

The basic idea of golf has been around for centuries, the first game originating with the early Romans. "Paganica" was the name of the Roman game, which they played in the streets during their occupation of Britain from approximately 40 A.D. to the 400s. This game used a bent stick and a leather ball stuffed with feathers.

The game as we know it, however, probably originated in Scotland. The first set of written rules was devised by the Honourable Company of Edinburgh Golfers in Edinburgh, Scotland in 1744. Ten years later, the Royal and Ancient Golf Club of St. Andrews, known as the Society of St. Andrews Golfers, set the standard for eighteen holes. Golf had been played in America, but the first clubs were not established until the 1880s, in the New England states.

Boys golf in Traverse City, in the early years, was an off-again, on-again sport. It is difficult to determine the exact year that the Senior High adopted golf into the athletic program; however, the first recorded team is from 1928. Any teams that existed before this date were most likely club teams. Gordon MacDonald coached the 1928 golf team of Joy (captain), Robbins, Bramer and Milhulka.

The first two official seasons for Trojan golf were very successful. In both 1928 and 1929 Traverse City walked away with the regional crown. A placing such as this warranted a trip to the state finals. The 1928 finals were held in Detroit and the 1929 match was in Ypsilanti. For the trip to Ypsilanti, the boys were able to travel by car thanks to donations from area businessmen. After these dates the team is absent from school

The newly instituted 1938 Trojan golf team under Coach Charles Crawford.

records until they resurfaced again in 1932.

In the years following 1932, due to lack of interest and most likely funds, Traverse City did not have anyone within their region to compete against. The team made its second comeback in 1939. Charles Crawford was named the first official coach of the team. He had earned the title of "Golf Artist" while studying at Western State Teachers College (now known as Western Michigan University).

Crawford coached the team through the 1942 season. During the course of his coaching, Traverse City consistently beat the same teams. Big Rapids and Manistee were the usual fallen opponents while Cadillac was always a tough match. The conference meet of Coach Crawford's final season in 1942 was cancelled due to lack of competition.

In 1943, Coach Crawford was inducted into the Navy, making it necessary for a new coach to come forward. Stepping up to fill his shoes was "Dutch" Kanitz. There was little competition for the Trojans in 1943. The teams that did maintain a schedule, however, were easily beaten by Traverse City.

DUE TO THE WAR it became increasingly harder for the Traverse City boys to find teams to contend with. The only other schools that continued teams in 1944 were Manistee and Elk Rapids.

Irv Menzel coaching the 1949 team of Jerry Overholt, Earl Felske, Zeke Solomonson, Robert Overholt, Eugene Dennis.

State and regional tournaments were halted until the end of the war. Many schools dropped their programs until the reinstatement of the tournaments. Beginning again in 1945, schools slowly began to re-enter competition.

Harold Andreas assumed coaching responsibilities for the 1946 season, which was the only information available for that year. Following, in 1947, was Irv Menzel who led the team for the next seven years, until 1955.

Under the guidance of Coach Menzel, the team consistently improved. In the years 1947 to 1949, the Traverse City boys improved from fourth in the regional meet to second. In 1949 came the first trip to the state tournament in a few years. The team finished sixth in a field of 24 teams.

Once again, in 1951, they advanced to the state meet and this time completed the season in fourth place. In 1952, the boys had their best shot ever at winning the state tournament. Unfortunately, they were disqualified from the meet when Ron Wooters missed a putt and picked up his ball, ending a promising season.

Coach Menzel left the team after the 1954 season. No information could be found about the team for 1955. Bob Weaver entered the program in 1956 but coached the team for only one year and was followed Vern Hawes.

Due to snow and other bad conditions in 1957, the boys season did not begin until May fourth. The most interesting mishap of Coach Hawes' career centered around regionals. There was confusion surrounding the date and the team missed the meet.

Ed Schuknecht assumed coaching responsibilites in 1958. It took until 1966 for the team to

The 1958 team, from left to right: John Beall, Nick DeYoung, Bill Hicks, Hugo Trepte, George Drew, Lance Neuman, Wayne Burrows, Bill Heidbreder, George McCarty, Coach Ed Schuknecht.

achieve the past status of the Traverse City boys golf program. In the years between 1958 and 1966 they had low finishes in the regional meet. Part of the reason for this was shortened seasons because of foul weather.

The Trojans won the LMAC Conference title in 1967, a sweet reward for new coach John Connell. They also had a perfect record of 11-0, finished third in the regional, and traveled to the state tournament. Even though they repeated their conference championship, the 1968 team did not make it to the state finals. The only opponent to better the Trojans was Traverse City St. Francis, by one stroke.

For the next couple of years the team kept getting different coaches. Larry Grow led the team in 1969, and Larry Schroeder in 1970. In 1971, Jim Raymond took over the team and remained coach for a number of years.

With the consistency of one coaching method, Traverse City began to improve their play. They started to have winning records and in 1974 they were 8-0. That was also the year that the LMAC conference match became a round-robin event.

After finishing third in the conference and second in regionals, the boys advanced to the state finals in 1977. In 1977 and 1978, the Trojans also broke a few old-standing school records. In 1977, they bettered the record for lowest team score in a meet twice, which the 1978 team broke again the next year.

Dan Young was the next coach for Traverse City, taking over in 1980. During the three years that he was coach, Traverse City had young players and limited competition. The team competed with only Alpena and Cadillac in 1982.

THE NEXT PERSON TO STEP IN AS COACH was Bob Lober, who is also the current coach. Under his coaching the Trojans continued to improve more and more each year. The number of matches the Trojans competed in increased greatly at the time Lober became coach. Lober also began the intramural team, allowing for more students to improve their skills.

The early to mid 1980s were dominated by Jason Bostwick '87 and Dave Rutkowski '88. In 1984, Bostwick was nominated for All-State hon-

The 1977 boys golf team. Front Row: Ron Franks, Tom Chandler, Mark Schafer, Brian Stricker, Bob Bell, Scott Alpers; Back Row: John VanWezel, Mike Smith, Jeff Geiger, Mike Meindertsma, Pat McDuff, Peter Clark, Tom Cizek, Loren Washburn, Don Piche', Chris Regan, Dave Milligan, Jeff Dow, Paul Wyatt, Jeff Farrell, Darren LaCharite, Coach Jim Raymond.

ors and the following year became the first Traverse City golfer to be named to the Class A All-State team. In 1986 Bostwick, again selected All-State, and sophomore Rutkowski, who was nominated for that honor, led the team to a fourth place regional finish. In 1987, Rutkowski was first medalist at regionals and third medalist in the state as the team took a 10th place state finish. Rutkowski became the first Trojan to be named to the All-State Super Team (the best five players in the state). As a senior with a 78.0 scoring average, Rutkowski led the team to a third place in the regionals, a repeat 10th in the state and another All-State selection.

Both 1989 and 1990 were disappointing years because each had excellent teams who were ranked as high as No. 3 in the state during the season but placed fifth at regionals, failing to make the state meet. At the 1989 Grand Blanc Tournament, four Trojan golfers (Sean Sommerfield, Dudley Smith, Jon Shaw and Scott Thompson) shot 79 or better for a total of 306. "That's the best score I can remember us shooting in a major tournament since I've been coach," praised Coach Lober. Also that year, freshman Mike Kramer was fifth medalist at regionals which qualified him for the state finals, "almost unheard of for a freshman," stated Lober. In 1990, Adam Warren, Kelly Robinson and Kramer led the team to four tournament wins. Despite the fact that the team did not qualify for state competition (although Warren did as an individual), the strength of this team was shown as Warren and Robinson were named All-State and Kramer, Honorable Mention.

The 1990s started out with a strong 1991 team that was ranked No. 1 during the season. Low scorer Kelly Robinson set a Traverse City record with a 69 on the Forest Akers course. With four tournament wins, six second places and a third, this was the "best ever" team according to Lober, at that time. The Gold team of Robinson, Adam Warren, Mike Kramer, Justin Keillor and Ryan Cerny won the regional meet for the first time and placed second in the state, the Trojans' highest finish. Robinson was fourth medalist in the state and was named to the All-State Super Team while Warren, who had had a fourth place regional finish, was honored as All-State. Coach Lober was named Coach of the Year after this successful year.

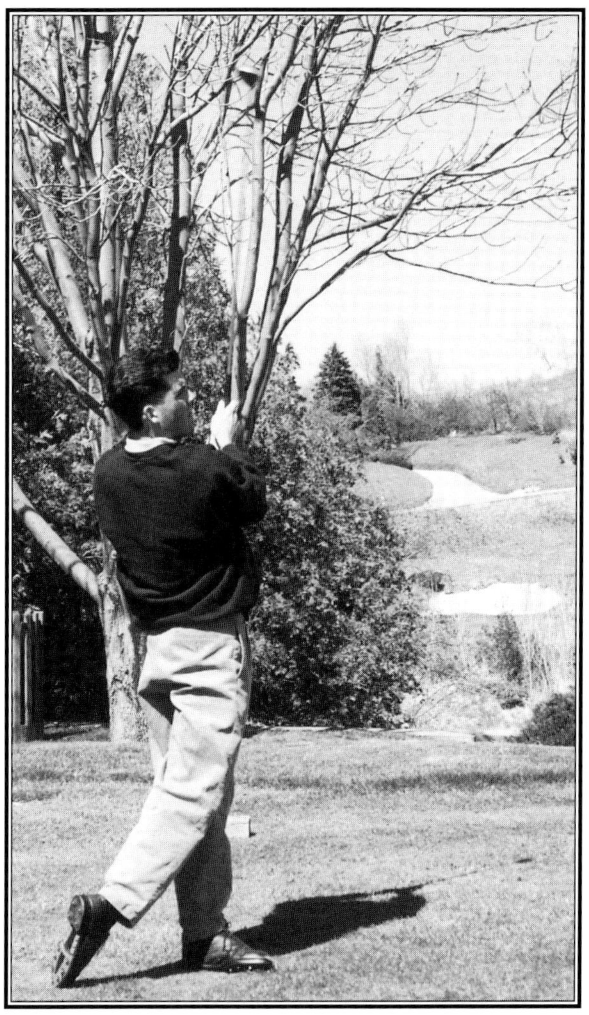

Super Team member Kelly Robinson tees off.

THE 1992 TEAM PRODUCED another All-State Super Team member in Mike Kramer and All-Stater Justin Keillor as they won regionals and placed eighth in the state. The following year had five tournament medalists (Mike Schultz, Keillor, Matt Kalat, Brett Anable and Kyle Tousain) although they did not qualify for states. According to Lober, the regional meet was played at North Kent, "a fairly easy course which leveled the playing field." Keillor, however, was selected All-State for the second year.

By 1994, the Trojans were on a roll. The team had a 22-0 record, were regional champions and state runners-up. The top five scorers were fractions apart in their scoring averages: Kyle Tousain (79.4), Matt Kalat (79.5), Kyle Kilcherman (79.6), Paul Berry (79.7) and Chris Stefanciw (80.3). Matt Kalat shot a 69 at Elmbrook to tie Kelly Robinson's school record. Berry was regional medalist and All-State. At the state finals, Brett Anable was fifth medalist and Kalat sixth.

The 1995 team seemed to progress even further as it became "the finest team in Trojan golf history so far," according to Coach Lober. The Gold team of Kyle Kilcherman, Brian Seipke, Kyle Tousain, Jacob Burden and Jan Smits won 11 of 12 tournament titles and took one second place. They went on to win regionals with Kilcherman the first medalist and Seipke second. Having been ranked as high as No. 1 in the state, the team was eight strokes behind eventual state champion Grand Ledge after the first day of state play. The next day the Trojans came back as the low scorers to finish third in the state. Seipke was fourth state medalist, with Kilcherman and Tousain both seventh. As a result of their performances, cousins Kilcherman and Seipke were both named to the All-State Super Team and Tousain to the Class A All-State team. Bob Lober was nominated for National Golf Coach of the Year with an impressive 254-26 record.

The 1996 Trojan golf team set a record in Michigan high school boys golf as they were undefeated in match play, won all 12 invitationals, captured the regional title and were state champions! Several team and individual records were set: team scoring average of 307; tournament record of 339-1 in 16 tournaments; varsity scoring average of 80.3 in 157 rounds; top five scoring average of 77.7; state champion medalist – Brian Seipke; individual scoring average – Kilcherman with 74.8; seniors' combined scoring average of 76.5 (Berry, Kilcherman and Seipke); and first hole in one in competition – Tom Brayton at regionals. Both Kilcherman, first medalist at regionals and third in the state, and first state medalist Seipke were again named to the All-State Super Team and were both up for the Mr. Golf award. Coach Lober, now with a 270-27 overall record, was named Boys Golf Coach of the Year as well as Class A Boys Golf Coach of the Year.

The state meet that year wasn't completely tense; there were some light moments. On Friday

The 1996 team, which won the first Trojan state championship golf title. Back Row: Head Coach Bob Lober, Carl Gagnon, Andrew Calcutt, Derrick Smith, Tom Brayton, Jamie Berry, Brian Seipke, Kyle Kilcherman, Chris Baic, Jay Cassens, Kelly Robinson. Front Row: Chris Kellogg, Casey Smits, Chris Rogers, Robbie Tighe, Mitch McDonald, Mike Dean, Joe Lihne.

Cousins Kyle Kilcherman and Brian Seipke cap off a championship year by both signing to play for the University of Michigan.

night, after the first day of the state tournament, Trojans Kyle Kilcherman, Brian Seipke, Jamie Berry, Chris Kellogg and Tom Brayton had a fairly comfortable eight-stroke lead. Both days of competition were played on the tough West Forest Akers course which was advantageous to the Trojans. The only trouble was on that Friday night, the toilet in the room shared by Brayton, Kellogg and Berry leaked all night. At 3:00 a.m., a hotel employee woke them up to find 1 1/2" of water in their room. After having to change rooms, they did not get much sleep that night. All the laughs they had over this "must have kept them loose," explained Coach Lober, as they won the state championship title the next day.

Over the past 11 years of the Traverse City golf team, the program has continued to improve. Five Trojans have been placed on the All-State Super Team, two of them twice. In just the past five years, Coach Lober's teams have been regional champions four times, state runners-up twice, third in the state once and finally, state champions. Traverse City now has established itself as a golf powerhouse in Michigan.

BOYS GOLF ALL-STATE SUPER TEAM

1987	Dave Rutkowski
1991	Kelly Robinson
1992	Mike Kramer
1995	Kyle Kilcherman
	Brian Seipke
1996	Kyle Kilcherman
	Brian Seipke

CLASS A BOYS GOLF ALL-STATE

	First Team	Honorable Mention	Nominee
1984			Jason Bostwick
1985	Jason Bostwick		
1986	Jason Bostwick		Dave Rutkowski

CLASS A BOYS GOLF ALL-STATE (continued)

	First Team	Honorable Mention	Nominee
1988	Dave Rutkowski		
1989		Sean Sommerfield	
		Kelly Robinson	
1990	Adam Warren	Mike Kramer	
	Kelly Robinson		
1991	Adam Warren	Mike Kramer	Justin Keillor
1992	Justin Keillor		
1993	Justin Keillor	Mike Schultz	
1994	Paul Berry		Brett Anable
			Matt Kalat
			Justin Keillor
			Kyle Tousain
			Kyle Kilcherman
1995	Kyle Tousain		Jacob Burden
1996		Jamie Berry	Tom Brayton
		Chris Kellogg	

ACADEMIC ALL-STATE

	First Team	Honorable Mention	Nominee
1991		Ed Maier	Adam Warren
1992	Chad Bigelow		
1994	Matt Maitland		Chris Stefanciw

TROJAN BOYS GOLF COACHES

1928	Gordon MacDonald
1939-1942	Charles Crawford
1943-1945	Dutch Kanitz
1946	Harold Andreas
1947-1955	Irv Menzel
1956-1957	Bob Weaver
1958	Vern Hawes
1959-1966	Ed Schuknecht
1967-1968	John Connell
1969	Larry Grow
1970	Larry Schroeder
1971-1980	Jim Raymond
1981-1983	Dan Young
1984 – present	Bob Lober

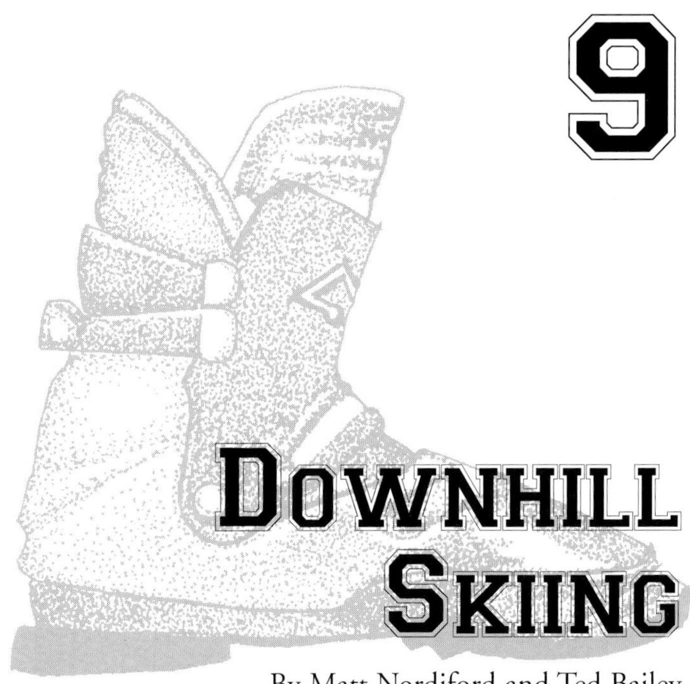

9

Downhill Skiing

By Matt Nordjford and Ted Bailey

"You can't depend on your judgement when your imagination is out of focus."

– Mark Twain

1954 was the inaugural year of a new interscholastic sport in Michigan. The Michigan High School Athletic Association officially recognized downhill skiing and sponsored a Lower Peninsula meet at Sugar Loaf with ten participating schools and 92 contestants. Coached by Jim Ooley, the Trojans formed both boys and girls ski teams that first year. At the Sugar Loaf meet, the girls took first honors, as they had in every meet they entered that year. Top skier Barbara Sherberneau won every meet in which she competed. The boys finished fourth with captain Larry Bensley taking first in the downhill. Later that season, the Trojan boys took first in downhill, slalom and cross-country over Midland and Cadillac.

With new coach Richard Hoag, the 1955 season had six dual and triangular meets not counting the Caberfae regionals (with Leelanau, Atlanta, Gaylord, Bay City Central, West Branch, St. Ignace, Boyne City and Grayling) and a winter play day for members of the Arrowhead Conference held at Hickory Hills. The boys team of John McGuffin, Jerry Meach, Russ Adams, Roy Arnoldt, Jim Beebe and Richard Zue won only two meets including a total upset over Leelanau at Sugar Loaf. Fortunately, Meach and Zue were the only seniors so most of the team members were returning the next year. Joey Cowell was the top skier for the Trojan girls until a bad fall at Sugar Loaf put her on the bench for the rest of the season and left teammates Joan Lovell, Susanne Gregory, Connie Meach and Meredith Raftshol without her. In February, the first meet held under lights in lower Michigan was held with Cadillac at Hickory Hills.

In 1956, former Trojan star Barbara Sherberneau returned to coach along with Richard Hoag to produce the top ski team in the conference. The girls team won all eight meets that season, while the boys only won five. Both teams had a tough time with injuries as Meredith Raftshol, Betty Shield, Jim Beebe and Roy Arnoldt all hurt their ankles during the season. Top skiers were Connie Meach and Roy Arnoldt until his injury, when John McGuffin took top honors. It had only been a few years since the first ski team at Traverse City and already it had become a very popular sport. The girls team won the state meet this year.

THE 1957 TRAVERSE CITY SKI TEAMS HAD A GREAT YEAR. Under new coach Art Schubert, the girls once again took first place at the state meet held in Leelanau, beating their long-time rival Cadillac. The top girl skier was Joni Lovell, who also won the title of being the top girl skier in the Lower Peninsula. John McGuffin, Traverse City's #1 skier, took the same honor for the boys team which took a third at the state meet. That year the boys team lost McGuffin, Bob McCall, Marshall Carr, Jim Palmer and Jon Beebe to graduation. On the girls side, only Betty Shield would not be returning.

The 1958 teams had another great season. The girls team once again proved themselves to be queens of the slopes. The girls team had outstanding members in Connie Meach, Meredith Raftshol and Joni Lovell. They were a powerhouse, winning all duals and regionals. Unfortunately, these top three skiers would be graduating. The boys team, all underclassmen, still took third in regionals. This was not a bad accomplishment considering there was only one returning racer from the 1957 year. This was a big rebuilding year for the boys team.

The 1959 ski season was supposed to be a rebuilding year for the girls ski team. They had been hit hard by graduation, but the girls didn't quit at the end of their season. After they had won every meet during the season, they then took first at regionals as they were led by All-Stater Sue Arnoldt. The boys team, led by Dick Swan, ended up placing second in the regionals. All in all, it was a good year.

The 1960 ski season was phenomenal! Traverse City definitely showed their school spirit on the slopes as they took three road trips to Leelanau, Gaylord and Thunder Mountain. The boys team of juniors Mike Merrill, Dick Swan, Dick Bohn, Bud Zue and senior Bill King along with Jim Frasier, Chuck Ferguson and John Stanek cleaned up at regionals with a winning margin of 86 seconds! This was a huge improvement from their second place standing the previous year. Sue Arnoldt won the regional title and with team-

Leading Trojan skiers of 1954, Barbara Sherberneau and Larry Bensley.

mates Sandy Shield, Mary Jo Williams, Sharon Raftshol and Mary Hunsberger won the state title by a slim margin. Coach Schubert had the most successful season since the beginning of this relatively new sport. Traverse City was finally recognized as the team to beat.

1961 proved to be a season of great change for the ski team. For the first time since the beginning of Traverse City skiing, the girls team placed second at regionals. Despite their loss, Sandy Shield (the only senior), Mary Jo Williams and Bonnie Stults skied well. The boys team, however, finished first again at regionals beating out such powerhouses as Cadillac and Leelanau, although their team of Mike Merrill (All-State), Jim Frasier, Ken King, Dick Swan, Dick Bohn and freshman Len Ligon (All-State) had four seniors graduating. Skiing against Harbor Springs, Ludington, Cadillac, Atlanta, Boyne City and Gaylord, this was also to be the last year for coach Art Schubert.

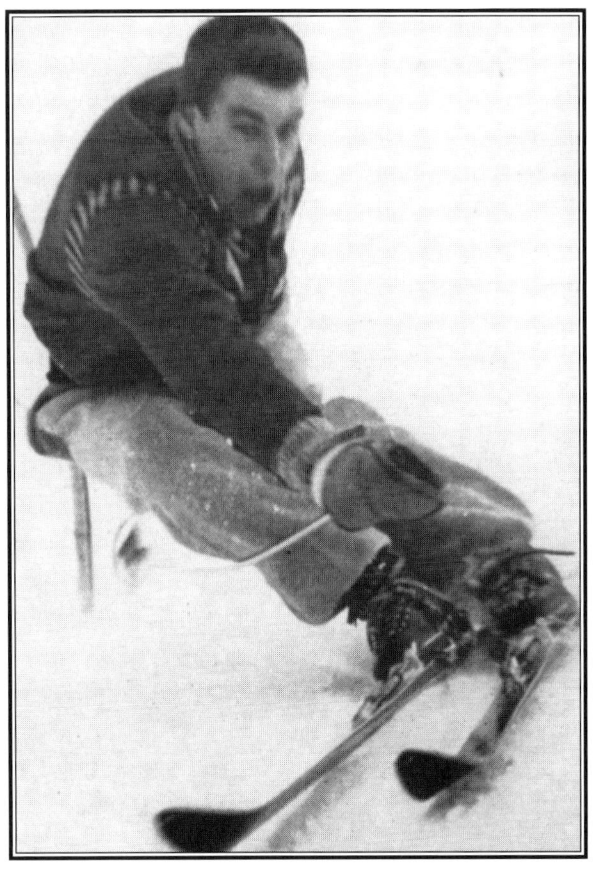

1957 racer John McGuffin in a reverse shoulder turn.

THE 1962 TRAVERSE CITY SKI TEAM WAS UNDER A NEW COACH, Russ Luttinen. Coach Luttinen's training was very rigorous; he expected only the best from his racers and rarely let them use a rope tow to reach the top of the hill. Walking up the hills was the best was to stay in shape, he thought. He believed skiing should be run like any other varsity sport. The team's determination and his hard work paid off, as both girls and boys teams won their state championships! They would also be strong contenders for the next year as the only leading seniors for the boys were Ken Lindsay and Ken King. Val Hays, Lorna Stulen, Bonnie Stults,

1962 boys team: Mgr. Chris Jones, Jim Milliken, Henry Clark, Jerry Kammerer, Jim Murner, Bill Milliken, Jim Merrill, Ken King, Len Ligon, Ken Lindsay, Jim Olson, Roger Downer, Ken Lynch, Gej Jones, Jack McAdams, Steve Cornwell, Coach Russ Luttinen.

Beth Perkett, and Francie Dorman were all underclassmen who won four of the first five places at the state meet. For her outstanding performance, Hays was named All-State.

Even before the 1963 ski season started for the Traverse City team, their training was well under way. The team had a huge reputation to live up to from the year before. For the girls team, it would be easy. The entire team remained intact from last years' championship team which was a major plus for them. Captain Bonnie Stults, along with other racers Val Hays, Jane Frasier, Lorna Stulen, Beth Perkett, Marilyn King, Francie Dorman, Pam Lantz and Roberta Kyselka, literally ran away with every meet they were in. The boys, however, had only three returning lettermen for the 1962-1963 year. Despite the team's obstacles, Traverse City prevailed. Both the girls and boys teams coasted to victory in the Lower Peninsula Ski regionals held at Hickory Hills. Losing only Steve Cornwell to graduation, the 1963 team under captain Jim Murner had plenty of experience to carry this year's victory through to the next year. Also returning would be Len Ligon, named All-State again this year as was Val Hays.

The boys and girls teams both looked forward to another successful season in 1964. Aside from losing four girls to graduation the year before, the girls team maintained their standard of excellence. They extended their winning streak to 42 wins since 1961 and for the third straight year swept all meets and the regionals. Captain Francie Dorman was the winner of the Lower Michigan Girl Skier of the Year Award while Val Hays received All-State honors for the third year. Rounding out this team were Pam Lantz, Marge VanderWall, Cherie Gibson, Luana Kyselka, Cary Thompson and Marilyn King. Led by All-State team captain Jim Merrill, the boys team continued its dominance of Lower Peninsula skiing with a perfect season. That year was their fifth straight winning season and the fifth regional crown in a row for them. Team members Len Ligon and Jerry Stanek (both All-State), Jerry Kammerer, Gej Jones, Jim Murner, Jim Rennie and Tom Shield made up the strongest ski team in ten years of interscholastic competition. The girls also had a perfect season.

COACH LUTTINEN ONCE AGAIN PROVED that Traverse City was the team to beat for the 1965 ski season. The boys team ended with a perfect 18-0 record. Key team members like All-Staters captain Jim Rennie and Jerry Stanek helped make the season a stupendous one which included their fifth consecutive regional win. The girls team also made a huge splash for this year's circuit. Led by All-State captain Cherie Gibson, this team won regionals for the fourth straight time. This year

1962 Trojan girls: Mary Thirlby, Sue Schrotenboer, Margaret Kysleka, Pam Thompson, Marilyn King, Jane Frasier, Francie Dorman, Bonnie Stults, Beth Perkett, Lorna Stulen, Val Hays, Pam Lantz, Coach Luttinen.

Coach Luttinen was awarded Coach of the Year by *The Detroit News.*

In 1966, the Trojan boys and girl skiers again proved unbeatable! That was probably the best season so far for the Traverse City ski teams. For the sixth straight year, in Coach Luttinen's sixth season, the boys team took first in the Lower Peninsula championships. The team, led by captain Jerry Stanek, ended with a perfect 13-0 score. Jerry Stanek, All-State for the third year, Jim Rennie, All-State the second time, Tom Shield and Jim Owens, named All-State this year, along with teammates Ted Thirlby, Chuck Ligon and Tom Bensley, had now compiled a 47-win streak. The girls team also had an impeccable season led by captain Cary Thompson and All-Staters Cherie Gibson and Cathy Paulos. Cherie Gibson was honored as Michigan Skier of the Year after leading the girls team to the Lower Peninsula championships. A mild season erased the opening meet at Hickory Hills, the second one at Sugar Loaf, and Sugar Loaf and Thunder Mountain meets in February. Coach Luttinen was named Michigan Ski Coach of the Year for the second time after one of the best teams in Trojan skiing history. Unfortunately 12 seniors left at the end of this season, leaving Traverse City with much rebuilding to do.

Despite this huge loss from graduation, the 1967 ski team had a very admirable year, starting the season off with a new coach, Lyndon Salathiel. At the end of the season, the boys team took a close second to Gaylord at the regionals while the girls took a disappointing fourth. During the regular season the boys team had only one loss, their first in 50 meets. Cathy Paulos was the only Trojan to be named All-State that year.

Traverse City once again proved superior during the 1968 ski season. Led by captains Glenn Hazelton and Cathy Paulos, the boys team of Bruce Beers, Chuck Ligon, Dan Kipley, Tom Lindsay and Rick Thirlby took first at the regionals by a slim margin while the girls, helped by Cindy Cottom, Tracey Long and Shelley Thayer on the other hand, placed third. One week before the regionals, Paulos fractured her ankle. Despite her disappointing injury, she was still named to the All-State ski team for her third and final year. Also selected as All-State was Barb Bohn. Other top teams at that regional were Cadillac, Gaylord, St. Francis, Grayling and Petoskey.

During the 1969 ski season, the Traverse City High School boys team posted another perfect season, despite the loss of senior Tom Lindsay due to a broken ankle. The boys team of Dan Kipley, Rick Thirlby, Jim Babel, Bill Hazelton, Chip Stulen,

Unbeaten 1966 Trojans: Mgr. Dennis Hoxsie, Chuck Ligon, Capt. Jerry Stanek, Ted Thirlby, Jim Rennie, Jim Owens, Tom Shields, Tom Bensley, Capt. Cary Thompson, Luana Kyselka, Marge Vanderwall, Cathy Paulos, Jeanne Feiker, Cherie Gibson, Coach Russ Luttinen.

Bob Werner and Ken Core went undefeated and won the regionals again, thanks to their superior depth. The girls team sadly lost two meets and placed second at the regionals. The only senior on the team, Barb Bohn, skied well throughout the season, as did Tracey Long, Lynn Hazelton, Shelley Thayer, Pat Nagy, Kathy Hayes and Meredith Parsons. Seniors Barb Bohn and Dan Kipley, three-year letter winners, were named to the All-State ski team, along with junior Rick Thirlby.

The 1970 ski team had a successful season. The boys were regional champions and placed second to St. Francis in the West Bloomfield Invitational, the first unofficial state meet. Traverse City High School and the Grand Traverse Ski Club hosted this meet, held at Timberlee for the top two teams in each region. Captain Rick Thirlby made the All-State team for the second year in a row. Tracey Long captained the girls team to a second place regional finish and a win at West Bloomfield. *The Detroit News* named coach Lyn Salathiel the Coach of the Year.

The 1971 girls team, led by All-Staters Rondi Wuerful and Jackie Core and helped by Cynthia Hazelton and Marlene Hines, won regionals with slalom finishes of second, third, fourth, fifth & sixth places. They lost the West Bloomfield Invitational, however, to Marquette by only .087 seconds. Taking third at regionals was the boys team of Tom Hazelton, Ken Core, Ted Kramer, Tom Wiley, Dave Webster, Tim Wiley, Bruce King and Pete Norcross.

THE 1972 SEASON WAS ABSOLUTELY PERFECT. It was the 11th regional crowning for the boys and the 13th for the girls since the meet originated in 1954. The regional meet was a fitting climax to the end of a wonderful season. The girls team placed third at the West Bloomfield Invitational at Timberlee. However, even with All-Stater Toubo Collings, the boys team did not place. In this first year of B team competition, these teams took close second places behind the A teams.

In 1973, both boys and girls teams won the first annual Northwestern Michigan Ski Conference meet at Sugar Loaf. Cynthia Hazelton captured both the slalom and giant slalom events for the girls, with Mary Jo Thiel taking a second and third. After winning regionals, the girls took second to Hancock at the West Bloomfield Invitational at Thunder Mountain where Julie Pelto was named All-State. The boys team was led by All-Conference juniors Jim Fredrickson, who won the giant slalom, and Tom Babel, taking top honors in the slalom. At the regional meet, Toubo Collings blew away all his competition in slalom, winning by a four-second margin, although the boys as a team came in fourth.

The 1974 ski team had a fantastic season. The boys' overall record was 10-3 while the girls clung to a 9-4 record. Both the boys and girls reigned as regional champs once again. Because of these wins, both teams competed in the unofficial state meet held at Timberlee. Here the boys team took fifth and the girls team placed second. Based on this meet, Kathy Ferrar, Julie Pelto, and Jim Frederickson were named to the All-State team.

The Trojan ski team of 1975 proved it was probably the best team ever to appear under the name Traverse City and even in the history of state high school competition up to this time. The racers had a flawless season as Don Dunsmore began as assistant coach to Lyn Salathiel. The girls squad never really had any competition from the other teams since they were just too fast. Before capping off their season by winning the first official state meet at Marquette, both boys and girls teams swept through all regular season competition, the conference meet and regionals. Losing Dick Kipley, Paul Wiley, Pat Nuyens, Paul Schneider, Cheryl Hutchinson and Lynn Mattern to graduation was made easier with all the young talent. Still around for the following year were Tammy Hagerty, Ann Alward, Jane Gilmore, Bill Bogley, Ted Lockwood, Keith Forton and Brian Hutchinson. Named All-State were Judy Kramer, Tammy Hagerty and Jim Wagener. Coach Salathiel was again named *The Detroit News* Coach of the Year after this highly successful season.

In the 1976 ski season, adversity appeared to be a key word for the Trojans. In a quest for their second consecutive state championship, Bill Bogley, Brian Hutchinson and Judy Kramer had problems with injuries while Ted Lockwood and Jim Wagener left with hopes for higher achievement in independent competition. However, these losses were offset by strong performances from Nick Nixon, Tammy Hagerty, Ann Alward, Julie Basta, Shane Evans, Keith Forton and Jane Gilmore as both teams repeated as champions in the regional and state meets. The girls team made a statement by beating Cadillac by a whopping 48-113 score. Hagerty and Kramer received All-State recognition for the second time and Nixon and Brian Hutchinson for their first award. Coach Salathiel received *The Detroit News* Coach of the Year honor for the third time.

Coach Salathiel led both the 1977 boys and girls teams to winning seasons. Both placed first in regionals while the girls took third at the state competiton and the boys fourth. Outstanding competitors were Tammy Hagerty, the most consistent skier on the girls team, Karen Hutchinson, Nick Nixon, (the best skier in Michigan, an All-State racer and one of the best in the central U.S.), All-Stater Bruce Hutchinson, Shane Evans and Bill Bogley.

THE 1978 TROJAN SKI TEAM HAD A VERY SUCCESSFUL SEASON. Under Coach Salathiel, the boys were co-champs with Cadillac in the Northwest Michigan Ski Conference and the girls took second. In the regional meet, the girls ended in second place while the boys won. Top finishers

The 1976 Trojans. Front Row: Bruce Hutchinson, Rich Core, Brian Hutchinson, Keith Forton, Nick Nixon, John Guba, Shane Evans. Second Row: Lynn Wright, Julie Basta, Tammy Hagerty, Judy Kramer, Ann Alward, Jane Gilmore, Heather Lockwood, Jill Mattern. Back Row: Bill Bogley, Coaches Don Dunsmore and Lyn Salathiel.

were Heather Lockwood, Shelley Wilson, Cindy Newhouse, Karen Hutchinson, Dan Elliott, Scott Thompson and Mark Music. Heather Lockwood was selected to the All-State team.

The 1979 boys team had an excellent season, capturing the state title over ten teams at Iron Mountain. The girls, on the other hand, had an off season, so to speak, taking a disappointing fourth. Pacing the Trojans were All-Staters Karen Hutchinson, Dan Lautner and Mark Dancer, along with Cae Madion and Patty Cartwright. Although the boys came in second behind Cadillac in the Northwest Ski Conference, captain Dan Elliott stated, "We were only following suit with the football team when we didn't win our conference."

Despite starting the 1980 season with no snow and having a young team, the boys team placed third in the state. Team members included All-Staters Dan Lautner and Cae Madion, Shelley Wilson, Patty Cartwright, Bruce Lockwood, Brad Schwarm, Don Hicks, Matt Madion (captain), Jody Becsey, Kelly Kerlin, Michelle McGuffin, Wendy Jerome, Paul Johnston, Mark Music, Mike Kibler, Olga Baic, Lori Lather, Dave Phelps, Matt Boushor and Dan LeHoullier.

Nick Nixon, one of the top Trojan skiers of all times.

The 1981 boys ski team had a tough season. John Maunders and Brad Schwarm showed consistent top ten finishes, earning them All-Confernce honors, with teammate Paul Johnston chosen for honorable mention, although the team as a whole did not score well at regionals. The girls team, on the other hand, placed second at the state meet, paced by Cae Madion who was named All-State for the second time.

The 1982 season was the year of snow storms and a lot of young skiers. Seniors leaving their mark were G.J. Newhouse, Mike Wilson, and exchange student Bjorn Hagglund, in addition to underclassmen Craig Fiebing, Kevin Nelson, Greg Bohn, Richard (Cricket) Crampton and Jon Elliot, on a team that finished third at state finals. The girls team struggled with injuries to Tammy Lautner, Susan Mikowski and Ann Stephen in addition to meet cancellations. Outstanding performances by Kathy Skendzel, Ann Stephen and Trina Fiebing helped the team to a fourth place regional finish.

1983 proved to be an outstanding year for Traverse City. The boys team once again proved to be the best in the state. All-Stater Greg Bohn, Scott Schwarm, Cam Shaw, Craig Fiebing and Dave Cunningham led them to another state title as they captured four of the state's top ten places. The girls team swept regionals and took second at states with outstanding performances from Trina Fiebing and Kathy Skendzel, who were both named All-State.

The 1984 girls team had a good season even though they placed third in regionals and didn't qualify for state finals. All-Conference selections were Megan Madion, Mary Beth Skendzel and freshman Mollie Schwarm. Romy Gingras and Susan Mikowski battled injuries throughout the season, but were helped out by Kristen Salathiel. The boys team, starring captain Scott Schwarm, Greg Bohn, Jon Elliott, Richard Crampton, Dave Stephen, Dave Cunningham, Jim Woodburne, Tim Woodburne and Eric Rohwetter, was a big success. However, after winning regionals by a large margin, placing second to Petoskey at the state meet was a disappointment. Schwarm and Bohn received All-State recognition for their performances. Both were three-year letter winners along with Elliott and Crampton.

In Coach Salathiel's last season, a dominant 1985 girls team never suffered a loss all year. Easily winning the state finals at Crystal Mountain for the first time in nine years were All-Stater Mollie Schwarm, Mary Beth Skendzel, Amy Colligan, Liz Chambers, Kristin Salathiel, Jennifer Dunsmore, Allison Stegenga and Leslie Davison. A young boys team also went undefeated through the state meet. Led by state slalom champion Jim Woodburne (named All-State), three others who also placed in the top ten were Tim Woodburne, Dave Cunningham and Tim Cairns.

In 1986, Traverse City was headed by two new coaches, Don Dunsmore as the boys coach and alumnus Jerry Stanek as the girls coach. Both teams pulled away with a perfect season and won state titles. A powerful boys team was led by Jim Woodburne in his third year as a varsity skier. He took first place in the slalom and giant slalom at both the regional and state meets. In a season in which Cadillac was the serious competition, other strong performers were Chris Bohn, Dan Culp, Scott Zimmerman, Kurt Bader, Matt Lambert, Vince Fochtman and Matt Robb. The girls team, "one of the strongest I've seen in recent years," according to Coach Dunsmore, took six of the top ten places at regionals, which to Dunsmore's knowledge had never happened before. In the state finals, Mollie Schwarm took second and Mary Beth Skendzel third, which earned them both All-State honors.

After winning the state championship two years in a row, the 1987 girls team took a surprise second-place finish to Harbor Springs. Coached again by Don Dunsmore and Jerry Stanek, they had a great year which produced a large number of All-Conference skiers: Mollie Schwarm, named All-State for her third year and the first Trojan to make the All-Conference ski team four years in a row, Liz Chambers, Chris Chirgwin, Allison Stegenga, Mary Beth Skendzel, Jennifer Dunsmore, with special merit to Leslie

The 1986 boys state champions. Front Row: Vince Fochtman, Jim Woodburne, Matt Robb, Matt Lambert. Back Row: Dan Culp, Chris Bohn, Scott Zimmerman, Kurt Bader, Coach Don Dunsmore.

Davison. The boys team, with All-Stater Matt Lambert, Chris Bohn, Tod Lautner, Vince Fochtman, Mike Simpson and John Rockwood, lost the state title to Petoskey by just half a point. That year, former coach Lyn Salathiel was named to the Michigan High School Ski Coaches Hall Fame in recognition of his nineteen successful years as Traverse City ski team coach.

In 1988, the girls team had a terrible upset. For the first time in 10 years, they did not qualify for the state meet. At regionals Jennifer Dunsmore fell as the very first racer and had to be taken off the hill by a tobaggon, needing knee surgery the next week. Needless to say, the accident really shook up the team and their spirits were shattered. "Ten days ago with a full team we beat both Harbor [Springs] and Petoskey. So after what happened earlier in the week [losing a skier to ineligibility], watching Jenny being taken off on a tobaggon was devastating. It was my worst day as a coach," said Jenny's father Coach Dunsmore. Out of the girls team of Dunsmore, Renee Huckle, Shelly Fochtman, Lyra Cockrum, Shannon Carlson, Erika Chirgwin, Chris Zoutendyk, Lisa Petty and freshman Amy Portenga, only Huckle and Portenga qualified for the state meet at Marquette as individuals. Jennifer Dunsmore was named All-State because of top finishes before her injury.

The 1988 boys, however, finished first at regionals where an important contribution came from co-captains John Rockwood who finished seventh in slalom after starting in the 80th position. At the state meet they edged Birmingham Brother Rice and Petoskey by using their depth. On this winning team were co-captains and All-Staters Matt Lambert and Tod Lautner, Mike Simpson, Matt Anderson, Steve Owens, John Rockwood, Mike Wells and freshman Chip Petty.

The 1989 boys season began with the loss of two racers, Chip Petty and Mike Wells, to eastern alpine academies in addition to the four who had graduated. The girls team benefitted from the return of Amy Robb from two years at Bay Race Academy and the transfers of Emily Fisher from New England

The 1986 state championship girls team. Front Row: Mollie Schwarm, Mary Beth Skendzel, Jennifer Dunsmore. Back Row: Coach Jerry Stanek, Liz Chambers, Leslie Davison, Allison Stegenga, Renee Huckle, Chris Chirgwin, Coach Don Dunsmore. Not pictured: Amy Robb.

and Heather Johnson from Manistee, but had to do without Amy Portenga for most of the season due to both knee and head injuries. Funds from the feeder program at Grand Traverse Ski Club allowed the Trojans to hire a third coach, Craig Fiebing, to work with the growing number of racers on the B teams, while Dunsmore concentrated on the boys team and Stanek the girls.

Leading the boys team were captain Mike Simpson, Matt Anderson, Jeff Owens, Tyler Blumenfeld, and sophomore Spencer Stegenga. After winning most of the races during the regular season, seniors Robb and Owens repeated as double winners at regionals. "In my 14 years of coaching, that's the first time I can recall two individuals from the same school sweeping both events," said Coach Dunsmore. At the state meet at Nub's Nob, both teams captured state crowns as the boys defeated Petoskey. The girls trounced Cadillac 51-110 as Robb became the state giant slalom champion and she, Shelly Fochtman, Jeff Owens and Mike Simpson were named All-State.

THE NEW DECADE STARTED with seemingly the same success as the 1980s. Both Trojan teams were ranked high throughout the 1990 ski season. Spencer Stegenga and Heather Johnson, the #1 skiers, paced the Trojans, winning a good share of all the races. The boys team edged Petoskey for the state title with Stegenga's third place in slalom the top finish. Even though the girls were conference champions, they had to settle for a very close second behind Cadillac at the state finals. Coach Stanek's girls team had not lost a meet all season

1989 state champion boys and girls teams. Front Row: Ben Ferris, Amy Robb, Spencer Stegenga, Amy Portenga, Libby Hoxsie. Back Row: Tyler Blumenfeld, Jeff Owens, Shelly Fochtman, Jamie Arnold, Tyler Blumenfeld, Terry Raven, Mike Simpson, Lisa Petty, Pat Robson, Coach Don Dunsmore, Renee Huckle, Shannon Carlson, Emily Fisher, Erika Chirgwin, Chris Zoutendyk.

until they met their match at the finals. Johnson prevailed as state giant slalom champion along with a third place in the slalom to take All-State honors with Stegenga. Coach Dunsmore was named the Michigan High School Coaches Association Coach of the Year.

The 1991 season proved to be another championship one with top racers Ben Elkins, Jeff Gregory and Amy Portenga, who was a frequent double winner for the girls team that season. Senior Spencer Stegenga started the season strong but left the team to take part in a national competition. The boys team captured their fourth consecutive state championship by beating Petoskey, where Elkins made All-State. The girls team of Portenga, Martha Huckle, Alexa Cockrum, Sara Benner, Libbie Hoxsie and Dani Barkel had a strong showing at regionals, although one half point kept them from making it to the finals. Qualifying as individuals to the state meet, Portenga tied for third in the slalom and was named All-State, while freshman Huckle placed fifth in the giant slalom.

The 1992 teams had a nice blend of youth and experience. Veterans Ben Elkins, Jeff Gregory, Jason Garver, Cam Leuenberger, Collin Salisbury, Justin Selby and Knute Zehner were given an added boost from freshmen Mike Mohrhardt and Nate Smith. The boys team showed its depth as they competed at the state meet without three of their top skiers and still defeated Leelanau School for its fifth straight title. However, the girls, without two top skiers, couldn't surpass Petoskey. Martha Huckle captured second in the slalom to lead the Trojans and earn All-State honors along with Jeff Gregory for his performance. Gregory also received the Michigan High School Athletic Association Scholar-Athlete (MHSAA) award for downhill skiing.

BY THE END OF THE 1993 SEASON, history had repeated itself. Both teams were regional champions, with the boys team again winning the state title and the girls taking second to Petoskey. All-State awards went to Mike Mohrhardt and state slalom champion Ben Elkins. Elkins was also

Ben Elkins, the 1993 Michigan High School Skier of the Year.

named the 1993 Michigan High School Skier of the Year. After eight years as head coach, Don Dunsmore retired after establishing himself as a dominant coach in Michigan high school skiing. No other ski teams in the state matched what Coach Dunsmore's boys teams had accomplished by winning seven state titles in eight years.

The boys were definitely on a streak, chalking up six consecutive state championships. In 1994, Jerry Stanek took over as head coach for both the boys and girls teams after having been involved in the Traverse City coaching program for 13 years. The boys beat Petoskey again for the state title as Cory Cassle was a double state champion. Earning All-State honors were top skiers Cassle, Mike Mohrhardt, Nate Smith, Nate Elkins, with a strong performance by Peter Wysong. The girls team, led by All-Stater Ellen Quirk, edged Petoskey by .004 of a second, probably the closest contest ever in the history of the state meet.

In 1995, a new format was introduced into Michigan high school racing. Class A schools began competing in their own regional and state meets with Class B, C and D schools having their own combined regional and state meets. That change had a big impact on Traverse City racers since they would no longer have to face their perennial rival

Petoskey at those important meets. Competiton for the Trojans at regionals shifted to Marquette, Cadillac and Grand Rapids Forest Hills Central. Leading both teams to state victories that year were All-Staters Mike Mohrhardt (slalom state champion), Nate Smith (giant slalom state champion), Ben Maier and Ellen Quirk. Former Trojan stars Ben Elkins and Mike Wells served as assistant coaches. Jill Gregory was the 1995 MHSAA downhill skiing Scholar-Athlete recipient.

For the first time in nine seasons, the 1996 Trojan boys were defeated at the state finals by Grand Rapids Forest Hills Central. The girls won the state championship for the second year in a row, led by team captain and graduating senior Ellen Quirk. Quirk won every high school race that season, including the regional and state meets, an unprecedented feat in high school racing. Earning All-State honors were Jim Stanley, Quirk for the third time, Marin Schulz and Brooke Schulz. Also this year, Don Dunsmore was honored by being named to the Michigan High School Ski Coaches Hall of Fame.

For the third straight year, the 1997 girls ski team claimed the No. 1 spot in Class A by beating Marquette. On the other side of the meet, the boys team didn't fare as well, losing to Marquette by four points. The road to the finals was an uphill battle for the girls team. Amanda Alward tore a knee ligament one week before states which necessitated surgery, Megan Bickel suffered a wrist injury and Kate Stevens had been dealing with a bad knee. Luckily, Bickel and Stevens were able to ski. After losing to Marquette at regionals, the girls pulled together to win the state title. Marin Schulz was state giant slalom champion, while sister Brooke won the slalom. The boys, who lost to Marquette in the regionals, also faced a loss to them at the state meet. Ben Belyea was the top finisher for the boys, placing second in the giant slalom. Earning All-State honors were Marin Schulz and Brooke Schulz, both for the second time, Megan Bickel, Ben Belyea and Justin Smith.

In 42 years of sanctioned high school ski teams, the Traverse City program has certainly been dominant. This is a tribute to the hard work of the racers, the high caliber of coaches the boys and girls have been fortunate to have had, and certainly the Grand Traverse Ski Club as a feeder program. As former coach Lyn Salathiel stated, the success of our high school ski teams "must be shared with the Grand Traverse Ski Club, which has been such an obvious force for ski racing in Northern Michigan." The Ski Club has been financially supportive of the Trojan team by helping with uniforms, equipment and funds for additional coaches which the school could not provide. Ski Club parents have helped staff regional and state meets when hosted by Traverse City, which could not have been done with just Trojan ski team parents. And finally, the cycle has been completed many times when former Trojan racers returned to coach for the Ski Club at Hickory Hills, where they got their start. There has been a strong familial trend in this sport as can be seen by the number of brothers and sisters who have skied for the Trojans, as well as children of former racers. If this trend keeps up, Traverse City should continue to have a wealth of ski talent in the future.

Trojan skier Ellen Quirk won every high school race her senior year, including regionals and states.

CLASSES A/B/C/D DOWNHILL SKIING ALL-STATE

	First team	Second team	Third team	Honorable Mention
1959	Sue Arnoldt			
1961	Mike Merrill Len Ligon			
1962	Val Hays			
1963	Len Ligon Val Hays			
1964	Jim Merrill Len Ligon Jerry Stanek			
1965	Cherie Gibson Jim Rennie Jerry Stanek			
1966	Cherie Gibson Cathy Paulos Jerry Stanek Jim Rennis Tom Shield			
1967	Cathy Paulos	Jeanne Feiker Bruce Beers Chuck Ligon		
1968	Barb Bohn Cathy Paulos	Bruce Beers Chuck Ligon Dan Kipley		Tom Lindsay Rick Thirlby Cindy Cottom Tracey Long Shelley Thayer
1969	Barb Bohn Dan Kipley Rick Thirlby	Tracey Long		
1970	Rick Thirlby	Rondi Wuerfel Lynn Hazelton		Bob Werner Bill Hazelton Tracey Long Meredith Parsons
1971	Rondi Wuerfel Jackie Core	Ken Core Cynthia Hazelton		
1972	Toubo Collings			
1973	Julie Pelto			
1974	Kathy Ferrar Julie Pelto Jim Frederickson	Cheryl Hutchinson		
1975	Judy Kramer Tammy Hagerty Jim Wagener	Cheryl Hutchinson Brian Hutchinson Keith Forton		Lynn Mattern
1976	Nick Nixon Tammy Hagerty Judy Kramer Brian Hutchinson	Shane Evans Keith Forton		Jane Gilmore Ann Alward Julie Basta

CLASSES A/B/C/D DOWNHILL SKIING ALL-STATE (continued)

	First team	Second team	Third team	Honorable Mention
1977	Nick Nixon Bruce Hutchinson			Tammy Hagerty Karen Hutchinson Bill Bogley
1978	Heather Lockwood			
1979	Karen Hutchinson Dan Lautner Mark Dancer			
1980	Cae Madion Dan Lautner			
1981	Cae Madion			
1983	Kathy Skendzel Trina Fiebing Greg Bohn			
1984	Scott Schwarm Greg Bohn			
1985	Jim Woodburne Mollie Schwarm			
1986	Mollie Schwarm Mary Beth Skendzel Jim Woodburne Chris Bohn	Jennifer Dunsmore Matt Robb Dan Culp		
1987	Chris Bohn Mollie Schwarm	Matt Lambert Allison Stegenga		
1988	Jennifer Dunsmore Matt Lambert Tod Lautner	Mike Simpson		
1989	Amy Robb Shelly Fochtman Jeff Owens Mike Simpson	Matt Anderson		
1990	Spencer Stegenga Heather Johnson	John Zimmerman Tyler Blumenfeld Shelly Fochtman		Amy Portenga Renee Huckle Terry Raven
1991	Amy Portenga Ben Elkins	Martha Huckle Jeff Gregory		
1992	Jeff Gregory Martha Huckle	Justin Selby Alexa Cockrum	Nate Smith	Paul Zoutendyk
1993	Ben Elkins Mike Mohrhardt	Martha Huckle Ellen Quirk Sara Benner Cam Leuenberger	Sara Chambers Jill Gregory Nate Smith Pete Wysong	
1994	Ellen Quirk Cory Cassle Mike Mohrhardt Nate Smith Nate Elkins	Martha Huckle Megan Simpson Sara Chambers Jill Gregory	Casey Cross Katie Jacobs	

CLASS A DOWNHILL SKIING ALL-STATE

	First Team	Second Team	Third Team
1995	Ellen Quirk	Megan Simpson	
	Ben Maier	Sara Chambers	
	Mike Mohrhardt	Marin Schulz	
	Nate Smith	Matt Jacobs	
		Neil Barkel	
1996	Ellen Quirk	Laura Wilbur	
	Marin Schulz	Heather Willson	
	Brooke Schulz	Neil Barkel	
	Jim Stanley	Collin Anable	
	Justin Smith		
1997	Marin Schulz	Laura Wilbur	Morgan Cox
	Brooke Schulz	Chris Geer	Alisha Raehl
	Megan Bickel		
	Ben Belyea		
	Justin Smith		

DOWNHILL SKI MEET SCORING

- Six skiers race in a varsity meet.
- Skiers are seeded 1-6, with #1 the best skier on the team.
- Two races make up a meet, slalom and giant slalom. In slalom, the gates (poles) are closer together, requiring more technical skill. In giant slalom, they are further apart with fewer turns on the course, generating more speed.
- Skiers are seeded separately for slalom and giant slalom. A skier's running order could be different for the two events.
- Points are earned according to the final standing of a racer. First place is one point, fourth place is four points, etc.
- Only a team's best four finishes are counted. The best team score possible is a 10, if a team placed racers in 1st, 2nd, 3rd and 4th places.
- The best four results are taken from slalom and giant slalom and then added together for a total. The team with the lowest score wins.
- In a meet, the #1 racers from all schools race first. Then all #2 skiers race; then the third seed, etc. In ski racing there is not a level playing field for all racers. As the race progresses, the course can get choppy and icy. While the #1 skiers get a fresh course, the lower seeds often have to ski ruts. Between seeds, the course is often "slipped" (a few skiers slip down sideways to try to level out the ruts).

TROJAN DOWNHILL SKI COACHES

Jim Ooley	1954
Richard Hoag	1955
Barbara Sherberneau	1956
Arthur Schubert	1957-1961
Russ Luttinen	1962-1966
Lyndon Salathiel	1967-1985
Don Dunsmore	1986-1993
Jerry Stanek	1994-present

10

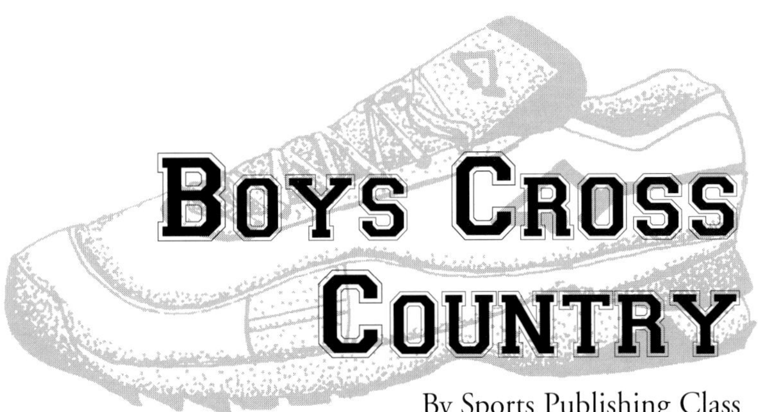

Boys Cross Country

By Sports Publishing Class

"You get out of cross country what you put in. By working hard you get good. Good runners are made, not born."
– ANDY HAYES '92, TROJAN ALL-STATE CROSS COUNTRY RUNNER

Cross country competitors run five kilometers (3.1 miles) on an outdoor course of varied terrain. In a varsity meet, teams run seven athletes, but only the top five runners' places count towards the score. A "sweep" is a team which has runners finish in first, second, third, fourth and fifth places for the lowest possible score of 15. The team with the lowest score wins the meet.

Boys cross country was introduced in fall of 1960 by track coach Dick Frank. After a 2-2 season, this team placed third in the LMAC and took sixth place at regionals.

The 1961 season started with only one returning letterman. This didn't worry Coach Frank, however, since he had a large turnout of underclassmen who ran well. The number one runner, Larry O'Heren, placed second in the regionals and 19th at the state meet. Robert Elliot took over as coach in 1962 and started the season with only two previous letter winners. Jim Oberling was the number one runner, along with teammates Tom Park, Jim DeWolfe, Dick Wollam, Jay Schneider, Eric Jones, Bob Park, Phil Boothroyd, Steve Swan, Terry Lautner, Tom Dyke, Jerry DeNoyer, Steve Ferrell and Bob House.

Dan Young was the new coach in 1967. His team of Rob Holt, Bennie Lautner, Pete Wiens, Joel Safronoff, Jim Deering, Don Thayer and Bill Oberling posted a 4-4 season and second place in the LMAC. In 1968, Joe Niehardt coached Bob Niswander, Joel Safronoff, Dave Chapman, Don Basch, Ben Lautner and Rob Holt to another second place LMAC finish despite a 2-6 season.

In 1973, the team had a different look. Diane Culp, the first girl to go out for the sport, joined the boys team since there was no girls cross country team yet. Some of her teammates that year were Gene Felton, Hunter Lang, Rich Evert, Dan Groszek, Dan Aja and Keith Forton.

BY 1975, THE TEAM FINALLY HAD A VICTORIOUS 14-0 SEASON. Helping the team in this effort were Tom Pelto, Dan O'Brien and Noel Schroeder. The 1976 team had another winning season, taking first in the LMAC. Starring that year and making All-Conference were John Elsenheimer, Jim Wise, Marty Hayward and Tony Beaverson. Elsenheimer qualified for the state meet that year.

"I'd like to have the seniors cloned!" stated coach Dan Young in 1978. The team placed second in the LMAC and sixth at regionals. Al Carpenter, the number one runner, qualified for the state finals. The rest of this successful team were Marty Hayward, Tim McMaster, Greg Biehl, Mauri Pelto and Mark Smith.

In 1980, an outstanding team won the conference for the first time since 1976. This was also the first time since 1966 that the entire team qualified for the state finals. Traverse City's Kurt Johnson, Ken Orchard, Tom McKaye, Karl Olson and Todd Beaverson formed half of the All-Conference team of ten members.

The 1981 team had an exceptional season under coach Wayne Hintz. Out of their twelve meets, they finished first in all but three. They won all three LMAC meets, which had strong competition. However, the winning streak ended at regionals, where they took second to Grand Rapids Union. At the state meet, they placed 15th out of 24 teams. Runners that year were Ty Scheiber, Mike Fielder, Karl Stegmeyer, Tony Wisniewski, Steve Mead, Perry Stoppa, Kurt Johnson, Gary Farley, Tom McKaye, Kurt Wilkes, Bjorn Hagglund and Ken Orchard.

In 1983, coach Dan Young was back again along with the only returning runner, Dan Fournier. That year, freshmen were allowed to compete on the high school team. Earning All-Conference honors were senior Jeff Hengesbach, junior Dave Cunningham and freshman Cory Freisen. Other Trojan runners were Tim Parker, Tim Preston, Greg Asiala, Mike Crain, Dave Grant and Craig Million.

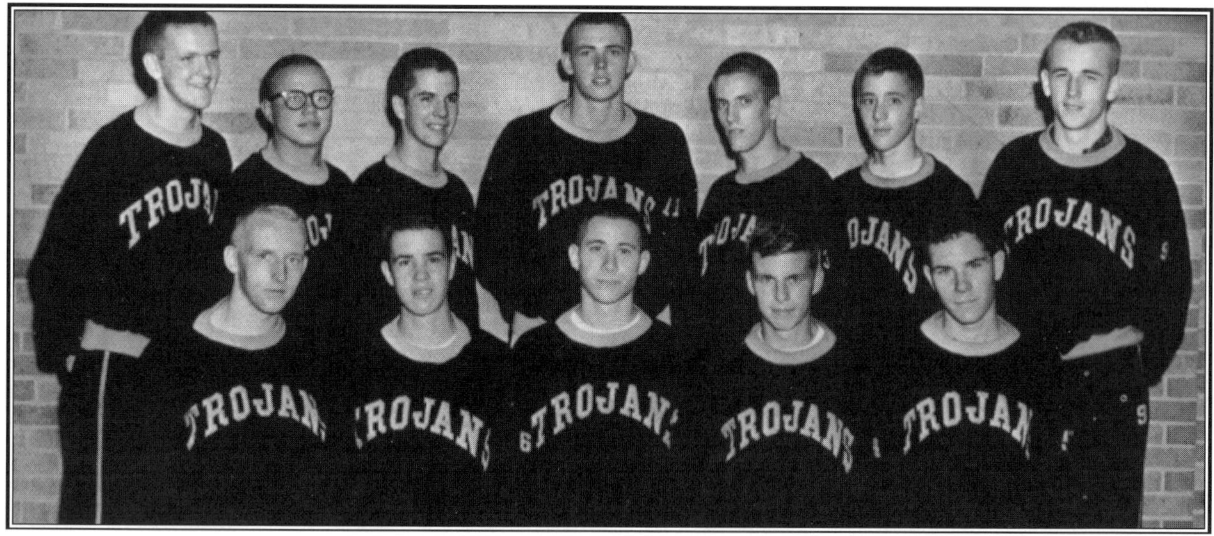

First Trojan cross country team in 1960. Front Row: Bob MacEachron, Ray Fifarek, Paul Steusel, Bob Rothermel, Larry Cummings. Back Row: Jim Frasier, David Lewy, Dennis Johnson, Larry Anderson, Gary Quick, Gordon Cornwell, John Knorr. Not pictured: Chum Schrotenboer, Coach Richard Frank.

Mark Fries took over for a year as coach in 1985. Although his record was 0-6, he commented, "We were a very young team with only Scott [Schwenter] coming back. We had a lot of fun, though, and you can never measure success by wins and losses. We grew as people and as runners." Troy Cannaday was the top Trojan finisher at regionals, in 41st place.

Just the next year, in 1986, coach Dan Young's team had probably the best season yet by taking first at regionals and sixth in the state. Pacing the win at regionals were Jeff Linger who took third, Derek Barg's fourth and Greg Million in sixth place. They were helped by Dan Mullins, Steve Fox, Troy Cannaday, Brent Manthei and Aaron Prevo. Barg's 19th place at the state meet led them to the sixth place finish.

In 1989, after almost thirty years of many different coaches, John Lober took over as boys cross country coach. Dan Young had coached for nine of those years, with his longest span in the 1970s. The 1989 runners Chad Bousamra, T.J. Eash, Andy Hayes, Jim Huber, Brent Manthei, Joe Panatella and Jeff Rizer placed third at regionals and 21st in the state. In 1990, the Trojans placed second at regionals and had improved to 14th in the state. State finals runners were Bousamra, Hayes, Ken Johnson, Mike Mathieu, Jay Namboothiri, Rocky Ray and Dan Siderman.

THE 1991 TEAM QUALIFIED FOR THE STATE MEET for the third year in a row. Andy Hayes was named All-State as a result of his outstanding running. During the state finals, Keith Stotts lost his shoe in the mud in the first mile and ran two more miles with one shoe on and one off. Other state runners were Mike Franko, Mike Decker, Chance Wadkins, Ryan Dear and Ben Meredith. The team finished in 19th place.

In 1992, 23 of the 32 on that team were freshmen and sophomores. "I like the young guys. They are very goal-oriented and are always improving.

1976 boys cross country team. Front Row: Bob Zientak, John Elsenheimer, Al Carpenter, Greg Biehl, Jim Wise, Tony Beaverson, Mike Cramer, Paul Rombouts. Back Row: Doug Watkins, Mauri Pelto, Coach Dan Young, Dave Lavalley, Mark Smith, Matt Courtade, Scott Decker, John Schlosser.

They are good guys and they are going to be state champs in 1994," predicted co-captain Mike Franko (which was almost prophetic since the 1994 team ended up third in the state). Running to an 18th place state finish were Ryan Dear, Franko, Dan Stafford, Mike Decker, Paul Follett, Paul Hastings and Kevin Brokaw. Brokaw was named Academic All-State.

The 1993 runners were probably the highest quality group Coach Lober had seen so far. Captained by Mike Williams and Mike Peters, the team had its best state finish to date, eighth. However, the following year surpassed even that. In 1994, John Browne, Eric Houghton, Kevin Brokaw, Mike Decker, Paul Hastings, Adam Wheeler and Charlie Wolf won the regional meet and finished third in the state. Wolf was honored as All-State, while Brokaw was named Academic All-State for the third year in a row and Wheeler for the first.

The 1995 team was not to be outdone. "This year's team won more invitationals than any team in Traverse City High School history and proved it was the best ever by winning the regional meet with a low score of 28 points and finishing third in the state meet," explained Coach Lober. Led by All-Staters Mike Cell, Eric Houghton and Robert Haveman, the other state runners were Mike Straubel, Jim Smith, Charlie Wolf and Joe Agostinelli. Houghton and Haveman were also named Academic All-State.

In 1996, the strength of the 1995 team was still evident. After taking first place in seven invitationals and second place in the other three, this team capped off its season with a win at regionals and a second place finish at the state finals. Earning All-State honors were Robert Haveman and Eric Houghton, both for the second year, and Chris Vranich. Houghton was also named Academic All-State for the second year in a row.

The all-time best Trojan runners are probably Andy Hayes, Mike Decker, Eric Houghton, Mike Cell and Charlie Wolf. These runners of the 1990s have the all-time bests of the eleven annual cross country contests in which the team takes part. These performances are a tribute to the growth of

1980 boys team. Front Row: Karl Olson, Todd Beaverson, Jon Forton, John Shaw, Chuck Ailsworth. Back Row: Coach Wayne Hintz, Kurt Johnson, Craig Denton, Ken Orchard, Tom McKaye, Eric Lerew.

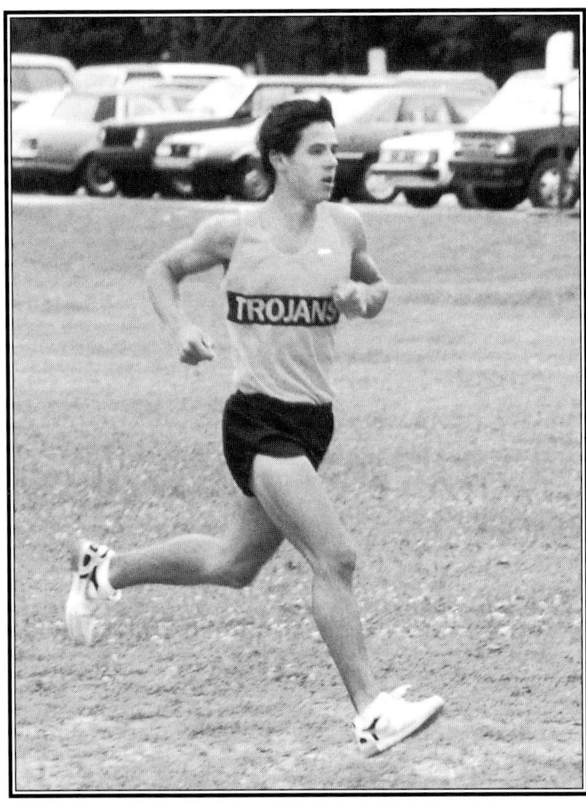

Andy Hayes, first All-State runner for Traverse City boys cross country.

the cross country program in Traverse City and the number of runners that the team attracts.

BOYS CROSS COUNTRY CLASS A ALL-STATE

1991	Andy Hayes
1994	Charlie Wolf
1995	Mike Cell Robert Haveman Eric Houghton
1996	Robert Haveman Eric Houghton Chris Vranich

BOYS CROSS COUNTRY ACADEMIC ALL-STATE

1992	Kevin Brokaw
1993	Kevin Brokaw
1994	Kevin Brokaw Adam Wheeler
1995	Robert Haveman Eric Houghton
1996	Eric Houghton

The 1995 "best ever" cross country runners. Back Row: Coach Don Lukens, Ben Woodward, Mike Cell, Nate Unkefer, Joe Agostinelli, Trainer Sarah Manthei, Steve Swaney, Eric Houghton, Mike Straubel, Kevin Vann, Coach John Lober. Middle Row: Noah Kamper, Aaron Wylie, Jason Whittaker, Chris Linsell, Charlie Wolf, John Browne, Dan Julian, Jon Hodge. Front Row: Steve Nielson, Adam Young, Tim Smith, John Lamb, Jim Smith, Scott Newman, Ryan Wheat, Sean Seekins.

BOYS CROSS COUNTRY COACHES and RECORDS

1960	Richard Frank			
1961	Richard Frank			
1962	Rovert Elliot			
1963	Robert Elliot			
1964	Dick Crampton			
1965	Ron Johnson			
1966	Ron Johnson	1st team to state finals		
1967	Dan Young			
1968	Joe Neihardt			
1969	John Swire			
1970	Dan Young			
1971	Dan Young			
1972	Joe LeMieux			
1973	Dan Young			
1974	Dan Young			
1975	Dan Young			
1976	Dan Young	1st in LMAC		
1977	Dan Young			
1978	Dan Young			
1979	Dan Young			
1980	Wayne Hintz	1st in LMAC	22nd in state	
1981	Wayne Hintz	1st in LMAC	2nd in regionals	15th in state
1982	John Benedict			
1983	Dan Young			
1984	Dan Young			
1985	Mark Fries			
1986	Dan Young	1st in regionals	6th in state	
1987	Dan Young			
1988	Dan Young			
1989	John Lober	3rd in regionals	21st in state	
1990	John Lober	2nd in regionals	14th in state	
1991	John Lober	2nd in regionals	19th in state	
1992	John Lober	3rd in regionals	18th in state	
1993	John Lober	2nd in regionals	8th in state	
1994	John Lober	1st in regionals	3rd in state	
1995	John Lober	1st in regionals	3rd in state	
1996	John Lober	1st in regionals	2nd in state	

11

Wrestling

By Marissa Taylor

"A chip on the shoulder is too heavy a load for any athlete to carry"
– Anonymous

Wrestling activity dates back to prehistoric times. In French caves, drawings and carvings 15,000 to 20,000 years old show wrestlers in a variety of positions. In 708 B.C., it became part of the Olympic Games in Greece. In America, the Indians wrestled among themselves before the arrival of the Europeans.

Even though wrestling is a team sport, each wrestler competes entirely on his own without the help of his teammates. It's an individual effort, with only the support of the teammates, the coach, and the onlookers. Wrestling is a sport where two opponents wrestle each other to earn points which are achieved by performing moves to gain control of the other opponent and lead to a pin. A pin is the final move where one opponent is able to hold both of the other opponents' shoulders to the mat.

Coached by George Boehm, Trojan wrestling began in 1970 at the end of football season with a team that consisted of approximately 15 boys. Because that was the team's first year, things were a little shaky and they didn't have a successful year. The team wasn't part of the LMAC (Lake Michigan Athletic Conference), but did do intramural meets. Traverse City won scrimmages with both Benzie Central and Frankfort, but any other records during the year are not known.

Unlike most of Traverse City sports, wrestling only had one year of intramural play before it went interscholastic. It began only as an intramural sport in 1970, but with the help of George Boehm, John Sonnemann and a rapid demand for the sport, it became interscholastic by 1971.

That year the team began real competition

against other schools, with George Boehm as head coach and John Sonnemann as the assistant coach. Although they had 33 boys try out, it was their first year and they didn't have much success. They placed sixth in the conference, with Gary Henschell and Mike Tiberg each placing fourth in their respective weight classes. With a record of two wins, 14 losses, and one draw they were hopeful for a better year in 1972.

And that they had. At the two-year mark and with a rookie coach, the wrestling team had an impressive record. Head coach Dave Rosendale and John Sonnemann as assistant coach led the team to a 9-9-1 finish and a fourth place in the LMAC.

The Trojan wrestlers continued their progress upward in 1974, as a team and as individual wrestlers. Grand Haven was the opposing team that tied them for second place in the LMAC competition. As for the individual wrestlers, Bruce Hooper had a three-year-record of 61 wins, and led the team in new records with 23 escapes, 27 two-point near falls, and the fastest pin of 11 seconds. Jeff Carlson and Joe Holt both had 14 pins, and Holt set a record of 53 wins. Bruce Hooper and Ken Haughn were elected co-captains, and Shaun Clark most improved.

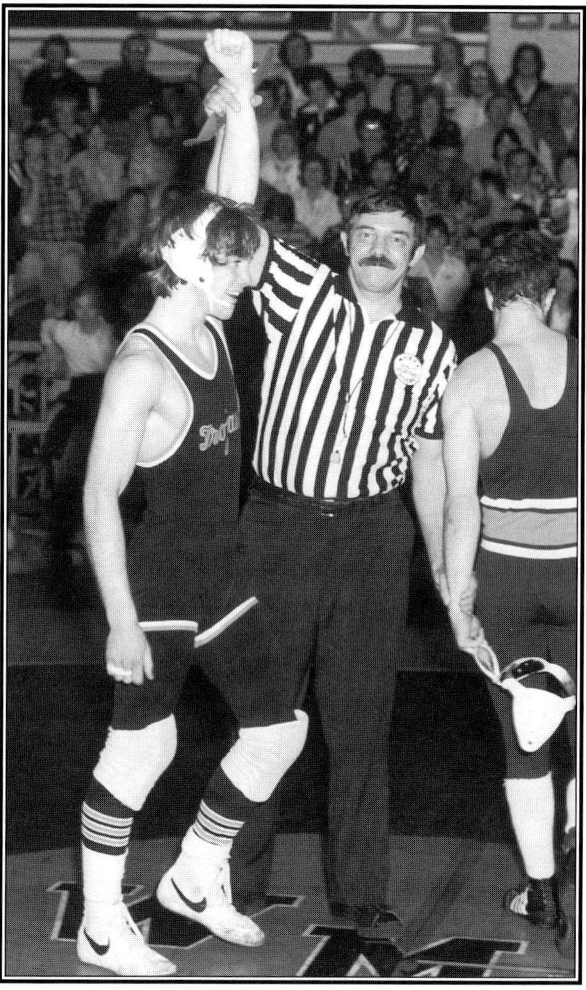

Hand is raised in victory for two-time state champ Larry Haughn.

IN 1976, THE TROJANS HAD THEIR BEST YEAR since the wrestling program's inception. With the help of a new head coach, Jack Clark, the team finished with a 12-3 dual meet record and won four tournaments while placing second in three others. The team took second in the LMAC, but went even further to place 12th in the Class A state competition. Sophomore Larry Haughn (119 lbs.) and seniors Charlie Hooper (126 lbs.) and Bruce McLachlan (155 lbs.) all won LMAC titles. Four Trojans advanced to the Class A meet where senior Ted Weber placed fifth at 138 lbs. and Bruce McLachlan finished second at 155 lbs. to earn them both All-State honors. McLachlan's second place finish was the best record to date for a Trojan wrestler.

Due to the lack of wrestlers, Traverse City suffered a loss of points on the mat during the 1976-1977 season. In every meet, they had to forfeit between 18-30 points because they couldn't fill all of the weight classes. But that didn't stop the team from having a satisfactory year, finishing with an 8-8 dual meet record. They made more of a statement in the state finals, taking 15th of all Class A teams. On an individual note, junior All-Stater Larry Haughn took the Class A state championship in the 119 pound weight class. Bill Smith and Mike Kerr were two other Trojan individuals who both finished eighth in the state.

Six seniors, six juniors, eight sophomores, and a new head coach made up the 1977-1978 Trojan wrestlers. Coach Ed Haughn (Larry Haughn's father) directed the team to a successful year. With a record of five wins and five losses, the team didn't appear to do very well; however, they only lost each match by a couple of points. They also hosted the Christmas Invitational Tournament in which they placed sixth. In addition to their record, they placed third in the LMAC tournament and won four of their five LMAC matches. Again, Larry Haughn made an impact on the team. He was the team's most outstanding wrestler, once again winning the Class A state championship title and All-State honors. By breaking many school and state records, being nominated for All-American honors and having a 42-1 individual record, he was considered the best on the team and on any prior team.

AT THE TURN OF THE DECADE, Trojan wrestling continued to progress and become more popular among the students. With 22 members on the 1980 team and Ed Haughn as the coach for his third year, they had a memorable year. Six wrestlers finished the season with twenty or more victories, while three wrestlers came out on top as LMAC champions: sophomore Eddie Smith in the 98 lb. class, junior Randy Scussel in the 145 lb. class, and senior Brian Johnston in the heavyweight class. Qualifiers for regionals that were held in Ottawa Hills included seniors Jeff Lasich, Brian Johnston, and Scott Strait with juniors Max Lint, Randy Scussel, and Randy Weber. The two Trojans who set the pace for the team throughout the year were Brian Johnston and Max Lint, both of whom qualified for state finals. Lint at 126 lbs. went on to place fifth in the state at the wrestling finals at Lansing Eastern High School that March and was named All-State.

In 1982, the wrestling team placed third in the LMAC finals, although their season record of four wins and 10 losses would not have predicted it. Despite that record, they had many accomplishments throughout the year. Highlighting the season was the performance of All-Stater Max Lint (126 lbs.) at the state level where he captured third place. Other LMAC champions who went on to

1978 Trojan wrestlers. Front Row: Bruce Hayes, Dan Hoyt, Les McCorkle. Second Row: Dave Hoyt, Larry Haughn, Dave Case, Rich Kundrata, Dan McQuade. Back Row: Frank Weber, Frank Vandervort, Al Weber, Butch Strait, Jim Hurst. Not pictured: Coach Ed Haughn.

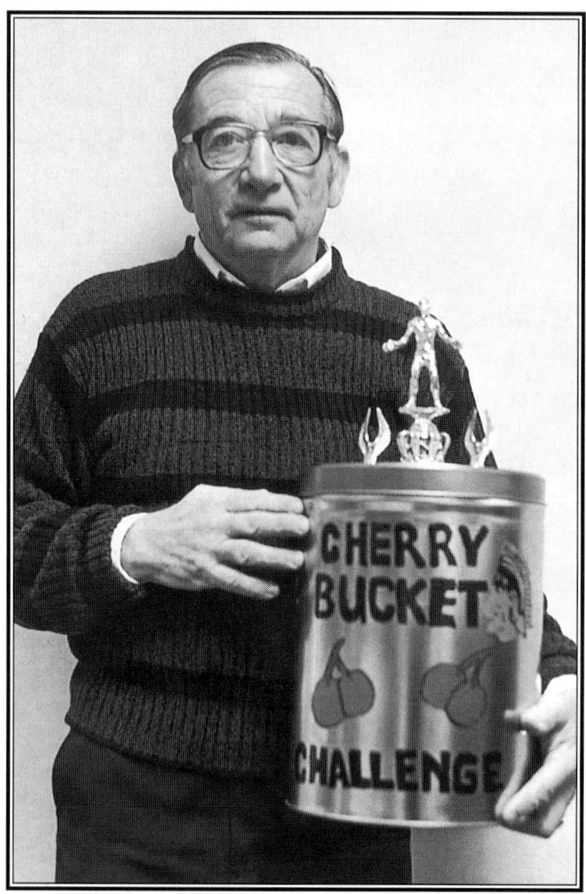

Coach Ed Haughn with Cherry Bucket trophy.

state finals along with Lint were Ed Smith (98 lbs.) and Dan Klingelsmith (119 lbs.). In what coach Ed Haughn called a "good learning situation," Lint set two new individual school records for a single season in achieving 75 takedowns and 42 three-point near falls. Lint also was the first Trojan wrestler to represent Traverse City as a regional champion two years in a row.

Trojan wrestlers had the LMAC in the palm of their hands during the 1983 season. In addition to winning the first ever LMAC championship for Trojan wrestlers, the team had five individual LMAC champions: Paul Roebke, Jason Klingelsmith, Dan Klingelsmith, Todd Springer, and Ross Landis. Overall, they had an outstanding year cleaning up at LMAC meets and also ending the season with a 9-7 record. "We were a close team," explained Coach Ed Haughn. "Everyone worked together and pushed each other to their limits." That attitude is what Coach Haughn attributed to the LMAC victories.

For almost every sports team, each year is going to be different than the previous one. It could be better or it could be worse. Wrestling waned from a great year in 1983 to a mediocre year in 1984. Although the team didn't have a large amount of wins, they still gave it their all. The team, with John Sonnemann then the head coach, finished the season by placing third in the LMAC conference meet and an outstanding second in districts. Trojans who wrestled exceptionally well during the 1984 season were B.J. Wolff, Jason Klinglesmith, Rance Pennington, and Chris Kocks. Kocks went on to qualify for the state finals at 132 lbs. where he placed third, taking All-State honors by winning three out of the four matches in Lansing.

"The 1986 season was a down year if you look only at our 3-10 dual meet record," said (once again) new head coach Ed Haughn, "but there certainly is more to it than wins and losses. Even though the team as a whole did not have many wins, there are certain individuals who did exceedingly well, and there are those who will be back in the future who gained much needed experience." Senior Tim Lamie earned All-State honors by completing the year with a 29-9 record which gave him a three year total of 81-36. Besides ending his career with an incredible record, he also ended up finishing in sixth place at the state finals. Other wrestlers with an impact on the team were senior Ken Kloosterman and junior Tim Smith who both had great years which aren't reflected in their records.

With a team composed of mostly underclassmen (four juniors, ten sophomores, and seven freshmen), the 1987 Trojans had a memorable year with statistics to show it. They had a 15-9-1 record, won the Sanford-Meridan Tournament and placed second at Greenville with an end-of-the-season power finish. "Our outstanding wrestler was obviously Tim Smith. Tim finished fifth in the state and had an excellent state tournament," assistant coach John Sonnemann said about the 119 lb.

senior. Placing fifth in the state meet and winning All-State honors when he managed to pin the prior year's state champion in 59 seconds were his major accomplishments for the year. Smith and senior teammate Steve Montez led the team with pins, each having 23, and sophomore Mike Nadlicki led the team in take downs (50) and escapes (25).

Mike Nadlicki remained top contender of the Trojan wrestlers with teammate Dondi Norton during the 1987-1988 season. Nadlicki did a great job on the mat with 42 wins and only seven losses in the 198 lb. weight division. The "N" boys both went on to the state finals where Nadlicki placed sixth, to be named All-State, and Norton was accepted to wrestle at Ferris State in his freshman year. Senior Andre Kuschell and junior Nate Alger also helped the team out with good records. The team's individual successes are what paced the team's overall standings.

The winter season of 1989 was a year of striving to put forth their best and meet individual goals among the Trojan wrestlers. Once again Mike Nadlicki did his best and finished out his senior year of wrestling by scoring his 100th career win at the Reed City Invitational, becoming only the second Trojan to attain that goal. Nadlicki and Dondi Norton were the only wrestlers to qualify for the state meet in 1989, where they earned All-State honors, Nadlicki for the second time. Junior Justin Vanderlinde simply had a goal to do better than the year before and continue to improve. Goals are what kept these guys going. Assistant coach John Sonnemann said the team was, "very youthful, and we had a good number of wrestlers who all wrestled good competition."

Placing second in the Mid-Michigan Wrestling League was the final accomplishment for the Trojan wrestlers in 1990. With the help of all the members, they were able to meet that goal. It took "self-discipline, dedication, and a great work ethic", said coach Ed Haughn. They had a successful year and looked forward to 1991.

"The hardest part of the season for me has been getting my mind set to go out on the mat and do

First LMAC wrestling champions, the 1983 team. Front Row: Steve Elzinga, Jim Eisner, Paul Roebke, Randy Seeley, Chris Kocks, Ed Joslin, Leo Grand. Second Row: Tony Harris, Scott Chile, Ross Landis, Dan Klingelsmith, Todd Springer, B.J. Wolff, Jim Diehl, Pat Swanstrom. Back Row: Coach Ed Haughn, Jeff Grenko, Jerry Hilborn, Joe Paupore, Dave Tokie, Laverne Wolfgram, Jason Klingelsmith, Coach John Sonnemann.

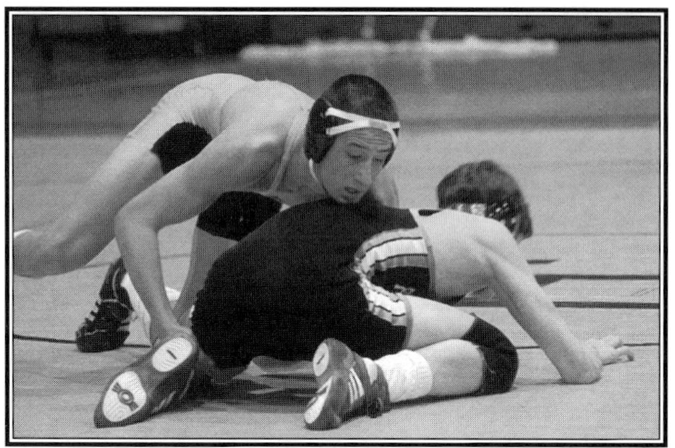

State champion Jeremy Gonzalez gets the upper hand on his opponent.

what I have to do to win," said junior Bill McDonald, a 1991 Trojan wrestler. Although it became difficult sometimes to stay focused and keep the "winning" mind set, the Trojans pulled through and placed first in the district meet at Grand Haven. Named All-State that year were Jason Norton and Dave Hudson.

The 1992 wrestlers felt that their year was better than the previous one. Junior Troy Petroskey said, "The team is doing better than last year because we all have more experience and we are working better." The team also gave credit to the fact that they had good coaches, Ed Haughn and son Larry Haughn. Larry was probably Traverse City Senior High's most outstanding wrestler in the history of the sport on campus, placing first in state finals in 1977 and 1978. Although the 1992 team didn't have a wrestler in the 103 pound class, or a solid heavyweight wrestler, they still finished with a winning season. Dave Hudson was a repeat All-Stater, with Chad Smith also earning the distinction.

According to senior Jason Kabot, "In wrestling, anyone can beat anyone no matter how good they are. If your mind isn't in it then your opponent will

1997 regional qualifiers, with a record six wrestlers going on to the state meet. Front Row: Ethan Smith, Adam Beers, Erik Johnsen, Nate Reynolds. Middle Row: Jason Ferris, Shawn Maison, Ben Zeits, Sean Morrissey. Back Row: Coach Toni Diola, Miles Gordon, Travis Banton, Troy Banton, John Szwalek, Coach Jeff Mosher.

take advantage of that and win." That was what Kabot and his teammates had to keep in mind when they were face-to-face with their opponents in 1994. Sophomore Jeremy Gonzalez kept that in mind when he had his final match to win first place in the state finals. He was awarded All-State distinction along with Alex Zakusylo, who went to the state finals with Gonzalez and placed eighth. Senior Jake Ubl finished his high school record with a 109-34 record. With the help of new coach Jeff Mosher, they had the best state of mind to meet their individual goals.

Heading toward the end of the millenium, things were looking pretty good for Trojan wrestlers. The season of 1995 had a great turnout with a few memorable accomplishments. The team overall had a record of 23 wins and 6 losses, and were named district champs. They fought hard for the team in regionals, but lost humbly to Grandville. This season had a few new records as well. Junior All-Stater Jeremy Gonzalez finished with the most takedowns in a season (133), as well as the most takedowns in a career (253). Jeremy also finished his season by placing eighth in the state finals. Another qualifier for the state finals who didn't place was junior Rob Pawloski. Overall, the 1995 team exhibited some excellent wrestling and helped pave the way for the returning 1996 team.

THE YEAR OF THE MOST ACCOMPLISHMENTS to date was undoubtedly 1996. The season ended with an impressive record of 20-5-1. Jeremy Gonzalez finished his high school wrestling career with 402 takedowns and 142 total wins for his senior year. The team had their first freshmen to ever qualify for regionals, Darren Smith and Troy Banton. They also had the most wrestlers to qualify for regionals, 11, and the most to qualify for state finals, five. Of the five wrestlers who advanced to the state finals, all five ended up placing and being named All-State. Senior Jeremy Gonzalez placed fourth, junior John Szwalek also placed fourth in his weight class, senior Rob Pawloski placed sixth, and juniors Miles Gordon

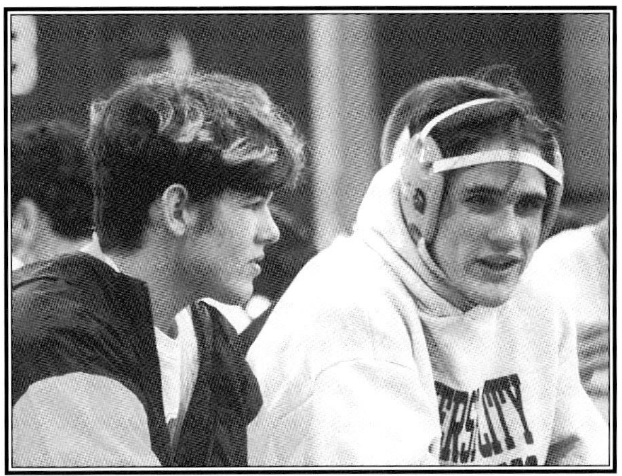

Ben Zeits and state champion Miles Gordon (right) wait for their turns on the mat.

and Shawn Maison both placed eighth in their individual weight classes.

Although the 1997 wrestling team as a whole did not advance to the state meet, they had a winning 25-4 season and were district champions. Two individuals emerged as regional champions, Miles Gordon at 145 lbs. and John Szwalek at 189 lbs., while the Trojans sent a record six wrestlers to the state meet, with one becoming a state champion. Seniors Gordon, Szwalek, Adam Beers, Shawn Maison and Sean Morrissey earned spots during regionals to compete at the state finals, along with Ethan Smith who became the first Trojan freshman to qualify. Morrissey, who had wrestled on the junior varsity team for the majority of the season, surprised himself by making it to state competition.

Miles Gordon captured the state title, becoming only the third Trojan state champion, after Larry Haughn who won in both 1977 and 1978 and Jeremy Gonzalez in 1994. Gordon then became the first Trojan wrestler to compete in Nationals. Indicative of the strength of the 1996-1997 team was the fact that four wrestlers, Miles Gordon, Adam Beers, Nate Reynolds and Shawn Maison, captured 100 career wins that season.

After the best showing ever at the state wrestling meet, five Trojans earned All-State honors: state champion Gordon, freshman Ethan Smith who placed sixth at 103 lbs., Adam Beers who placed eighth at 135 lbs., and John Szwalek and Shawn Maison, who also placed at the state meet. Coach Mosher offered praise, saying, "As individuals we .... represented the team, wrestled for the team." The success of the 1997 Trojan wrestlers was especially gratifying to Jeff Mosher. After having coached this group in junior high, he began as varsity coach the same year these seniors started tenth grade. It was evident that their years of working together had paid off.

CLASS A WRESTLING ALL-STATE

Year	Name	Year	Name
1975	Shawn Clark	1991	Jason Norton
1976	Ted Weber		Dave Hudson
	Bruce McLachlan	1992	Dave Hudson
1977	Larry Haughn		Chad Smith
1978	Larry Haughn	1993	John Ockert
1979	Dave Hoyt		Dave Sivits
1980	Max Lint	1994	Jeremy Gonzalez
1981	Max Lint		Alex Zakusylo
1982	Ed Smith	1995	Jeremy Gonzalez
1984	Chris Kocks	1996	Jeremy Gonzalez
1986	Tim Lamie		Miles Gordon
1987	Tim Smith		John Szwalek
1988	Mike Nadlicki		Shawn Maison
1989	Dondi Norton		Rob Pawloski
	Mike Nadlicki	1997	Miles Gordon
			Adam Beers
			Ethan Smith
			John Szwalek
			Shawn Maison

TROJAN WRESTLING COACHES

George Boehm	1970-1971
Dave Rosendale	1972-1975
Jack Clark	1976-1977
Ed Haughn	1978-1993
Jeff Mosher	1994-present

TROJAN WRESTLING RECORDS

SEASON RECORDS			CAREER RECORDS	
Takedowns	149	Jeremy Gonzalez 1996	402	Jeremy Gonzalez 1993-96
Reversals	48	Dan Klingelsmith 1983	126	Dan Klingelsmith 1980-83
Escapes	49	Scott Strair	67	Dave Hoyt 1976-79
2Pt Nearfalls	31	Charlie Hooper	60	Larry Haughn 1975-78
3Pt Nearfalls	42	Max Lint 1981	85	Larry Haughn 1975-78
Pins	29	Sean Flanagan 1976	67	Rob Pawloski 1993-96
Tourney Champ	11	Larry Haughn	24	Larry Haughn 1975-78
Fastest Pin	:08 :08	Bill Milton 1991 John Szwalek 1996		
Consecutive Wins	41	Larry Haughn		
Wins	142	Jeremy Gonzalez 1993-96		
First Freshmen to Qualify for Regionals		Darren Smith (1996) Troy Banton		
First Freshman to Qualify for States		Ethan Smith (1997)		
Most Wrestlers Qualified for Regionals	11	(1996)		
Most Wrestlers Qualified to States	6	(1997) Miles Gordon Stan Szwalek Shawn Maison Sean Morrisey Adam Beers Ethan Smith		
Most Wrestlers to Place in States	5	(1996) Jeremy Gonzalez John Szwalek Rob Pawloski Miles Gordon Shawn Maison		(1997) Miles Gordon Ethan Smith Adam Beers Stan Szwalek Shawn Maison
State Champions		Larry Haughn 1977 Larry Haughn 1978 Jeremy Gonzalez 1994 Miles Gordon 1997		

WRESTLING SPECIFICS

LENGTH

Dual Meet	Three two-minute periods
Tournament	Three two-minute periods If tied, there is a two-minute sudden death period. If still tied, there is a 30-second sudden death period from the referee's position.

Time is stopped if the wrestlers go out of bounds, if there is an injury or technical violation, or if a situation becomes dangerous to either wrestler.

SCORING

Individual Match

Takedown (2 points)	One wrestler gains control of his opponent from a neutral situation.
Reversal (2 points)	One wrestler is being controlled by his opponent and reverses the situation so that he now controls his opponent.
Escape (1point)	One wrestler is being controlled by his opponent and breaks away from him into a neutral position.
Nearfall (2 points)	One wrestler holds the shoulders of his opponent at a 45-degree angle, or less, from the mat for 2-4 seconds.
Nearfall (3 points)	One wrestler holds the shoulders of his opponent at a 45-degree angle, or less, from the mat for more than 5 seconds without pinning the opponent.
Nearfall (4 points)	Scored if the offensive wrestler has met the 3-point nearfall criteria and the defensive wrestler requires injury time for an injury sustained in a legal move. New in 1996-1997 season.
Penalties (1 or 2 points)	One wrestler is awarded the point(s) because his opponent is being penalized.
Cautions	A wrestler is given a caution for improper starting position. Points are awarded for each caution after the second. Receiving six cautions in one match results in disqualification.
Warning	A wrestler is warned for "stalling" if he is not wrestling aggressively. Points are awarded for each stalling call after the warning. Five stalling calls will result in disqualification.

TEAM SCORING

	Dual Meet	Tournament
Pin	6 pts.	2 pts.
Forfeit/DQ	6 pts.	2 pts.
Technical Fall (+15)	5 pts.	1.5 pt.
Mjr. Decision (8-14)	4 pts.	1 pt.
Decision (<8)	3 pts.	
Advancement		1 or 2 pts.

12

GYMNASTICS

By Sarah Wahl

"The gymnastics team had many special qualities, including working together and over-all friendship..."

– AMY BELOVICH

In 1974, girls gymnastics hit the mat as a varsity sport for the first time after Greg Barner pushed for adding this to the roster of athletics available to Traverse City students. Cartwheels and flips were on their minds. It was not a big sport then; great crowds of people did not fill the stands. That all changed with the 1976 Olympics when a young Romanian named Nadia Comanici received seven perfect tens and turned the media spotlight onto gymnastics.

After that initial 0-8 season, the team of 1974-1975 had a record of five wins and five losses. With Coach Barner, four girls qualified for the state tournament: Kristi School, Deb Kromer, Sue Nyland and Gayle Miller. In those years, the girls performed on wrestling mats which caused injuries, but now they use softer gymnastics mats which have reduced injuries. Sue Nyland was the first gymnast to win a partial scholarship for gymnastics.

Some of the basic stunts performed were walkovers, splits and handstands. More difficult ones were the balance beam, uneven parallel bars, vault and the floor exercises. In 1977-1978, the team consisted of five sophomores, two juniors and two seniors, all returning from the year before. By the end of the season, they had their best record in recent years with 12 wins and only five losses. Also in 1978, they went to their very first regionals. Only Pam Lynch, who placed first on the balance beam, qualified for the state finals where she was fourth on the beam. Bill Jacobs, who had previously coached the YMCA team, was now coaching the Trojan girls. Something special the girls had was a mascot, "Biff the Bear," which they said gave them luck.

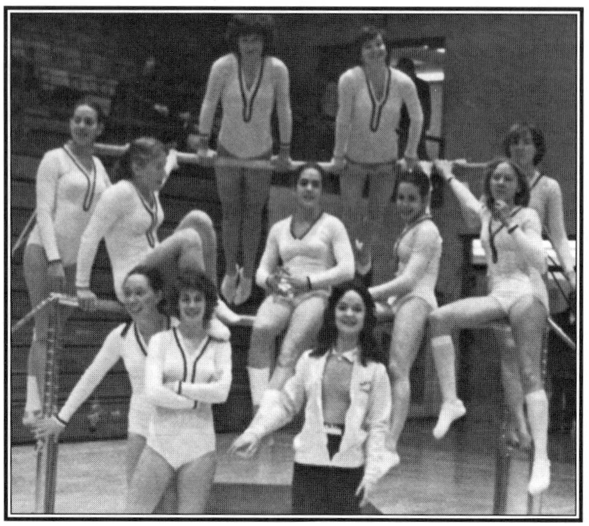

One of the earliest Trojan gymnastic teams, 1976-1977. Front Row: Chris Schopieray, Tracy Richardson, Coach Nancy Kerr. Second Row: Sandy Zimba, Lynne Richards, Kelly Shink, Shelly Shink, Pam Lynch, Kelly Crammer. Third Row: Sue Harris, Gail Miller.

In 1978-1979, the girls gymnastics team didn't do as well, but coach Bill Jacobs believed in his team as they ended their season with a 4-11 record. They really didn't care what their wins and losses were, just that they would qualify for regional competition. Things weren't easy for them because they had a small team with only two seniors, Pam Lynch and Lynne Richards. To get to regionals they had to reach a score of 84 or better at four meets. They just made it! At regionals no one on the team made it to the level of state competition.

AT THE START OF A NEW DECADE they had a fresh team which had a really great year. In 1979-1980, their performances and victories were impressive. However, in 1980-1981, they again had a small team with only five girls: Marena Sabo, Renee Bye, Barb Brooks, Stacie Roney and Steffie Watson. With the shortage of girls, they had to cancel all but one meet. That wasn't the biggest problem though; many injuries and illnesses plagued the small team.

The 1981-1982 season became shortened when three of the 10 meets were cancelled for various reasons. Still, Steffie Watson qualified for regionals while Renee Bye had three qualifying scores before suffering a knee injury. At regionals, Watson narrowly missed the state meet by .005 of a point on the balance beam.

By the next year, the team had an outstanding year due to its depth. Ending the season with a 36-4 record, the 1982-1983 team placed second at regionals, sending the Traverse City team to the state finals for the first time in a long time. Leading this team to a fourth place state finish were Steffie Watson, Karen Howe, Biz Gaff and Stefi Reed. Howe qualified for Senior Nationals, a national meet for seniors only.

The following year, 1983-1984, they did even better with second place in the state even though they were a small team of nine members who were

The Trojans' Ta Scala concentrates while performing on bars.

mostly first year varsity performers. Leading the Trojans to a 33-5 record were: sophomore Ta Scala with a sixth place all-around finish in the state; Karen Howe, the season's top scorer with 362 points and an eighth all-around in the state; and Biz Gaff, Jerilynn Straitiff and Kathy Schubert who also competed in the state meet. That year, Scala earned the right to go to Senior Nationals.

In 1985, they placed third in the state. "The season went pretty well," stated Bill Jacobs. "We blew our chances for taking a state title, but I was happy with the season." That year there were some tougher schools, one of which was Freeland. Even though the team was young, they still did well.

Senior captains Missy Goddard, Kathy Schubert and Christie Crewes led the 1985-1986 team to a sixth place state finish as injuries sidelined Ta Scala with a bad back and Jerrilyn Straitiff because of an injured knee. State performers were Schubert who took third in the state; Mandy Samuelson, fifth all-around; and Michelle Lautner, fifth in floor.

The team was not as successful in 1985, but they were close. It was said that one less wiggle or one less slip would have placed them in the finals. As it was, the Trojans missed the state meet by just .05 points. Junior Michelle Lautner and sophomore Mandy Samuelson individually qualified for states with fifth and sixth place respective regional finishes. Lautner placed second in the state on uneven bars and beam. That year Coach Jacobs said, "We're a very young team with no seniors, so we're proud of ourselves, but we're not ready for the season to end."

Michelle Lautner was the hero in 1988. She was one of about 87 people around the country to compete in Senior Nationals, which she earned by placing fourth overall in the state finals. Her achievement is a reflection of what this team accomplished in winning the state title. Mandy Samuelson clinched the championship for the team with her outstanding performance. Lautner was voted Most Valuable Gymnast on bars and beam and teammate Samuelson was Most Valuable on floor and vault.

Entering the new decade in 1990, the 1989-1990 team went through many challenges. They

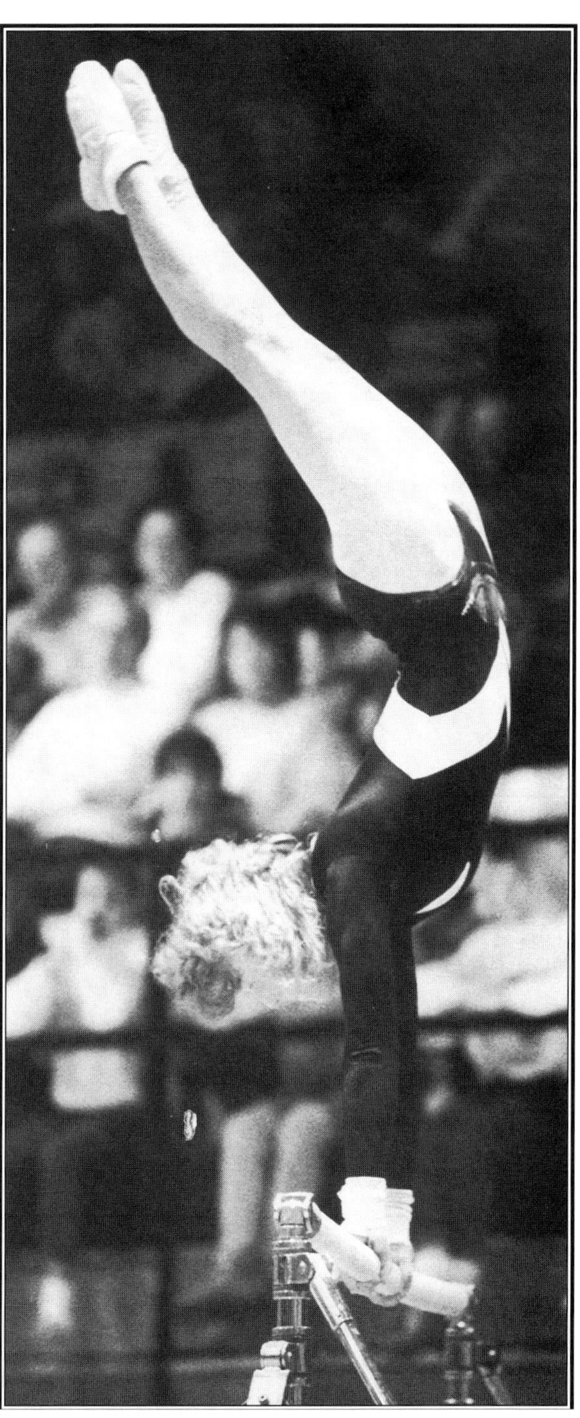

Michelle Lautner, showing the form that earned her the chance to compete in Senior Nationals in 1988.

1988 Trojan gymnasts, Class A state champions. Front Row: Mandy Samuelson, Julie Hofmeister, Amy Shumsky. Second Row: Coach Bill Jacob, Jill Timberlake, Stacie Hansen, Leslie Paupore, Capt. Michelle Lautner, Deb Theodorovich. Back Row: Laura Nelson, Lisa Downey, Julie Johnson, Diane Stoeckel, Michelle Bauer, Lori McWhirter, Margie Kinney.

had practices many hours of the day and had to have special diets. Laura Nelson said, "Gymnastics is one of the most difficult and dangerous sports." She was one of the two seniors in the team. Then Laura added, " We work as hard [as other sport teams], if not harder. It's too bad we are not recognized." However, gymnastics had come a long way. Even with all the freshmen and sophomores, they still had high scores because of the two seniors, Nelson and Kim Johnson. Moreover, the younger girls improved greatly throughout the season.

After a 1990-1991 team made up entirely of underclassmen, Greg Barner returned to coach the gymnastics team in 1991-1992. Barner stated, "Coaching a team like gymnastics is much different from a game like basketball or football. You emphasize the team idea, not the individual, so everything that is done, is for the whole team. We have a different strategy but the same spirit and philosophy." However, they suffered a big loss with an injury to top scorer Kristi Lewallen midway through the season. "The best thing about gymnastics is that it has taught me how to set realistic goals and achieve them," concluded Heather Bogard.

In 1992-1993, seniors Lewallan (having recovered from her previous year's achilles' tendon injury) and Bogard (who battled an ankle injury early that season) led the team. "Next year it's going to be hard to replace both Kristi [a four-year varsity gymnast] and Heather," commented Coach Barner.

The 1993-1994 team was small, but had committed gymnasts Autumn Hansen, Shannon Arterburn, Megan Carstens, Heidi Bogard, Jill Orlikowski and Christina Snyder. The girls worked very hard in the 1994-1995 season, with practices Monday through Thursday for three hours each day. The team consisted of three sophomores and four juniors.

In 1996, the team qualified for the state meet where they placed eighth. As a result, Autumn Hansen became just the fourth Trojan gymnast to go to Senior Nationals. After finishing fourth at regionals, the 1996-1997 team, unfortunately, did not qualify for the state finals. However, the team's only two seniors, Kristy Eldredge and Rachel Dowdney, both had strong showings as individuals. Eldredge was sixth all-around in the state, while Dowdney took tenth on the bars.

A FEW GYMNASTS WENT ON TO COLLEGE LEVEL COMPETITION, such as Sue Nyland, Mandy Samuelson, Dayna Samuelson, Michelle Lautner and Julie Hofmeister. Mandy Samuelson said that high school gymnastics was more fun than college. She said that the team does not get enough support and added that, "It's not one of those big sports... and it is so expensive." The better equipment costs a little more. One example is the mats. Samuelson said that an exciting time was at states when everyone was falling, but on the last exercise, the floor exercise, she got a high enough score for the team to win the state title, the first Trojan gymnastics team to achieve that honor. She was very proud of that moment.

QUALIFIERS FOR SENIOR NATIONALS

Michigan high school gymnastics does not award All-State recognition. Instead, an honor for top gymnasts in the state is to qualify for Senior Nationals, a national meet only for high school seniors. In the history of gymnastics as a varsity sport at Traverse City Senior High, four girls have achieved this distinction.

1983	Karen Howe
1984	Ta Scala
1988	Michelle Lautner
1996	Autumn Hansen

TROJAN GYMNASTIC COACHES

1974-1976	Greg Barner
1977	Nancy Kerr
1978-1990	Bill Jacob
1991-present	Greg Barner

GYMNASTICS SCORING

- The top four scores in each event are added together for the final score. The highest score wins.
- To qualify for regionals, a team must reach a cumulative score of at least 115 at four meets during the season.
- Ten is the highest score for each event.
- High school gymnasts do not have to do all four events (as do Olympic athletes); they can specialize.
- Scores are based on technique, composition and difficulty.

13

Girls Track and Field

By Sports Publishing Class

"Don't just stand there! Run! Run! "

– Author Unknown

The girls track team started off with a bang in 1974 under head coach Larry Grow. The 30-girl team won its first meet with Manistee and St. Francis and continued this pattern for most of that first season. They won nine meets, lost to Cadillac by three points, and then placed sixth in the State Meet Pentathlon at Michigan State University. At that meet, Jo Drake, Cathy Clarke and Jane Gilmore placed in the top twenty scores in five events: 60-yard hurdles, 220-yard dash, long jump, high jump and shot put. Jo Drake placed second in the meet, with Clarke 12th and Gilmore 17th. Drake was a versatile team member, competing in the long jump, 880 medley relay and the 220-yard dash. Senior Diane Culp was a mile runner on that team.

The 1975 girls track team recorded an undefeated season, capped off by a 30 point victory at the LMAC meet where they placed six athletes in the state meet. For the most part, they overwhelmed their competition that year and were in a good position with most of the girls being underclassmen.

The 1976 team had its second undefeated season in only its third year of existence and won the Class A regional by one point. In the shot put event, Polly Prouty finished first, Carolyn Keesor, second, and Julie Strong, third. Sally Zook finished first in the two-mile with a new school record of 11:32.4 and earned All-State honors in the 3200. Second places went to Keesor in the discus, Jane Gilmore, hurdles, and Barb Richards, the mile. In

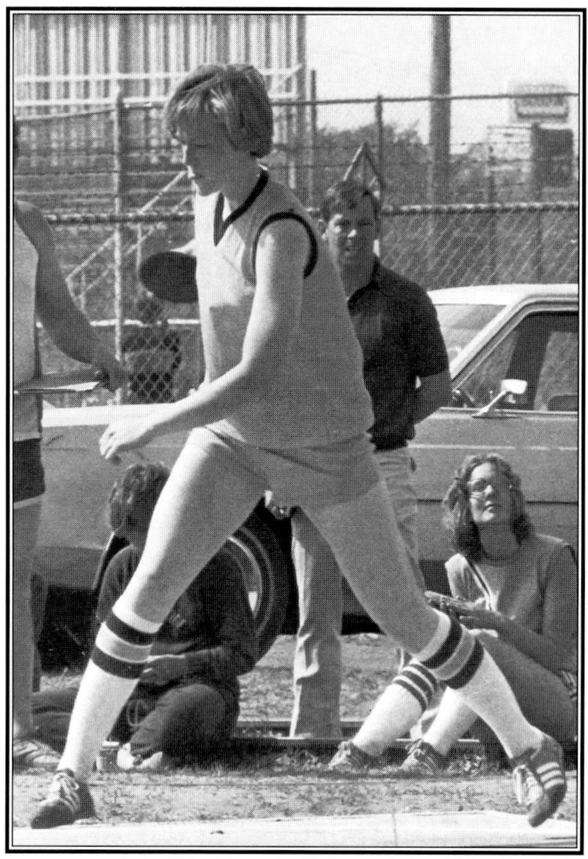

Polly Prouty, All-State in shot put and discus.

fourth place was the 880 relay team, setting a school record of 1:49.0.

In 1977, the success continued as three varsity athletes qualified for the state meet, including two regional champions. Sally Zook won the 3200 at regionals and finished third at the state meet, earning repeat All-State honors. Polly Prouty won the regional shot put title and finished second to teammate Carolyn Keesor in the discus. At the state meet, Prouty was named All-State in the shot and discus and set a new school record of 40'1" in the shot. Keesor set a new school record in the discus at 119'1". At the Honor Roll Meet, the Traverse City girls won nine of the 14 events and set records in four of them.

Running for the last season at Thirlby Field, the 1978 girls track team had an 8-3 record to take third in the LMAC. Besides competing in the regular conference meets, they ran in several multi-team competitions: the Ferris State Indoor Invitational, Petoskey Relays, and hosted the North Country Relays where they took three firsts. One of the highlights of that season was the setting of two new school records: Barb Becker in the 440-yard run with a time of 61.6 and the 440 relay team of Terri Meeves, Gina Pulcipher, Kathy Dohm and Deb Hinds with a time of 51.3. The 1978 team also had three girls qualify for the state finals: Barb Richards (880-yard run), Sally Rogers (two-mile run) and Julie Strong (discus). The second highlight of that season was the beginning of the new all weather track at the Senior High.

In 1979, former Trojan track team members Diane Culp and Julie Strong returned to help the coaching staff along with new head coach Mike Bee. The team ended with a 3-3 season and a win at the Petoskey Relays. Although no new school records were broken, there were six new sophomore records including a time set in the new event, 220 hurdles. The Outstanding Performer for the season was senior Lynne Richards.

The following year, four varsity records were broken during their 3-3 season. These records were: the 1600 meter relay, run by Kristen Zimmerman, Eileen Callaghan, Martha Snow, and Patty Cartwright in 4:07.22 minutes; the 400 meter relay by Lori Peek, Zimmerman, Shelly Bell and Janet Bowerman in 50.85; 200 meter low hurdles in 31.03 by Gina Pulcipher; and the shot put by Patty Roush with 35'3". In addition, four sophomore records were also broken, for a total of eight new records that year. The team placed fourth in the LMAC and 12th at regionals. For the third year in a row, the Trojans won the Petoskey Relays and finished with another 3-3 season.

In 1981, the girls improved to a second place LMAC finish after a season that saw three new school records. Kristin Zimmerman set a new record in the 400-yard dash (60.58), Patty Roush in the shot put with 36', and sophomore Lynda Fuller with 30.16 in the 200 low hurdles. MVP's that year were Patty Roush and Lynda Fuller, while

Kristin Zimmerman won the Outstanding Performance and Thoroughbred Awards.

The 1982 team had the problem of having only 20 girls on the team which meant that the whole team had to participate in both varsity and junior varsity meets. However, participating in all the extra events seemed to have a positive effect as all the girls saw a definite improvement. Outstanding performances that year were given by Danielle Daniels and Lori Peek in a variety of events, Allys Dwyer and Debbie Rode on long distances; and Lynda Fuller, Molly Piché, Kelly Burkholder and Natalie Breithaupt in sprints and relays.

In 1984, former star Kristen Zimmerman took over as head coach. Her first team did well, placing third in the LMAC and just missing second place by 2 1/2 points. Distance runners were the core of the team with state qualifiers being: Debbie Rode and Katherine Kopp in the one- and two-mile runs; Lynn Remillard and Wendi Scott in the two-mile relay; and Lisa Schramm in the 100 meter low hurdles. Coach Zimmerman stressed personal bests that year, which gave the runners a chance to win in their own minds, if not at the finish line.

After a 1985 season with only 23 members, the 1986 team under coach Polly Prouty-Meredith expanded to 56 girls actively competing. With these numbers, depth became a factor. There also were four coaches that year, which Meredith said, "was the best thing that could have happened to us." With extra help from Bonnie Gottshall, Laurie Cook and Ivanka Baic, the girls were able to get much more individualized coaching. Sophomore Anne Mudgett and exchange student Satu Pitkaabo qualified for the state finals, where Mudgett placed sixth in the 3200m run and Pitkaabo tied for sixth with a high jump of 5'3". That height set a new school record, as did Jodi Gaff's time of 15.4 in the 100m hurdles. Also, freshman Nikki Kulik set a new ninth grade long jump record of 16'1". MVP that year was Mollie Schwarm.

By 1986 and 1987, the number of girls participating in track continued to increase. The 1987 team of 65 girls had a very successful season and placed third at regionals after finishing 13th and seventh the previous two years. Beth Winninger was a standout in the high jump and 400m. Lisa Burkholder and Cammy Potter were the core of a great group of distance runners. Jenny Payne set a new team record in the two mile run while exchange student Camilla Heier had a record 400m time. Jodi Gaff won the 100 and 300m hurdles as well as the high jump in the Honor Roll Meet. Amy Klingelsmith became the first Trojan in 10 years to throw the discus over 100 feet.

In 1988, the team had the biggest number of girls who finished the season, 70, after 100 mem-

All-State two-miler Jenny Payne.

1991 state championship 3200m relay team with coach Mark Fries: Karlene Kurtz, Marlo Mata, Stephanie Walton and Jenny Peters.

bers began the season. Standouts were Jodi Gaff who tied school records for hurdle and high jump and Jenny Payne who broke the school record for the two-mile to earn All-State honors. Six Trojans qualified for the state meet: Payne, Gaff, Amber Mariage, Allison Dodge, Meg Wilson and Erika Moon. Moon, Dodge, Wilson and Payne finished tenth in the state in the two-mile relay.

In 1989 and 1990, there was a group of 13 juniors who were the core of the team. They had an outstanding work ethic and enthusiasm, according to coach Polly Walker. The outstanding sprinters/hurdlers included Tammy Smith, Robyn Eley, Kandi Kent, Dana Steckley, Libby Hoxsie and Nicki Biggs. Field event specialists included Jayna Greiner, Rebecca McGarry, Robyn Eley and Becky Fleis. Distance standouts were Stephanie Walton, Marlo Mata, Rachel Benedick, Kerry Mead, Jenny Peters, Karlene Kurtz and Lori Klingelsmith. This team performed well all year and continued to work hard over the summer in anticipation of the upcoming year.

THE 1991 TEAM HAD AN OUTSTANDING SEASON. In an exciting year for Trojan girls track, they won every invitational and dual meet they entered. The group of seniors led the team to its first regional championship since 1977. Thirteen athletes qualified for the state championship as the team finished in third place at the state meet, the highest place of any boys or girls team in the history of Traverse City High School track to date. Earning All-State honors were Jayna Greiner in the shot put; Stephanie Walton, Marlo Mata, Karlene Kurtz and Jenny Peters in the 3200 relay which captured first place at the state finals with a school record 9:37; and Karlene Kurtz who finished second in the 800. Tammy Smith, Robyn Eley, Dana Steckley and Kandi Kent finished fourth in the 800 relay and set a new school record. Erika Schimik finished fourth in the 3200, while Jenny Peters placed sixth in the 1600. Also competing in the state meet were Becky Fleis in the high jump and Lori Klingelsmith in the 3200. That year Greiner set a new record in the shot put by beating Julie Strong's 1978 record of 39'10 1/4" with 42' 1/2".

After losing 13 four-year varsity athletes to graduation, the 1992 team had a huge hole to fill. Nicki Biggs, Robyn Eley, Rebecca McGarry, Amy McEvoy, Karlene Kurtz, Jenny Peters and Lori Klingelsmith became the team leaders and top

The Trojans' Jayna Greiner, who was ranked No. 6 nationally in the shot put in 1991.

point earners. The team won the Saginaw Valley Invitational, Scottie Classic, Alma Relays and the McDonald's Relays and finished the season with a third place finish at regionals. Ten girls qualified for the state finals where Kurtz once again earned All-State honors in the 800 with her third place finish.

In 1993, Mark Fries became head coach after serving as the team's distance coach for five years. This year's quad was very large, with over 80 girls, and also very young. Coach Fries spent much of his time developing this talent and guiding the girls into the events which would most benefit the athletes and the team. The 1993 team had a very successful season, winning five invitationals and qualifying 10 girls for the state finals after the team placed third at regionals. The team was led by three-time All-Stater and school record-holder Karlene Kurtz, probably the most successful female Traverse City track athlete. Robyn Eley, the other star of that team, was an exceptional sprinter, hurdler and long jumper who holds records in the long jump and high hurdles. State meet qualifiers included Kurtz, Eley, Kerry Mead, Becky McGarry, Rebecca Mann, Amber Andresen, Holly Weber, Erika Schimik, Teya Smith and Kelly Weber. Kurtz placed second in the 800 with a time of 2:18. Eley placed eighth in the 100 meter dash and seventh in the long jump. The 3200 meter relay of Kurtz, Mann, Andresen and Holly Weber finished sixth.

In 1994, second-year Coach Fries continued the rebuilding process with much success. The team won five invitationals and was regional runner-up, giving eventual state champion Bay City Western all it could handle. The team qualified 11 girls to the state finals: Holly Weber, Amanda Smith, Teya Smith, Jenny Baynton, Emily Montie, Jill Orlikowski, Kelly Weber, Angel Wolf, Holly Ufer, Sara Sudekum and Jill Gregory.

The 1995 team was the best in school history, according to Coach Fries, as it overpowered all competition and had no weakness. The squad scored over 100 points in every invitational and finished the season undefeated. The team blew away the field at regionals, scoring an incredible 145 points to a distant second 54 points for Midland. The team recorded over 200 points (214) at the Traverse City Invitational. Two school

1995 girls track distance runners. Captain Amanda Kiessel (second row, second from right) was the top distance runner.

1995 throwers with Coach Jerry Ruskowski: top shot putter Jamie Martin (second row from bottom, far left) and Holly Ufer (second row from bottom, second from left), who set school discus record.

1995 hurdlers and jumpers. Heidi Bogard (second row on right) holds school record in hurdles.

records were set that year: Holly Ufer in the discus at 128 feet and Heidi Bogard with 47.95 in the 300m hurdles. The team qualified an amazing 13 girls for the state finals: Ufer, Bogard, Jackie Edginton, Jamie Martin, Angel Wolf, Sara DeBruyn, Amanda Smith, Heather Willson, Kelly Weber, Jill Orlikowski, Marin Schulz, Michelle Williams and Amanda Kiessel. Mark Fries was named 1995 Regional Coach of the Year for this successful season.

The girls track team continued on a roll when it finished the 1996 outdoor season undefeated, winning eight invitationals. It scored 114 points to claim its second regional title in a row, leaving Bay City Western far behind with 52 points. Two new school records which were set were: the 1600m relay with a new time of 4:01.0 by Kelly Weber, Marin Schulz, Marcie Pahl and Rachel Sturtz; and the 400m relay in 50.25 by Kelly Weber, Schulz, Katie Willis and Sheena Stokes. At the state finals, the 1600m relay placed fourth and the 3200m relay seventh. Coach Fries earned his second consecutive Regional Coach of the Year honors.

Traverse City girls track has emerged as a force in regional competition as it has increased its numbers and maintained high quality and dedicated team members. Even with the addition of the second high school, the future looks bright for Trojan track.

CLASS A GIRLS TRACK & FIELD ALL-STATE

1976	Sally Zook	3200m
1977	Sally Zook	3200 m
	Polly Prouty	Shot put
	Polly Prouty	Discus
1988	Jenny Payne	3200m
1991	Stephanie Walton	3200m relay
	Marlo Mata	3200m relay
	Karlene Kurtz	3200m relay
	Jenny Peters	3200m relay
	Karlene Kurtz	800 m
1992	Karlene Kurtz	800m
1993	Karlene Kurtz	800m

Sheena Stokes (bottom row on right) led the 1995 sprinters with a school record in the 400m relay.

TROJAN GIRLS TRACK SCHOOL RECORDS

Event	Name	Mark	Year	
100 meter dash	Kim Morey	12.1	1975	
200 meter dash	Kim Morey	25.4	1974	
400 meter dash	Kandi Kent	59.18	1990	
800 meter run	Karlene Kurtz	2:17.9	1991	All-State
1600 meter run	Sally Zook	5:11	1978	
3200 meter run	Jenny Payne	11:00.7	1988	All-State
Long jump	Robyn Eley	17'7"	1993	
High jump	Jodi Gaff	5'4"	1988	
	Becky Fleis	5'4"	1990	
Discus	Holly Ufer	27'3"	1995	
Shotput	Jayna Greiner	42' 1/2"	1991	All-State
100m high hurdles	Robyn Eley	15.16	1992	
300m low hurdles	Heidi Bogard	47.95	1995	
400 meter relay	Kelly Weber Marin Schulz Katie Willis Sheena Stokes	50.25	1996	
1600 meter relay	Kelly Weber Marin Schulz Rachel Sturtz Marcie Pahl	4:01.06	1996	
3200 meter relay	Karlene Kurtz Jenny Peters Marlo Mata Stephanie Walton	9:37.0	1991	All-State

TROJAN TRACK HEAD COACHES

1974-1978	Larry Grow
1979-1981	Mike Bee
1982	Jon Knowles
1983	Dan Young
1984	Kristin Zimmerman
1985-1992	Polly Walker
1993 – present	Mark Fries

14

Hockey

By Greg Stroh

"Losing is never fun, but if you've played well you can be proud and it's a lot easier to take."

– Eric Guttenberg, Former Trojan Coach

Although hockey came to America in the late 1800s, it did not make its grand appearance onto the Traverse City Trojan sport roster until 1975, when it was played as a club sport. Hockey is still today as it was then, played interscholastically at the Senior High School. There are no in-house feeder programs for hockey, unlike football which used to have programs going as far back as the fifth grade. Most of the hockey players were coached by personal coaches and trainers or they were involved in amateur leagues around the area. However, a strong youth area hockey program, the Grand Traverse Hockey Association, is now providing talent for the high school team.

The biggest reason for the delay of hockey to Traverse City was the lack of a permanent year-round enclosed facility until the late 1970s. With the construction of Glacier Arena, Trojan hockey began as a club sport which immediately drew large crowds for its games. Ross Childs, a former standout hockey player at the University of Michigan, got the Trojan hockey program underway as coach for the two years it was a club sport from 1975-1977.

Continuing into their first varsity season in 1977-1978, Ross Childs coached the Trojan hockey team to a 9-9-2 record. Team captain Dan Higgins was named the team's Most Valuable Player. Other players on the very first varsity hockey team were: Larry Green, Bruce Carpenter, Arne Sarya, Tom Chandler, Randy Jamison, Mike Wagoner, Neil Jones, Jeff Geiger, Darren LaCharite, Jeff Livingston, Tom Kelly, Wes Hernden, Bob Gleason, Dan Ferguson, Don Piche', Steve Armour, Bob Houle, Mike Drilling and Rob Murner. Considering it was the first

Trojan team, it was quite an accomplishment to end up with a .500 record. That first year they continued to have a surprising number of fans.

The 1978-1979 season was much like their first. Under a different coach, Denny Meyers, the Trojan hockey team went 11-11-3. During the course of the season the Trojans compiled 143 goals. On Tuesday, March 5, 1979, an amazing 48 goals were scored in one game against Saginaw; that is a little over a goal a minute! Jeff Armour, whose record still stands, scored an incredible nine goals in the slaughter.

The Trojans in the 1979-1980 season improved their record to 12-10 with Denny Meyers in his second year of coaching. They started the season slowly, but they didn't quit and came back from a 2-7 start to win 10 out of their last 13 games. John Detar was awarded Most Valuable Player.

IN THEIR 1980-1981 SEASON under a new coach, Ken McPhail, the Trojans had a disappointing 6-16 record. The biggest reason for that win/loss ratio was they were plagued with injuries. Most Valuable Player was Jim Gable. By this time, the team unfortunately no longer had Glacier Arena as its home and instead played in the enclosed bubble at the Civic Center which did not lend itself to spectators.

In 1981-1982, the first year of the 5 1/2 season reign of coach Eric Guttengerg, the Trojans went 3-16-2. The following year, 1982-1983, proved to be much the same for the Trojans with a record of 3-10. They only had one home game throughout the whole season.

With the new Civic Center Ice Arena as a home rink in 1983, Guttenberg brought the Trojan team out of a slump with their first winning season since Denny Meyers. Two records were broken that year:

Trojan hockey as a club sport. Back Row: Dan Ferguson, Dan Bell, Jeff Armour, Dan Higgins, Bill Robinson. Middle Row: Mgr. Don Ferguson, Tom Chandler, Tim Thomas, Jerry Clous, Jeff Livingston, Arne Sarya, Bruce Graham, Kevin Stewart, Coach Ross Childs. Front Row: Bob Houle, Wes Hernden, Teri Hibbard, Mike Wagoner, Terry Loveland, Kevin Ewing, Larry Green. Seated: Mascot Scott Childs.

the team had more wins than any previous Trojan hockey team and team captain Dave Detar broke brother John's record in earning the most points in a season with 63. The Trojans beat Alpena for the first time in an exciting overtime victory. Dave Detar made All-State Honorable Mention as well as Most Valuable Player and later went on to play hockey at Miami of Ohio. Also, Brandon Look was named best Student-Athlete.

It was not until the mid 1980s that Trojan hockey was really advertised and announced. At that time a billboard was placed on US 31 North that read, "Traverse City Senior High Hockey....The Hottest Ticket In Town." In addition to the billboard that same year, some of the Trojan games were announced during the Detroit Red Wings games. A little PR always lifts a sport.

Coaching his fourth year in 1984-1985, Eric Guttenberg led the Trojans to another winning season, taking them to a 12-9 finish. However, they had a disappointing loss in the first round of the playoffs to the Alpena team. The Most Valuable Player for the Trojans was Vince Stevens. Chris Hathaway received All-State Honorable Mention, as well as team Most Valuable Forward. With his 40 goals and 20 assists, Hathaway broke the old school record of 60 points in a season. He was also one of 38 boys to be picked to participate in an Olympic training camp in Colorado.

For the 1985-1986 season, the Trojans had joined a new conference, The Great Northern Hockey Conference. They unfortunately had a rough start, ending the year at 10-11-1, since they played good high quality teams like Sault Ste. Marie, Escanaba, Marquette and Alpena. However, they distinguished themselves by becoming the first team to beat Sault St. Marie in the Soo. This was also the third year in a row that they won the Big Rapids tournament. Chris Hathaway led the entire league in number of goals.

Eighteen losses and two wins marked the 1986-1987 "rebuilding" season. Eric Guttenberg decided to come out of retirement to coach for half of a year and then hand the reigns over to Jim Martin for the rest of the season. When they started the season with eleven sophomores, it was obvious then that victories would be tough in coming. A quote from the *Detroit Free Press* was that "goalie Mike Wood saw more rubber than I-75." He averaged around 40-50 saves every game, pretty much holding the team together throughout the season.

The 1987-1988 season was a little better than the one before. Under Coach Bill Stevens, the Trojans had a record of 7 wins, 14 losses. The most valuable players included Mike Wood, Vince Opper, Rob Garvin, and Matt McCullough. There

1983-1984 Trojan hockey team in its first winning season. Front Row: Mike Ripper, Jeff Lobdell, Joe VanAntwerp, Vic Bliss, Coach Eric Guttenberg, Todd Spaulding, Tom VanAntwerp, Dave Detar, Rod Herndon. Back Row: Mgr. Dan Smith, Pat Smith, Mark Wood, Terry Jones, Bryan Marger, Brandon Look, Kurt Coesens, Dave Sarya, Chris Hathaway, Dave Luzac, Kevin Barrett, Dave Peterson, Vince Stevens, Marty Lobdell.

Traverse City's Chad Fournier whips the puck toward the goal.

was another up and down season in 1988-1989 with a less than spectacular record of 10-12-1. Dave Rutkowski was named All-State for his strong playing that year.

With only three seniors, the Trojans had a great deal of rebuilding to do in their 1989-1990 season. After third-year coach Bill Stevens resigned eight games into the season, Jim Martin, Dick Murphy, and Eric Guttenberg took over the reigns for the remainder of the season. It was a very rough year for the Trojans as they had the worst record in their history, 0-21. The crazy thing about hockey in Michigan is that a team can make the playoffs regardless of their record, even with a record like 0-21.

IN 1990-1991, NEW HEAD COACH JUDE CUMMINGS led the Trojans to a slightly improved season, with a 3-17-1 record. Junior Mike Colenso said, "There was a definite change in our team's attitude. A couple of wins really boosted our morale. We kept with the other teams;

1994 Trojan hockey team, the first Great Northern Conference champions. Back Row: Trainer Sarah Valade, Ass't. Coach Chris Givens, Cory Kattelus, Matt Martell, Troy Keipper, Brock Ballard, Brent Straitiff, Ben Schnurr, Brooks Holland, Mgr. Tony Balcezak, Head Coach Jude Cummings. Middle Row: Ass't. Coach Ed Kattelus, Jim Warner, Scott Harvey, Anders Kelto, Dave Joynt, Derek McLeod, Duane Sudol, Kyle Smith, Ken Runyon, Ass't. Coach Bob Kattelus. Front: Charlie O'Hearn, Jason Martin, Steve Turner, Brad Schultz.

that is what we really wanted to do." The major reason for the poor record was because of all the penalties and game suspensions.

Second-year coach Jude Cummings improved the Trojans' record in the 1991-1992 season to 9-12, losing in the first round of the playoffs to Alpena 2-5. Instead of going out just to get into fights, they went out to win. WTCM started announcing more games on AM 580 which brought the morale up, as well as improved attitudes.

Once again the Trojans improved their record from the previous year. Coach Jude Cummings led the team to a 14-8-2 record in the 1992-1993 season. Despite the good record, however, they did not go all the way to the championship. The team's Most Valuable Player was Chad Fournier who also made All-State and the Dream Team. Also named All-State was Eric Keipper; Honorable Mentions went to Pat Erway, Chris Jackson, and Chad Lorenz.

Finally, in the 1993-1994 season they did it; the Trojans won the first Great Northern Conference championship in school history. They placed two games ahead of Alpena by beating Sault St. Marie 6-3 to end the season with the best ever record of 17-6. Scott Harvey had his second year as conference scoring champion and was the Most Valuable Player. He also finished second in voting for Michigan's Mr. Hockey. Assistant Coach Chris Givens said, "My most memorable player was Scott Harvey because he was so fun to watch because of the level of intensity that he played at and he was a great player to coach." The Trojans also set another school record of nine consecutive wins from January 21-February 28. Matt Martell said, "Our coaches changed the style of our hockey so that it was more fun to watch."

Scott Harvey was named All-State in 1994 after his outstanding season. Receiving All-State Honorable Mention were Kyle Smith, Brooks Holland, Matt Martell, Anders Kelto, Charlie O'Hearn, Troy Keipper, Jim Warner, Brock Ballard, Duane Sudol and Derek McLeod. Such a high number of skaters receiving All-State honors is indicative of the strength of the 1993-1994 team. A further honor for the 1994 Trojans was to have Jude Cummings named as state Class A Coach of the Year.

Scott Harvey, second in voting for the 1994 Mr. Hockey.

They had another playoff season in 1995, with a 12-11-1 record. The Trojans made it into the second round of the playoffs, getting past Sault St. Marie by a score of 7-1, which advanced them on to play Marquette in the district finals. It took Marquette four overtimes to conquer Traverse City and knock them out of the playoffs. "This was by far my most memorable game and will always stick with me," Chris Givens said. Defensive player Mike Wolf planned to try out for Junior Hockey in Canada, then move on to the minor leagues. Brock Ballard was named Most Valuable Player.

The Trojans finished their 1995-1996 season 12-9-1. Jim Warner was named Most Valuable Player, won the league scoring title and was All-State Honorable Mention along with Anders Kelto, Mike

Perdue, and Derek McLeod. This was Chris Givens' first year as head coach of the Trojans. He said, "The biggest rivalry so far for me is Alpena."

This quote from Coach Givens proved prophetic in the 1996-1997 season, as Traverse City finished the year with a loss to No. 2 ranked Alpena. Hugo Marsan, a French exchange student, sparked the team on and off the ice with his mastery of the game and good sense of humor. Sophomore Josh Thompson led a group of six fellow sophomores as third leading scorer. Older brother Justin spurred the team on as well.

1996-1997 was the last season with a hockey team representing only one high school. The Trojans finished with a 10-11-1 record, losing to Alpena 6-1 in their final game. This prevented Traverse City from advancing to the tournaments but put the Trojans tenth in the state. "We ended up on a bad note. But despite that, overall we had a good season," said team captain Toby Northway. Fifteen of their 22 games were either lost or won by only one goal. The team notably included one freshman and six sophomores. Hugo Marsan led the team with the most goals scored. Kevin O'Hearn was second and Josh Thompson was the third highest scorer, a feat unusual for a sophomore. All-State Honorable Mention went to O'Hearn, Northway and Marsan; O'Hearn also received All-Conference honors, with All-Conference honorable mention going to Northway and Marsan. Toby Northway was Most Valuable Player. Kevin Perdue received credit for playing the last game with an injured knee.

Trojan hockey has had many up and down seasons, poor years and great years. But this is still an up-and-coming program, building gradually year by year. It is getting stronger with time and undoubtedly some day will bring home the title of "State Champions". The 1996-1997 season marked the twentieth year of Trojan hockey with their total record being 165 wins, 229 losses and 12 ties. The Trojan hockey team has gone through nine coaches, four in one year.

Perhaps, in years to come, with a strong feeder program and the new Centre I.C.E. arena which just opened, the biggest rivalry will be across town rather than across state. Cheers, hockey fans!

HOCKEY ALL-STATE DREAM TEAM

1993	Chad Fournier
1994	Scott Harvey

CLASS A HOCKEY ALL-STATE

	First Team	Honorable Mention
1984		Dave Detar
1985		Chris Hathaway
1989	Dave Rutkowski	
1993	Eric Keipper	Pat Erway Chris Jackson Chad Lorenz
1994		Brock Ballard Brooks Holland Troy Keipper Anders Kelto Matt Martel Derek McLeod Charlie O'Hearn Kyle Smith Duane Sudol Jim Warner
1996		Anders Kelto Derek McLeod Mike Perdue Jim Warner

TROJAN HOCKEY COACHES

1975-1977 (Club Sport)	Ross Childs	
1977-1978	Ross Childs	9-9-2
1978-1980	Denny Meyers	23-21-3
1980-1981	Ken McPhail	6-16
1981-1986	Eric Guttenberg	41-55-3
1986-1989	Bill Stevens	19-44-1
1989-1990	Eric Guttenberg Jim Martin Dick Murphy	
1990-1994	Jude Cummings	55-75-4
1995-present	Chris Givens	12-9-1

15

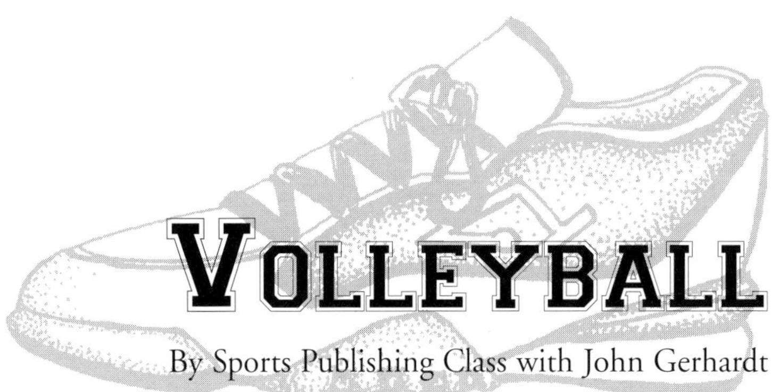

VOLLEYBALL

By Sports Publishing Class with John Gerhardt

"Volleyball is a sport where communication is a very important part of the game. If your team isn't close, then there isn't going to be any communication."

– KRISTI RYON '90

Volleyball was invented in 1895 by William G. Morgan, a physical education teacher at the YMCA in Holyoke, Mass. Since then, volleyball has grown to be an official Olympic sport and about 170 countries belong to the Federation International de Volleyball. Although Title IX was passed in 1972, legal haggling over what it meant kept most girls sports on the back burner until the late 1970s. At that time, schools began to add more girls sports, one of which was volleyball.

The inaugural 1978-1979 season of girls volleyball at Traverse City Senior High was a humbling one for the team. Newly named coach John Gerhardt said his total volleyball experience equated to "squadron volleyball in college and squadron volleyball in the Air Force." At tryouts in the gym they made do with a makeshift set-up where a net was tied to the bleachers. Coach Gerhardt asked Mike Kinney, the Leland Class D state champion coach, to bring his team over for a scrimmage and to show everyone some skills such as overlapping and serve reception patterns. Ironically, the season opened with a game against Leland that Gerhardt says lasted about 10 minutes and that thankfully no one can remember the score. Their record for the season was 5 wins and 13 losses. Senior Cathy Nichols was voted as the team's Most Valuable Player. In the district finals, Midland Dow defeated Traverse City 15-6 and 15-12, but the victory was not easy. Coach

Gerhardt observed, " My clearest memory is that their girls seemed to come out of the rafters and hit the ball with sledge hammers." Dow was ranked in the top ten in the state at the time.

The team's record improved in the 1979-1980 season as the girls brought their first trophy home from the Leland tournament. Coach John Gerhardt led his team to a 10-14 season in which they twice defeated Leland, the defending state champions. He fondly remembers those early players: Kim Hinsenkamp, Amy Dunscombe, Cindy Newhouse, Kim Leider, Shelley Wright and Linda Blodgett. Coach Gerhardt recalls, "One of the highlights of 25 years of coaching occurred that year up in Petoskey. They had beaten us every time we had played and I was tremendously frustrated because I felt we should have been beating them. Our girls, however, seemed resigned to losing and we lost the first game of the match something like 15-2 in about 10 minutes. As we gathered together, I looked at the Petoskey girls and they were laughing and joking and carrying on like the match was a foregone conclusion. I became infuriated, incensed, and I suppose, a little out of control. I remember screaming at the girls, 'Look at them – they're laughing at you; they think they can't lose!' Whatever it was I said, it struck the right chord and I can't remember coaching a more fired-up team. I think we beat them 15-1 in about five minutes... I think Knute Rockne would have been proud of that half-time speech, and I know I've never approached anything like it since."

The next season, the team again improved their record to 16-4, which was their first winning season since the team's inception. Shelley Wright and Linda Blodgett were chosen for the LMAC first team, and Kim Leider was named to the All-Conference second team. Coach Gerhardt noted

1979 Trojan volleyball team. Back Row: Jody Bescey, Carol Bringman, Cathy Nichols. Middle Row: Shelley Wright, Gina Pulcipher, Kim Hinsenkamp. Bottom Row: Linda Blodgett, Sue McGeorge, Sue Rickard, Amy Dunscombe, Coach Gerhardt, Jill Coffey, Cindy Newhouse, Sara Skrubb. Not pictured: Rosie Fleis and Sue Gavigan.

that part of the improvement came about because they began attending clinics in the summer. He went to coaches clinics as well. It was like boot camp for volleyball where college coaches "beat up on us just like we were their own players..."

"Our team was better than the record showed," commented senior All Conference athlete Stephanie Fraley, reflecting on the team's 12-13 record for the 1982-1983 season. Despite the losing season, the Trojans were victorious in the LMAC tournament even after being seeded last. "Obviously, we won three straight to win the tournament," Coach Gerhardt commented. "I remember one point where Stephanie Fraley made three consecutive blocks at the net, finally getting a point on the third one. It was awesome and the girls went bananas."

Several aspects of the game were troublesome for Coach Gerhardt."Probably the two most frustrating parts of the game for me were serving and aggressiveness. Serving is so important... I can remember screaming, 'There are 900 square feet of court out there and all you have to do is hit one of them!'" Gerhardt added, "One girl who did master the art of serving was Judy Bay, whose career ended with an intact record of 340 consecutive serves without a miss ... I would venture that Judy's mark is probably a state and maybe even a national record."

THROUGHOUT THE 1980S, the Traverse City volleyball team had a pretty consistent record with a winning percentage a little above 50 percent most of the time. Coach Gerhardt stated, "Winning the league tournament in 1983 and then the league championship in 1984 was a big step forward for our program." The Trojans, led by seniors Sherry Domres, Amy Hurst, Molly Piche' and Pam Squires, bagged their first LMAC title in 1984 with a record of 17-15. Coach Gerhardt recalls the championship tournament, "We broke out our new Darth Vader uniforms (all black) for the tournament. The girls had never seen the uniforms and didn't even know that I had them. After the first match, which we won, I gave them a box with the uniforms and sent them into the locker room to see what was in it. They came out of that

Volleyball's first conference championship team in 1984. Front Row: Kim Peek, Denise Johnson, Debbie Deacon, Kelly Donner. Back Row: Molly Piche', Sherry Domres, Michelle McManemy, Pam Squires, Amy Hurst, Karen Nelson, Kim Hondorp, Coach Gerhardt.

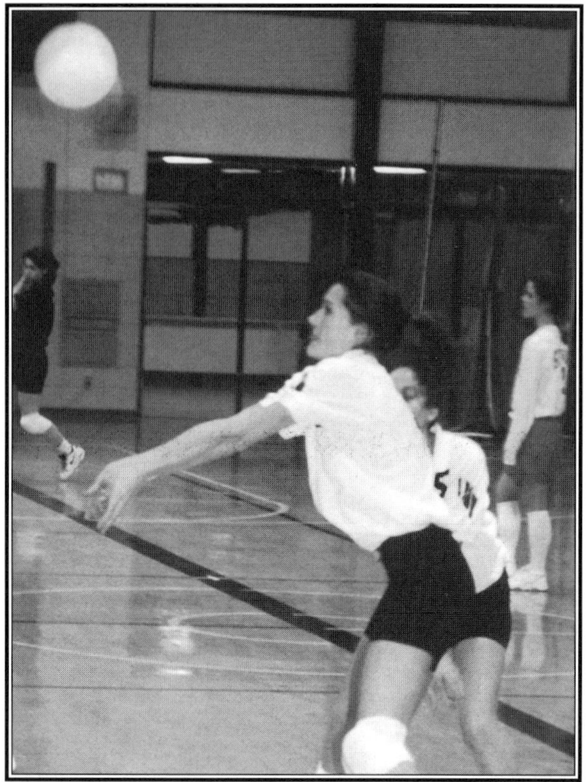

All-Region Dream Team pick Charla Holmes reaches for a shot.

locker room so fired up, it was unbelievable." Traverse City finished the season without ever losing all three games in a match. Gerhardt added, "Winning the league championship was a special accomplishment for the Trojans and for me. It meant that Traverse City was the only league member to win at least one championship in every sport, and, to the best of my knowledge, I am the only Trojan coach to win league championships in two totally different sports [volleyball and baseball] ... I'll always be proud of that."

Gerhardt's last two years of coaching volleyball were spent grooming the eventual district champs. However, with 75% of his team as new sophomores, the going was tough to begin with. Coach Gerhardt noted that this youthful bunch never quit and that the foundation was being laid for their senior year. "With captain Kim Hondorp as the only senior, and juniors Suzy Merchant, Laura Aylsworth, Amy Gee, Angie Stone, Chris Rose and Laura Holmes, the team went 16-11 the second year... and I said in the yearbook, 'Wait until next year!'"

SEVERAL LARGE CHANGES OCCURRED that next year. In 1987, one change was the addition of a new coach, Tim Keenan. The second, was a pretty new trophy which declared the Trojans as district champions! Compared to the previous two seasons' records, 9-23, and 16-11, respectively, that year's 56-9 record showed what having veterans on a team could do. Traverse City beat Flint Powers, 14-16, 17-15, and 15-10, and finally placed second in the regionals, after traveling over 4000 miles that season. Former Coach Gerhardt concluded, " The girls were wonderful and made me feel part of their success. After nine years, the team had made it to the elite in the state, and remembering where we had come from, I felt satisfied and proud."

The objective of the 1989 season was simple: win the district championship. The team carried a record of 21-19 into districts, but fell shy of their goal.

Since that time, the team has been coached by Laurie Glass, who played against the Trojans when she was a player for Leland in the very first matchup for Lady Trojan volleyball, and Kelly Neu, the current coach. The 1995-1996 season ended with a 42-21-5 record in which the team was the Glen Lake tournament champion. Julie MacIntosh and Trisha Ansorge were All-Region players while Charla Holmes made All-Region Dream Team.

The 1996-1997 season was even better at 51-17-0 with tournament wins at Roscommon and Cadillac. A first place win at the East Kentwood Invitational in the silver bracket and a second place in the South Haven Tournament silver bracket rounded out the season. Returning seniors Alison Carrier, Trisha Ansorge and Abby Mansfield summed things up this way, "Our goal as team leaders is to succeed victoriously together, but only if we have consistent positive attitudes, exceptional communication and 100% emotional/physical dedication and determination..."

The 1996-97 Trojan volleyball team. Back Row: Mgr. Melinda Harrigan, Allison Chamberlain, Laura Billette, Jenny Donaldson, Terah Maison, Emily MacIntosh, Susan Kashazta, Coach Kelly Neu. Front Row: Stacey Keegstra, Trisha Ansorge, Allison Carrier, Abby Mansfield, Darcy McClure.

VOLLEYBALL COACHES

1979-1986	John Gerhardt
1987-1990	Tim Keenan
1991-1994	Laurie Glass
1995	Mark Daniels
1996-present	Kelly Neu

16

Girls Cross Country

By Sports Publishing Class

"This is basically a simple sport – you work and you get good results; you loaf and nothing happens. Its rewards come from within, and only individual improvement leads to team success."
– Dan Young, Girls Cross Country Coach, 1984 – 1985

Cross country competitors run five kilometers (3.1 miles) on an outdoor course of varied terrain. In a meet, teams can run as many athletes as they want, but only five count toward the score. The team with the lowest score wins the meet.

Cross country became a sport at Traverse City Senior High in 1960. For 17 years, cross country was only for boys. That changed in 1973. Diane Culp was the first and only female to ever run on the boys team. In 1975, the government issued detailed regulations based on Title IX, outlawing discrimination based on sex in admissions, course offerings, hiring and athletics. Cross country is now enjoyed by a large number of girls.

The Traverse City Senior High's girls cross country team has become one of the most successful programs in the state. The team has won the regional championship seven times and the state championship in 1991 and 1992.

In 1978, Larry Grow was named the first cross country coach and he assembled a team of 12 girls. Success came quickly to the young program. Even though Traverse City was not a conference team that year, it competed in LMAC meets with Grand Haven and Mona Shores, having a 3-1 record before regionals. This group of schools gave out medals to the top ten finishers for the season. Traverse City had four girls receiving these medals: Carol Bringman, fifth place, Eileen Stoppa, seventh, Lynne Richards, ninth and Sue Hoffman, tenth. The team took third in regionals and qualified for the state meet, finishing 23rd out of 24 schools. According to Coach Grow, it was a real success just to have qualified for the state finals that first year.

By 1980, the team placed second at regionals, sending three members to the state finals, Allys Dwyer, Lori Dreves and Sue Hoffman. Dwyer had the fastest three-mile on the team (19.48) and the fastest 500 m (20.24). Each team member improved by at least one minute that season.

By 1981, the Trojans, under the leadership of first-year coach Carol Roehrich, were regional champions. The team had only seven members but had a strong season. Sophomore Debbie Rode earned MVP honors by placing first in every dual meet, was second at regionals and broke the course record twice with 20.58. The rest of the team included captain Sonja Simon, Allys Dwyer, Charlotte Ingersol, Kellie Wilson, Rosanna Laughter and Cheryl Ingersol. The entire team went to the state meet for the first time, where they placed 20th.

By fall of 1982, there were only two or three runners for the most part, so they did not receive any scores as a team. Noa Tabackman and Kellie Wilson battled injuries, leaving Trina Fiebing and Debbie Rode to do most of the competing. Fortunately, Debbie Rode had an outstanding year. She was named All-Conference after placing second in the conference, qualified for the state meet as an individual where she placed seventh, and was named MVP for these successes.

Senior Debbie Rode was the only returning cross country runner the following fall. She had another excellent season as she took many first places and broke seven out of 11 course records. She earned All-Conference honors with teammates senior Colleen Kelly, junior Kathy Kopp and freshman Cammy Potter. These runners were LMAC conference champions for the first time, quite a feat for a young and inexperienced team. After a second place regional finish, they qualified for states. There were two major changes this year: Larry Grow returned after two years to coach again and freshmen were allowed to join the high school team for the first time.

FORMER BOYS CROSS COUNTRY COACH DAN YOUNG took over in 1984. That year the team finished 17th in the state meet. In 1985, top runners Cammy Potter, Sharon Hicks and Jennifer Cook each set and broke individual goals and records.

In 1986, Mark Fries changed from boys coach to girls. This team had an undefeated regular season, won four invitationals and placed second at the other invitational. The team finished first at regionals and sixth in the state. Led by All-Staters

First Trojan girls cross country team running in 1978. Left to Right: Sue Hoffman, Kathy Nesvacil, Eileen Stoppa, Lynn Richards, Mgr. Patti Payne, Shelley Frye, Amy Sander, Kathy Sullivan, Amy Vrondran, Amy Wilhelm, Lori Dreves, Wanda Pillow, Carol Bringman and Coach Grow.

Anne Mudgett and Jenny Payne, others on Fries' first girls team were Sharon Hicks, Cammy Potter, Renee Cobb, Camilla Heirer, Linda Garvin, Jessica Ferry, Angie Myer, Kris Wilson, Erika Chirgwin, Jenny Roser and Bonnie Babel.

The 1988 team had a 4-0 record in dual meets and four invitational wins. With only one injury, to Jessica Ferry, they again won regionals. The team of Allison Dodge, Stephanie Walton, Rachel Benedict, Leah Bennett, Angie Myers, Myria Simmerman and Lori Klingelsmith placed eighth in the state where Dodge made All-State.

With many of the same runners returning, the 1989 season also went 4-0 in duals, repeated as regional champs and ended up seventh in the state. Runners on the state finals team were Lori Klingelsmith, Marlo Mata, Steph Walton, Myria Simmerman, Angie Myers, Erika Schimik and Rachel Benedict.

In 1990, the team finished the year undefeated, were regional champions and fourth at the state meet. Led by captain Marlo Mata, other team members were Karlene Kurtz, Stephanie Walton, Erika Schimik, Jenny Peters, Lori Klingelsmith, and Rachel Benedick. According to Coach Fries, this outstanding team was "maybe the best in the school's history." They were a "threepeat" as regional champions and placed fourth at the state meet. Sophomore Kurtz took sixth in the state and was named All-State.

The momentum of the 1990 season carried over to 1991, an exceptional year for the team. Led by All-Staters Karlene Kurtz, Erika Schimik and Lori Klingelsmith, along with Sara Jefferson, Kerry Mead, Sonya Mahoney and Libby Hackett, this team placed first at regionals and then won the state girls cross country title. To add to their honors, they were also Academic State Champions.

Amazingly, the 1992 team was not to be outdone. Living up to the expectations from the previous year, this team repeated all the 1991 team's accomplishments. First, they won the regional title for the sixth consecutive year. Then, after having been ranked second all year, they upset #1 ranked Brighton by 60 points to cruise to their second straight state championship. The 1992 girls were even named the Academic State Champions again. Karlene Kurtz, who is considered by many to be the most successful distance runner in school history, was named All-State for the third year and Erika Schimik for the second time. Other runners on the state finals team were Sara Jefferson, Libby Hackett, Kerry Mead, Sonya Mahoney and Amber Andresen.

In 1993, in Coach Fries' last season, Jefferson,

1991 girls cross country state champions. Front Row: Sara Jefferson, Sonya Mahoney, Shelby Bergeron, Lindsay Pascoe, Megan Simpson, Erika Schimik, Kerry Mead, Karlene Kurtz, Heather Adams, Raquel Smith. Middle Row: Jessica Hayes, Jaimee Ford, Libby Hackett, Jenni Hunt. Back Row: Erin VanWingerden, Jessica Werner, Meghan Martin, Jenny Baynton, Jenny Peters, Coach Mark Fries, Lori Klingelsmith, Becky Froehlich, Jessica Steed, Ali Hoxsie, Jessica Hill.

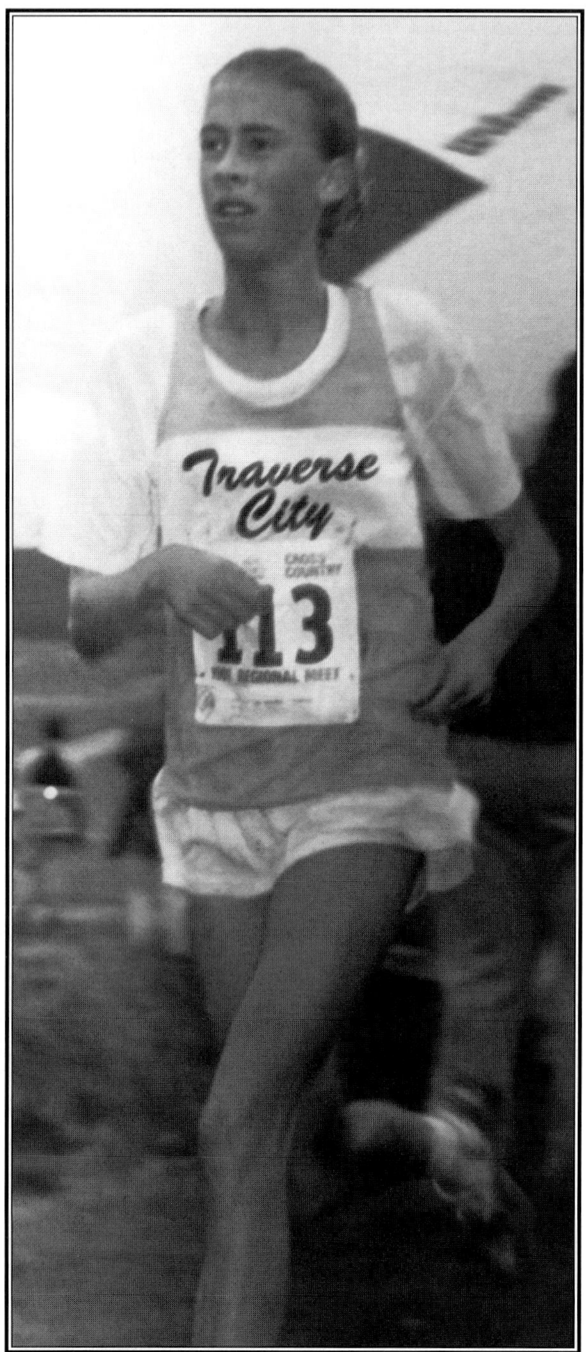

Three-time All-Stater Karlene Kurtz.

Hackett, Andresen, Becky Froehlich, Amanda Kiessel and Sara Torbet unfortunately didn't qualify for the state meet. However, over his eight years as head coach, Mark Fries led the girls teams to six regional titles and two state championships. The two state championship teams, 1991 and 1992, were also Academic Champions with grade point averages of 3.81 and 3.87 respectively. Coach Mark Fries received Coach of the Year honors in both 1991 and 1992.

In 1994, Lisa Taylor, a high school 3200 meter state champion and Big Ten standout at Michigan State University, took over head coaching duties for the Trojans. The roster was 30 strong, featuring the Top 7 talents of seniors Jessica Hill, Ali Hoxsie and Amanda Kiessel; junior Amanda Smith; sophomores Jessica DeKuiper and Michelle Williams; and freshman Sara DeBruyn. The number one position for most of the season was shared by Williams and DeBruyn, which promised a great outlook for the next few years.

AT THE CLASS A STATE CHAMPIONSHIPS, the Trojan team finished 17th overall and earned seventh place for Academic All-State with a team grade point of 3.76. Amanda Smith and Amanda Kiessel shared the distinction of running a sub-20:00 5000 meter time.

In 1995, the team returned all but two of its Top 7 from the 1994 season and increased its roster to 36 runners. The Top 7 was highlighted by juniors Stephanie Barker, Jessica DeKuiper and Michelle Williams, sophomores Sara DeBruyn and Kati Krikke, and freshmen Rachel Sturtz and Elizabeth Stallman. The Trojan team won four invitationals and qualified DeKuiper and Sturtz for the Class A championships, where both placed in the top 50. Jessica DeKuiper earned Academic All-State honors. Holding the number one position for most of the season was junior Michelle Williams, who cracked the 20:00 5K barrier two times. Freshman standout Rachel Sturtz showed great promise for the season ahead.

In 1996, the entire Top 7 returned, vowing to once again qualify the entire team for the state championships. The roster maintained at a high of 36, including at least 12-15 girls who committed to a full summer of base training, an act which paid off in regional competition and a fourth place Class A state finals showing. The Top 7 shuffled a bit to include senior standouts Michelle Williams and Jessica DeKuiper, juniors Sara DeBruyn and Katie Krikke, sophomores Mollie Cornwell and Rachel Sturtz, and freshman newcomer Becky Witkop. Sturtz was a runaway regional champion, leading the regional race from start to finish without a challenger. She then went on to earn All-State honors with a tenth place state finals finish including a sub-19:00 5K performance. Sub-20:00 5K performances became common among the Top 7, including a team best of 18:56 by Sturtz. Senior Stephanie Barker was selected as Michigan High School Girls Cross Country Scholar-Athlete for her outstanding leadership abilities.

New Trojan standards were set by an outstanding 1996 team which had committed to a summer training program. It became clear that to be Top 7, Trojan runners would train year-round. The team also made a commitment to finish with a successful season in the year before the new high school would split the team.

Girls choose to run cross country for different reasons. Some run to get in shape since in an average week of practice a cross country member will run 25 miles. Some participate in cross country to make friends. The 1990 captain Marlo Mata said, "There are a lot of fun days. We had water balloon fights and ran as a group at a lot of the meets." Former runner Lori Klingelsmith added, "It's all laughs until the race. Then you take care of business and it's right back to the laughs." Others choose cross country for future benefits. Erika Schimik said, "Competition is life and I expect to find it valuable in almost everything I do."

CLASS A GIRLS CROSS COUNTRY ALL-STATE

1986	Anne Mudgett Jenny Payne
1988	Allison Dodge
1990	Karlene Kurtz
1991	Karlene Kurtz Erika Schimik Lori Klingelsmith
1992	Karlene Kurtz Erika Schimik
1996	Rachel Sturtz

ACADEMIC ALL-STATE

1995	Jessica DeKuiper

TROJAN GIRLS CROSS COUNTRY COACHES

Larry Grow	1978-1980
Carol Rourke	1981-1982
Larry Grow	1983
Dan Young	1984-1985
Mark Fries	1986-1993
Lisa Taylor	1994-present

17

Swimming

By Nathan Wildman

"It is not the going out of port, but the coming that determines the success of a voyage."

– Henry Ward Beecher

Our earliest evidence of swimming dates back to 2,000 B.C. In its origin, swimming was not a sport (at least not organized) but a way to get around in the water, The science of carbon-dating of hieroglyphics and picture scriptures from the walls of ancient Egyptians shows evidence of figures in water, using similar movements such as the doggie paddle and a crude form of the breast stroke.

The organization of swimming in competition came around some time in the late 1800s. It was first allowed into the 1890 Olympics as a race type of a competition, where only men were allowed to compete.

Since that famous Olympic date, swimming has been a well-known activity and enjoyed sport. Due to the popularity of the Olympics, it is now coming into the competitive sport scene and gaining spectators.

On the local level, swimming became a competitive sport at Traverse City Senior High in 1978 for both boys and girls. Lynn Ebinger was coaching the Poseidon Swim Club when a group of parents approached her and she in turn went to the school board asking for swimming as a high school sport.

BOYS

"We might have been losers on paper but we were winners at heart", explained Dave Ford.

Surely this was a clear vote of confidence for the 1978 swim team and this kind of statement was not a rare one. The Trojan boys swim team had many ups and downs in their early history of competition. There were many seasons when the team was short on members, along with having little support from the school and fans. However, this did not in any way hinder the boys from achieving to the best of their abilities.

For example, the first team in 1978-1979 was a young one with mostly sophomores and juniors. One reason for their 0-5 season was that this team was out-numbered two to one in many meets so each Trojan had to compete in several events. Leading this first team were captains Jeff Brubaker and Dan Sondee, MVP Rob Harrington, Todd Beaverson and Dave Ford.

By 1981, with Lynn Ebinger as coach, much improvement could be seen as two new pool records and seven new school records were set in spite of a 1-6 season. New pool records were: Jeff Mead in the 200 yd individual medley relay and Al Clarke, Mike Brownley, Rob Harrington and Mead in the 400 yd freestyle relay. New school records were made by: Mead, Mark Crossley, Rick Anderson and Clarke – 200 yd medley relay; Mead – 200 yd individual medley; Clarke – 50 yd freestyle; Mead – 100 yd freestyle; Crossley – 100 yd breaststroke; 400 yd freestyle relay which was also the pool record; Pete Piche' with a diving score of 194.7

In 1982, Pete Piche set a new pool and school record with a 248.55 diving mark (still the top diving record today) and placed 19th in the state. Don Ackerman set a new school record in the 100 yd breaststroke and Scott Gest, Rick Anderson, Jim Aprea and Ackerman had a new school record in the 400 yd freestyle. Despite these strong performances, the team posted a 2-6-1 season.

The 1983 team was led by Brian Baker, who still has the fifth best Trojan diving record, and Don Ackerman, with the #3 overall 100 breast-

Coach Chuck Lendrum's first team in 1986-1987. Back Row: Doug Seeley, Bill Exo, Eric Jensen, Chuck VanPeenan, Mike Kurt, John Horton. Row 3: unidentified, Jason Clark, Grant Kellogg, Jeff Linger, Aaron McDonald, Don Smart, Mike Woods. Row 2: Managers Tina Chapple and Kelli Woodrow, Jason Parks, Joel Sanderson, Brett Lyon, Bill Werthman, Andy Marek, unidentified, Jeff Bush, Head Coach Chuck Lendrum, Diving Coach Pete Piche. Front Row: Dave Crewes, Kyle Rixom, Mike Braden, Paul Turner, Shawn Milarch, Mark Belovich, Jim Fields.

stroke time. The team was not in the LMAC, so swimmers had to place individually in the regional meet. Only Brian Baker placed, at 23rd. In 1984, the team consisted of only 14 members. Since they were competing against teams of 25-30 members, their 4-7 season was pretty admirable.

PROGRESS WAS EVIDENT as the 1985 team posted a winning 8-4 season and placed sixth in the conference. Swimmers from that team had records that are still in Traverse City's top 25 times. Ed Ackerman broke brother Don's 1983 100 breaststroke record which is still the #1 time. Rob Harrington has the current #2 500 freestyle record. Tim Trussell is the third best in the 100 butterfly. Dave Aprea has the #7 time in the butterfly and the #10 100 freestyle record. Ackerman, Aprea, Trussell and John Waslawski set a new record in the 200 medley relay.

Only two years later, in 1986, they were again short on members and slipped back to a 1-11 season. Only about ten members competed, due to sickness, injuries or other ailments. Yet that was not the only thing hindering the swimmers of 1986. The school stopped funding the sport, so the members had to either raise the money to rent pool time or pay for it out of their own pockets. Because of this, they had less time in the pool than the other teams they were competing against. As Dave Crewes reflected on overcoming the lack of swimmers and available pool time, "We will definitely be back next year, stronger than last."

Crewes' prediction almost proved correct; the team came back, stronger than ever, although it took two to three years. But that was not the only thing for them to smile about. In 1988, they broke two home records, including the 100 backstroke by Paul Turner and the 400 freestyle relay by John Horton, Jim Fields, Mark Belovich and Doug Seeley. Other finishes from that year that still stand well are Seeley's 200 individual medley and Dave Crewes' and Jeff Linger's performances in diving.

The 1988 season was an excellent one for the boys. Not only did they have new hair cuts (mohawks), they also had a new coach, Chuck Lendrum. He showed the boys how to swim more effectively, and in no time they were swimming like dolphins. He held the torch that led them to victory, which was placing third in the conference out of seven possible places.

The following year was another good one with a 9-5 record. Ten Trojan times from 1989 still have records in the top 25. Jim Fields had a part in six of those records. He has the #two 200 freestyle record, #6 100 freestyle and 500 freestyle times, is seventh in the 100 butterfly and part of two relays. The 400 freestyle relay team of Fields, John Horton, Doug Seeley and Mike Hogue now has the #4 overall record, and the 200 medley relay with Seeley, Aaron McDonald, Fields and Horton is still the fifth best. Horton set records in both the 50 and 100 freestyle, now the #2 and #3 times. McDonald has the seventh best time in the breaststroke and Mike Diehl is the all-time #9 diver. The conference meet, however, was iced out which was unfortunate for the Trojans since they should have made a good showing that year.

IN 1990, THE SEASON IMPROVED TO 8-3 and a third-place conference finish. Sergio Silva starred that year with four events in the current top five times: 200 individual medley, 500 freestyle, backstroke and butterfly. He was also part of the 200 medley relay which has the #10 time, along with Ryan Fajardo, Jason Smith and Jon-Eric Burleson. Joe Thomas has the current third highest diving points; Doug Seeley scored the fifth best butterfly and seventh best 200 freestyle times; and Seeley, Mike Hogue, Mike Braden and Matt Medler have the #8 time in the 400 freestyle relay.

In 1991, after a 7-3 season, the team also took third in the conference. 1992 kept up a winning season, with a 7-4 record and a fourth place in the conference. Top times then were set by Matt Medler, the current second best time in the 100 freestyle, #5 time in the 200 freestyle, and #10 in the 50 freestyle. Ryan Fajardo set what is now the #2 time in the breaststroke and is ninth best in the

50 freestyle. Others with current top 10 records were Mike Hogue, Chris Collins, Greg Seyler, Marc Kropf and Phil Collins. Diver Noel Ellsworth is still the #2 diver. Since then, no diver has broken into the Trojan top 10.

In 1993, Kevin Fajardo finished his fourth year on the varsity team. Although the team finished with an 0-9 record, Fajardo had a great season. He is today the #1 swimmer in the 100 backstroke, #2 in the 200 individual medley and the fifth best in the 100 freestyle.

The 1994 team improved again to 7-3. For the first time, Traverse City had a joint team with St. Francis to try to lower costs and increase the team size. Sean Quinn and Ryan DeMarsh from St. Francis joined the team, which placed second in the conference.

The 1995 team again placed second in the conference, thanks to a number of strong swimmers. At the top were Brian Adams, who has the #1 time in the 200 freestyle and set the #4 overall time in the backstroke. Marc Kropf has the #3 time in the 500 freestyle and Sean Quinn set the #3 backstroke record. Others with times still in the top ten were Jon Burian, Ryan DeMarsh, Chris Burian, Travis Gray, and Phil Collins.

In 1996, Coach Lendrum brought the team to a 7-2 overall season and their fourth consecutive second-place victory in the conference. The strength of the Trojan swim team was definitely emerging. Twenty-two of the season's times remain in the current top ten overall best. Brian Adams had a part in 12 records that are still in the top ten. Close behind him are Chris Burian, Jon Burian, Chris Clark and Matt Isaacson, along with Phil Collins, Marc Kropf, Ryan DeMarsh, Shane McClure, Travis Gray and

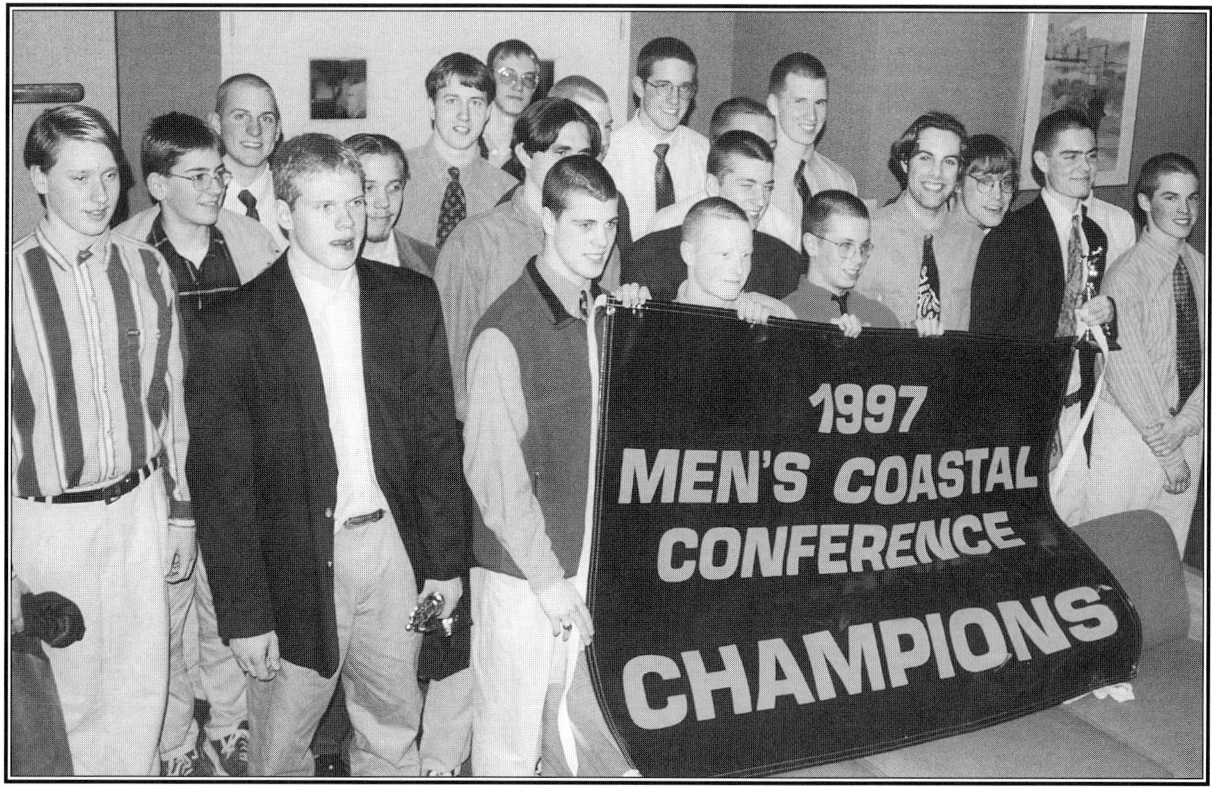

First Trojan conference swim champions. Front Row: Ken Iverson, Dean Adams, Jeff VanDalson, Pat McGarry, Mike Tubbs, Jared Powell. Second Row: Chris Daniels, Dan Kennedy, Phil Jewell, co-captain Jon Burian, Ben Collins, Ryan DeMarsh, Matt Isaacson, Travis Hillier. Third Row: co-captain Brian Adams, Jeremy Clark, Chris Clark, Pat McManus. Fourth Row: Scott Reichert, Ben Woodward, Andy Magoun.

Scott Reichert. The strength of this team is shown in the fact that five of the top ten times in both the 50 freestyle and the 200 freestyle relays are held by 1996 team members.

A first-ever conference title led the list of accomplishments for the 1997 boys swim team when they won the West Michigan Coastal Swim Conference. With this win they not only dethroned long-time league power Holland Christian by an impressive 345-299 score, but also finished the season undefeated. The team sent a record high seven swimmers to the state meet: Brian Adams, Chris Clark, Ken Iverson, Matt Isaacson, Ben Collins, Jon Burian and Mike Tubbs. Although the 200 freestyle relay team was seeded fourth, they did not make it to the finals. Iverson was the only Trojan swimmer in the finals, placing 11th in the 100 butterfly which earned him All-State honors.

Brian Adams finished his Trojan swimming career with three individual school records (in the 50, 100 and 500 freestyle) and was an important part of four relays. Assistant coach John Horton saw his own 1989 Trojan 50 freestyle record of 22.27 broken when Brian bettered that with a time of 22.14. Ken Iverson won the 100 butterfly, 200 individual medley, set times that are now #6 in the backstroke and breaststroke and #8 in the 200 freestyle, and was also in two of the top 10 relays. Ben Collins set the #2 breastroke time, remains fifth in the 200 individual medley and helped in two top relays. Chris Clark swam the #2 time in the backstroke, fourth best in the 100 freestyle and set the #10 200 freestyle time, plus two relays. Ryan DeMarsh set the fourth best 200 freestyle time, Matt Isaacson has the #5 breaststroke time, as well as part of the #1 200 freestyle relay, while Jon Burian and Scott Reichert also posted times in the current top ten.

The 1997 relay teams were especially strong. In the 200 medley relay, combinations of 1997 team members Adams, Collins, Iverson, Clark, Isaacson and Pat McManus hold the #1, 2 and 6 spots. In the 400 freestyle relay, the #1, 2 and 5 records are held by Adams, Iverson, Collins, Clark, Jon Burian and DeMarsh. the 200 freestyle relay team of Adams, Isaacson, Jon Burian and Clark hold both the #1 and #2 times. Combined with Collins, Iverson and Mike Tubbs, they also have the third and tenth records.

Brian Adams, top Trojan swimming record-holder.

Brian Adams is undoubtedly the top swimmer of the 1997 team, and possibly the best Trojan swimmer of all time. Of the 11 high school swimming events, Adams holds seven first place records, four individual and three in relays. Another 1997 swimmer, Danish exchange student Ken Iverson, holds four firsts, two individual and two in relays. A look at the progression of the Trojan swim team shows a clear dominance by the 1996 and 1997 teams. Of the 11 swimming events, 1997 team members hold 28 top 10 records; 1996 members have 22. The 1995 team has 11 of the top ten times and the rest of the teams have less than that. The only exception is in diving, where most of the top ten scores have come from the 1980s teams.

GIRLS

"Despite the lack of fan support, we've managed to kick some butt," summed up Libby Behm '90 and Steph Newman '90.

Girls swimming began in the fall of 1978 at Traverse City Senior High, and for the girls it was a good way to start off their high school swimming career. Lynn Ebinger took on the position as the first girls swim team coach, assisted by Marsha Haley. The girls placed fifth out of seven teams at the Alma Invitationals. Along with placing fifth there, junior Kelly Gest also ranked tenth in the state in the 100 yd backstroke. They participated in the Alma Invitationals because there was not a specialized league for the swim team like the LMAC. For their first season, the team ended up with a 1-8 record. "We did great for our first year," commented coach Lynn Ebinger. Senior captains were Sue Rosely and Barb Bell, with Rosely taking MVP honors.

This original group of swimmers has proved to be a strong one. From the first two girls swim teams in 1978 and 1979, nine girls records still remain in the Traverse City top 25 best times over the life of the swim team: Sue Rosely in both the 50 freestyle and 100 freestyle; Barb Bell, 100 breastroke; Gail Lehman, diving; Janice Mackkonen, 500 freestyle; Kelly Gest, 100 butterfly; Katie Kilburg, 100 freestyle; Leslie Davison, 100 freestyle; and Lynn Brisson, 200 individual medley.

In fall of 1980, six new records were set in the 5-4 season. Junior Patty Clarke, voted Most Valuable, broke records in the 50, 100 and 200 freestyle. Kelly Gest set a record for the 100 yd backstroke, while Stephanie Watson had a new diving record. The 200 medley relay team of Gest, Brisson, Clarke and Heinrici also set a new record, which is still the eighth fastest school time.

The following year, the 1981 team set several new records. Senior Patty Clarke had another good season with a new record in the 500 yd freestyle

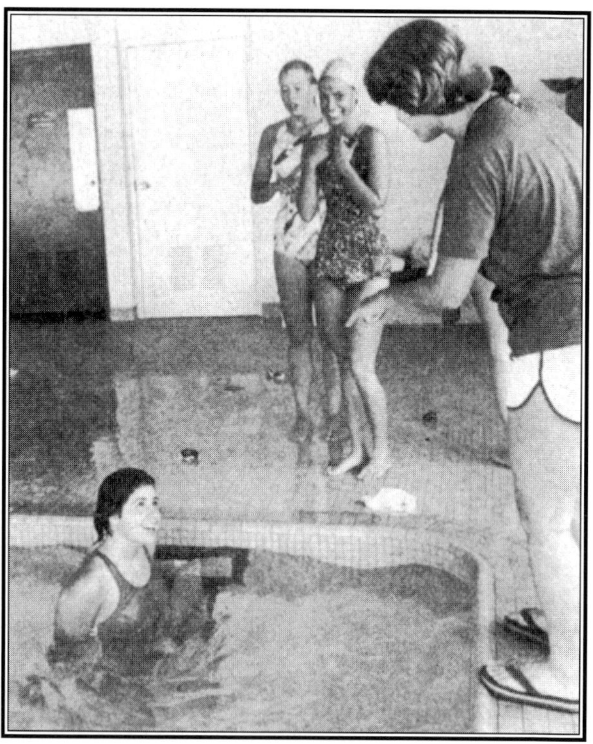

In the pool, swimmer Patty Clarke gets instructions from Coach Lynn Ebinger.

while Trisha Samuelson set a new record in the 100 yd breaststroke. A new 400 freestyle relay record was also made by Kirsten Beyer, Lynn Brisson, Clarke and Samuelson. Steffie Watson capped off a successful diving season with a 15th place at regionals. Clarke finished seventh at the state meet where she broke the 100 yd backstroke record.

The 1982 team established a few more school records. Patty Clarke set a new record in the 100 backstroke, which is still today the #2 time. Steffie Watson set a new school diving record at 238.45, and was backed up with strong diving performances from Shelly Bates and Wendy Schieber. Teammates Jennifer Ebinger, Kirsten Beyer, Missy Holmes and Trisha Samuelson set a new school record in the 400 freestyle relay. After a 5-6 season, Watson placed tenth at regionals with a score of 324.25 which qualified her for the state meet.

In 1983, no new records were set, but four team members still have times in the school's top 25. Jenny Ebinger led the team in the 100 butterfly, 100 breaststroke, 100 backstroke and 100 freestyle. Also turning in strong performances that year were Katie Kilburg, Andrea Miller and Lisa Williams.

The 1984 team had the largest turnout of swimmers so far, 24, due to the new freshman eligibility rule which helped add much depth to the team. A sizeable number of team members had school times that are still ranked. Kim McTaggart led this group with two new school records: the 500 freestyle which is still the #3 time today, and the 200 freestyle, the sixth best Traverse City time to date. Two divers still maintain top scores. Elizabeth Gaff is the #3 all-time best diver while Karen Howe holds the #5 spot. These performances were stronger than their 4-5 season indicated.

The next year, the 1985 team had a greatly improved 9-3 season. Losing once to Holland Christian and twice to Ludington, they placed fourth in the conference. Katie Kilburg established a new record at 1:14.05 in the 100 breaststroke.

In 1986, a new 400 freestyle relay record of 4:05.97 was set by Leslie Davison, Kim McTaggart, Angie Beall and Katie Kilburg. Kilburg also set two new records herself: 200 individual medley record, which still stands as the school's #6 time, and the 100 freestyle which is still the fifth best time. Providing strong assistance in that same event, Jenny Ebinger's time is #7, while Beall's is 12th. Kendra Lutes set times still recognized in the 500 and 200 freestyle and McTaggart did the same in the 50 freestyle.

The swim team did exceptionally well in 1987. Again, with no pool of their own other than the Civic Center, their record was memorable. For the first time, 14 of the swimmers had times in the top 12 at the conference meet while the team came in fourth. Divers Jennifer Dunsmore and Leslie Paupore qualified for regional competition and still remain the school's eighth and tenth place divers. The Traverse City tradition of the "mass shave" had developed by this time. At the conference meet, shaving cream was given out and all the swimmers sat down to shave their arms and legs.

The 1988 and 1989 teams began to show how far the Trojan girls swim program had come. Led by Sarah Abbott, Stephanie Newman, Monica Bullard and Aimee McDonald, the 1988 team placed third in the conference while the 1989 team took a second. Top swimmer Sarah Abbott set a new school record in the 200 individual medley which remains the #5 time. Abbott's other top 25 times are in the 100 butterfly (also the fifth best Traverse City time), 50, 100 and 500 freestyle and 100 breaststroke. Newman set times which are still in the top 25 in the 100 backstroke, 100 butterfly, 200 and 500 freestyle (#6 time) and 200 individual medley.

The 1990 swim team was led by Heather Heffner, who had four finishes which are still in the top 25 times (100, 200 and 500 freestyle and 200 individual medley) and Tonya Thompson who is still the #1 Trojan girls diver with 248 points. Leya McVicker had a good year in both the 100 breaststroke and 200 individual medley. One way that coach Chuck Lendrum decided to use to boost morale was to hang pink plastic pigs around the swimmers' necks. PIGS were Pretty Intelligent Girl Swimmers. That's how they swam, intelligently, because they had a 10-2 season thanks to PIGS. The girls wore them before meets and after victories, so that their opponents would know who they

Sarah Abbott in the 100 yard butterfly.

were. Again taking a second place in the conference, 1990 was one of the best teams yet.

The 1991 team compiled a successful 9-2 record and took a third consecutive second place conference finish. Lindsey Seyler had an outstanding year with one new school record and seven finishes which still rank high in the school's top 25 times. Seyler's new record in the 100 butterfly remains the #2 Trojan time. Her other top times were fourth in the 100 breaststroke and the 500 freestyle, fifth highest 200 individual medley result, #7 200 freestyle finish, eighth highest 100 freestyle time, 50 freestyle (#9), as well as five high relay performances. Several relay teams were especially strong that year. Setting a new record were Julie Riddle, Seyler, Sarah Abbott and Kelli Schroeder in the 200 medley relay, still the #7 time. Those four swimmers, plus Tammy Baker and Willow Bartruff, combined for five current top relay times. Abbott, in her fourth year on the varsity team, had strong finishes in the 100 backstroke (#6 time) and 200 freestyle.

IN 1992, THE TEAM HAD A GREAT SEASON with an 8-2 record, two invitational wins, and a repeat second place in the conference. The strength of this team is shown by the fact that 17 swimmers had finishes that are still among the top 25 of all time. Leading the way was Tammy Baker with a new school record in the 500 freestyle which now stands as the #2 time. Baker also placed well in the 100 freestyle and 200 individual medley. Amy Curry had a successful year in the 200 and 500 freestyle (#7) and 200 individual medley. Six relay teams comprised of Riddle, Karen Brege, Kat Rheem, Kelli Schroeder, Joni Sturgeon, Baker, Chessa Schenk, Emily Dornbos and Lindsay Burleson also are still in the top 25. Commented Willow Bartruff, "We did really well at conference this year [second]. Holland Christian is our main

1991 girls swim team. Front Row: Melissa Risinger, Erica Hornby, Sarah Abbott, Karen Kevwitch, Karen Brege, Kelli Schroeder, Lori Warmbold, Kelly Wood, Cherie Spaulding, Lindsey Seyler, Jeni Sachtleben, Rachel Gloshen. Middle Row: Courtney Padgett, Tammy Baker, Kathy Szwalek, Kerrie Grow, Stacie Reamer, Kat Rheem, Torie Bunn, Bethany Renfer, Amy Currie, Francesca Schenk, Elizabeth George. Back Row: Lyle Powers, Mandy Wagner, Amy Johnson, Willow Bartruff, Julie Riddle, Nicole Gamble, Jodi Butzow, Coach Chuck Lendrum.

competition and we came a lot closer to them. Next year we'll have the most seniors on the team, so we can beat Holland Christian."

Although they didn't live up to this prediction, the 1993 team did have a strong season, winning eight contests and again placing second at the conference meet. Although 20 freshmen were on the team, this was the year for Joni Sturgeon and Laura Fajardo to shine. Sturgeon set new records in the 100 breaststroke, still the #1 time, and the 200 individual medley, the #3 time. She also had top finishes in the 50 freestyle, 100 butterfly and 100 backstroke. Fajardo recorded seven individual times that are still in the top 25: 50, 100, 200 and 500 freestyle, 200 individual medley, 100 butterfly and 100 backstroke. Tammy Baker recorded the current #3 time in the butterfly.

Ashley Shaw, Katie Cutler and Tammy Baker dominated the 1994 season in which several new records were broken. Shaw set the top time in the 100 butterfly and the 500 freestyle, the second best time (a new record then) in the 200 freestyle, and the #3 time in both the 50 and 100 freestyle. Cutler set new records in the 50 freestyle (the #1 time) and the 100 freestyle, now the #2 time, and has the eighth best time in the 200 freestyle. Baker holds top spots in the 50 (#5) and 200 (#4) freestyle. The best 200 freestyle relay team is still that of Baker, Dornbos, Shaw and Katie Cutler. Another second place conference win capped a 9-1 season.

After again placing second at the conference meet, the 1995 girls swim team qualified for the state meet where they came in 34th. Four new records set during the year remain as the #1 times in their events: Ann Townsend in the 100 backstroke, Ashley Shaw in the 200 individual medley, Ritchie, Townsend, Jessica VanDalson and Shaw in the 400 freestyle relay and the 200 medley relay team of Townsend, Shaw, Jessica Ritchie and Katie Cutler (which also has the #2 time in the 200 freestyle relay). This was the year of very strong relay teams.

In the 400 freestyle relay, different combinations of swimmers that year hold nine of the top 25 times, including the #1, 3, 5, and 9th spots.

1996 state qualifying relay team: Ann Townsend, Jessica VanDalson, Jessica Ritchie, Ashley Shaw.

Team members on those relays were Ritchie, Townsend, VanDalson, Shaw, Cutler, Julie Stock and Christina Hutchens. Townsend was one of the strong swimmers who paced the team with individual performances, also holding top times in the 100 and 200 freestyle and the 100 breaststroke. Ritchie set the second fastest time in the 200 individual medley and seventh in the 100 butterfly.

The 1996 team had an overall 3-5 season, finishing third in the conference and 31st in the state. Jessica Ritchie starred that season, setting two #1 times in the 100 and 200 freestyle, the second-best in the 50 freestyle and a third fastest 100 backstroke. She was also part of relays holding two second- and one third-best times, accomplishments which earned her All-State honors. Others with especially good seasons were Ann Townsend in the 200 individual medley and 50 freestyle and Jessica VanDalson in the 100 and 500 freestyle, as well as high relay performances for both. Top divers in 1996 were Rachel Dowdney and Kristy Eldredge.

A good share of the top 25 girls' swim records were set in the 1990s, especially in the last few years. The all-time top performer is Ashley Shaw who holds either a first, second or third place record in ten of the 11 swimming events. Jessica Ritchie is a close second in holding those credentials in eight of the 11 events. However, in diving, four of the top five spots belong to the 1980s, with top diver Tonya Thompson from the 1990 team.

CLASS A SWIMMING ALL-STATE

1996	Jessica Ritchie
1997	Ken Iverson

TROJAN SWIM COACHES

Girls

Lynn Ebinger	1978-1988
Chuck Lendrum	1989-present

Boys

Lynn Ebinger	1978-1981
Mike Haley	1980-1981
Steve Fortney	1982
Marcia Haley	1983
Tom Roos	1984
Blake Vance	1985
Jane Regenmorter	1986
Lynn Ebinger	1987
Chuck Lendrum	1988-present

DIVING COACHES GIRLS & BOYS TEAMS

Marcia Haley	1978-1989

SWIM TEAM SCORING

Three individuals are allowed to compete in each event for points. There are a total of six places per event. First place is given six points, second is given four points, third is given three points, fourth two points, fifth one point, and sixth zero. Invitationals are scored as follows (consecutively from first to twelfth place): 16, 14, 13, 12, 10, 8, 6, 5, 4, 3, 2, 1. For relays, points are doubled (first – 32 points, second – 28 points, third – 26 points and so on).

TROJAN BOYS MEET AND SEASON TEAM RECORDS (1978-PRESENT)

TRAVERSE CITY TROJANS BOYS SWIMMING TOP 25 1996-97 Page 1

200 Medley Relay

	Relay	Time	Year
1	B.Adams,B.Collins,K.Iverson,C.Clark	142.04	1997
2	P.McManus,B.Collins,Iverson,Isaacson	1:45.34	1997
3	B.ADAMS,ISAACSON,C.BURIAN,GRAY	1:46.23	1996
4	B. ADAMS, ISAACSON, C. BURIAN, C. CLARK	1:48.61	1996
5	Seeley, Mc Donald, Fields, Horton	1:49.36	1989
6	P.McManus,Isaacson,Iverson,B.Collins	1:49.72	1997
7	B.ADAMS,REICHERT,C.BURIAN, C.CLARK	1:49.78	1996
8	Quinn, Kroph, C. Burian, Gray	1:50.52	1995
9	Waslawski, Ackerman, Trussell, D. Aprea	1:50.55	1985
10	Silva, R. Fajardo, J. Smith, Burleson	1:51.09	1990
11	P.McManus,Reichert,J.Burian,Isaacson	151:11	1997
12	Quinn, Isaacson, C. Burian, Gray	1:51.16	1995
13	K. Fajardo, Kropf, C. Burian, Elmer	1:51.22	1993
14	Quinn, Kropf, C. Burian, Gray	1:51.60	1994
15	Quinn, Isaacson, C. Burian, B. Adams	1:51.66	1995
16	Quinn, Kropf, C. Burian, Isaacson	1:51.81	1995
17	D. Aprea, E. Ackerman, Trussell, Kevwitch	1:52.00	1985
18	B.ADAMS,ISAACSON,GRAY,REICHERT	1:52.29	1996
18	SCHLITT,ISAACSON,D.ADAMS,GRAY	1:52.29	1996
18	Quinn, Isaacson, J. Burian, C. Burian	1:52.29	1995
21	Adams, Pierson, C. Burian, Isaacson	1:52.48	1994
22	Silva, R. Fajardo, Seeley, Hogue	1:52.60	1990
23	B. Adams, Pierson, C. Burian, P. Collins	1:52.60	1995
24	C. Collins, R. Fajardo, Hogue, Medler	1:52.82	1991
25	Quinn, Kropf, C. Burian, P. Collins	1:52.96	1994
	STATE QUALIFYING TIME	1:43.19	1997

200 Freestyle

	Name	Time	Year
1	BRIAN ADAMS	1:49.83	1995
2	Jim Fields	1:54.88	1989
3	JON BURIAN	1:54.89	1996
4	Ryan DeMarsh	1:55.65	1997
5	Matt Medler	1:56.00	1992
6	Rob Harrington	1:56.23	1981
7	Doug Seeley	1:56.51	1990
8	KEN IVERSON	1:58.20	1997
9	Phil Collins	1:58.83	1994
10	CHRIS CLARK	1:59.15	1997
11	Wilson Elmer	1:59.26	1993
12	Jason Clark	2:00.04	1988
12	Greg Million	2:00.04	1987
14	Kevin Fajardo	2:00.14	1993
15	Greg Seyler	2:02.02	1992
16	SHANE MCCLURE	2:02.34	1996
17	Ed Ackerman	2:03.10	1983
18	Rick Anderson	2:04.22	1982
19	Mike Kurt	2:04.25	1989
20	Ryan Fajardo	2:04.29	1992
21	Chris Burian	2:04.47	1993
22	Mike Braden	2:04.51	1990
23	Tim Lyon	2:04.80	1993
24	Sergio Silva	2:04.84	1990
25	Marc Kropf	2:05.64	1993
	STATE QUALIFYING	1:49.19	1997

200 Individual Medley

	Name	Time	Year
1	KEN IVERSON	2:04.75	1997
2	Kevin Fajardo	2:06.95	1993
3	Brian Adams	2:07.85	1996
4	Sergio Silva	2:07.93	1990
5	BEN COLLINS	2:08.18	1997
6	Jeff Mead	2:10.60	1981
7	Mark Kropf	2:15.58	1995
8	Phil Collins	2:16.14	1995
9	Scott Reichert	2:20.66	1996
10	Doug Seeley	2:17.38	1988
11	Mike Hogue	2:17.81	1990
12	Jon-Eric Burleson	2:18.29	1990
13	Sean Quinn	2:19.46	1995
14	Chris Clark	2:21.17	1996
15	Mark Belovich	2:22.20	1988
16	Ed Ackerman	2:22.22	1983
17	Paul Turner	2:23.97	1988
18	Tim Lyon	2:24.15	1994
19	Matt Isaacson	2:24.37	1996
20	Andy Pierson	2:25.05	1993
21	Rick Anderson	2:25.24	1982
22	Scott Gest	2:25.24	1983
23	Jason Clark	2:25.90	1988
24	DAN KENNEDY	2:26:16	1997
25	Rob Harrington	2:27.09	1978
	STATE QUALIFYING TIME	2:04.19	1997

TRAVERSE CITY TROJANS 1995-96 TOP 25 Girls Swimming Page 1.

200 Medley Relay

	Relay	Time	Year
1	Townsend, Shaw, Ritchie, K. Cutler	1:57.47	1995
2	Townsend,Angela Kostrzewa,Shaw Ritchie	1:57:94	1996
3	Stock, Shaw, Baker, K. Cutler	1:59.87	1994
4	Townsend,Ritchie,Angela Kostrzewa, Amy Edson	2:00.56	1996
5	Townsend,Ritchie,Shaw,Hansen	2:01.61	1996
6	Townsend, Shaw, VanDalson, K. Cutler	2:02.30	1995
7	Riddle, Seyler, Abbott, Schroeder	2:02.89	1991
8	Gest, Heinrici, Brisson, Clarke	2:03.20	1980
9	Townsend,Shaw,Ang.Kostrezwa, VanDalson	2:03.22	1996
10	Riddle, Seyler, Abbott, Baker	2:03.23	1991
11	Stock, Kostrzewa, Baker, K. Cutler	2:03.87	1994
12	Riddle, Brege, Rheem, Schroeder	2:04.19	1992
13	Townsend, Shaw, Stock, K. Cutler	2:04.23	1995
14	Ebinger, Kilburg, McTaggart, Davison	2:04.27	1984
15	McTaggart, Kilburg, Beall, Davison	2:04.27	1986
16	Townsend,Ritchie,Ang.Krostrezwa, McIntosh	2:04.44	1996
17	Stock,Ritchie,Shaw,Amy Edson	2:04.68	1996
18	Otto, Baker, Sturgeon, Burleson	2:04.71	1993
19	Riddle, Sturgeon, Brege, Schroeder	2:05.11	1992
20	Clarke, Kilburg, Brisson, Samuelson	2:05.30	1981
21	Riddle, Sturgeon, Brege, Burleson	2:05.40	1992
22	Townsend, Kostrzewa, Stock, K. Cutler	2:05.52	1995
23	McTaggart, Kilburg, Beall, Davison	2:05.85	1985
24	Glenn, Shaw, Ritchie, Hutchens	2:06.29	1995
25	Glenn, Shaw, Baker, K. Cutler	2:06.83	1994
	STATE QUALIFYING TIME	1:57.09	1996

200 Freestyle

	Name	Time	Year
1	Jessica Ritchie	2:03.19	1996
2	Ashley Shaw	2:03.99	1994
3	Ann Townsend	2:05.75	1995
4	Tammy Baker	2:06.26	1994
5	Jessie VanDalson	2:07.95	1995
6	Kim McTaggart	2:08.62	1984
7	Lindsey Seyler	2:09.85	1991
8	Katie Cutler	2:10.01	1994
9	Sarah Abbott	2:10.54	1991
10	Stephanie Newman	2:11.93	1989
11	Katie Kilburg	2:13.85	1984
12	Patty Clarke	2:14.00	1980
11	Joni Sturgeon	2:15.45	1992
14	Amy Curry	2:15.79	1992
15	Heather Heffner	2:16.55	1990
16	Chessa Schenk	2:17.14	1992
17	Angie Beall	2:17.61	1985
18	Kendra Lutes	2:17.70	1986
19	Tricia Samuelson	2:17.86	1981
20	Mandy Hitesman	2:18.57	1996
21	Jennifer Edson	2:18.59	1995
22	Emily Dornbos	2:19.19	1993
23	Laura Fajardo	2:19.27	1993
24	Kristen Beyer	2:19.82	1982
25	Nicole Gamble	2:19.99	1992
	STATE QUALIFYING	2:01.09	1996

200 Individual Medley

	Name	Time	Year
1	Ashley Shaw	2:18.57	1995
2	Jessica Ritchie	2:23.47	1995
3	Joni Sturgeon	2:24.03	1993
4	Ann Townsend	2:24.38	1996
4	Sarah Abbott	2:25.69	1988
5	Lindsey Seyler	2:26.40	1991
6	Katie Kilburg	2:27.45	1986
8	Jennifer Ebinger	2:31.64	1986
9	Tammy Baker	2:32.61	1992
10	Julie Stock	2:33.05	1995
11	Laura Fajardo	2:33.34	1993
12	Angie Beall	2:34.18	1986
13	Lynn Brisson	2:34.79	1979
14	Heather Heffner	2:37.13	1990
15	Angela Kostrzewa	2:37.51	1996
16	Jennifer Edson	2:38.31	1995
17	Kat Rheem	2:38.56	1991
18	Julie Riddle	2:38.71	1992
19	Stephanie Newman	2:39.50	1989
20	Courtney Padgett	2:39.81	1992
21	Leya McVicker	2:41.03	1990
22	Jessie VanDalson	2:41.54	1995
23	Aimee McDonald	2:42.14	1989
24	Amy Curry	2:43.50	1992
25	Jennifer Sachtleben	2:44.04	1993
	STATE QUALIFYING	2:19.09	1996

TROJAN BOYS MEET AND SEASON TEAM RECORDS (1978-PRESENT)

TRAVERSE CITY TROJANS Boys` Swimming TOP 25 1995-96 Page 2

50 Freestyle		
1 Brian Adams	22:15	1997
2 John Horton	:22.27	1989
3 Chris Clark	:22.94	1996
4 Matt Isaacson	:23.01	1996
5 Chris Burian	:23.12	1996
6 Shane McClure	23:25	1996
7 Travis Gray	:23.30	1996
8 Mike Hogue	:23.30	1992
9 Ryan Fajardo	:23.40	1992
10 Matt Medler	:23.42	1992
11 David Aprea	:23.80	1985
12 Jim Fields	:23.88	1989
13 Todd Milarch	:24.27	1984
14 Doug Seeley	:24.29	1990
15 MIKE TUBBS	:24.51	1997
15 Al Clarke	:24.63	1981
16 Derek Pronger	:24.82	1985
17 Don Ackerman	:24.90	1984
18 Jim Aprea	:24.94	1983
19 Ed Ackerman	:24.96	1985
20 Chris Seeley	:25.00	1985
21 Mark Werrtman	:25.03	1994
23 Dave Schlitt	:25.25	1995
25 BEN WOODWARD	:25.28	1997
STATE QUALIFYING TIME	:22.69	1997

Diving		
1 Pete Piche	248.55	1982
2 Noel Ellsworth	226.55	1992
3 Joe Thomas	216.45	1990
4 Dave Crewes	211.65	1988
5 Brian Baker	203.80	1983
6 Jeff Linger	191.20	1988
7 Kevin Lippert	186.40	1980
8 Pat Robertson	183.00	1986
9 Mike Diehl	176.55	1989
10 Troy Cannaday	170.55	1987
11 Jim Grzesiak	163.95	1982
12 Ty Schieber	163.30	1983
13 Matt Medler	163.10	1989
14 Pete Clark	161.55	1990
15 JARED POWELL	144.20	1997
16 PAT MC GARRY	141.65	1997
17 John Korhonen	141.30	1994
18 Levy Frey	140.60	1996
19 John Block	136.24	1987
20 John Coffman	132.13	1984
21 Mitch Bulman	130.30	1990
22 Dave Johnson	129.95	1986
23 Shane McClure	129.15	1995
24 Tim Gallagher	129.05	1992
25 Grant Kellogg	128.50	1988
STATE QUALIFYING TIME	TOP 12 AT	REGION

100 Butterfly		
1 KEN IVERSON	:52.85	1997
2 Chris Burian	:57.78	1996
3 Tim Trussell	:59.00	1985
4 Sergio Silva	:59.11	1990
5 Doug Seeley	:59.26	1990
6 Jon Burian	:59.31	1995
7 Jim Fields	1:01.17	1989
7 David Aprea	1:01.17	1985
9 Rick Anderson	1:01.60	1982
10 Mike Hogue	1:02.62	1992
11 Phil Krumm	1:03.72	1983
12 Andy Pierson	1:04.30	1994
13 DEAN ADAMS	1:04.56	1997
14 MIKE TUBBS	1:04.62	1997
15 Todd Milarch	1:05.50	1984
16 Jason Smith	1:05.69	1990
17 David Ford	1:05.71	1980
18 Mark Belovich	1:05.75	1988
19 Dave Murdick	1:06.00	1980
20 Mike Lake	1:06.82	1993
21 Don Ackerman	1:07.00	1983
22 Tim Kevwitch	1:07.00	1985
23 Rick Utter	1:08.17	1990
24 Eric Jensen	1:08.17	1988
25 Bill Werthman	1:08.33	1988
STATE QUALIFYING TIME	:55.59	1997

TRAVERSE CITY TROJANS Girl's Swimming TOP 25 1995-96 Page 2

50 Freestyle		
1 Katie Cutler	:24.32	1994
2 Jessica Ritchie	:24.56	1996
3 Ashley Shaw	:25.60	1994
4 Ann Townsend	:25.79	1996
5 Tammy Baker	:25.99	1994
6 Patty Clarke	:26.05	1980
7 Joni Sturgeon	:26.54	1993
8 Kim McTaggart	:26.54	1986
9 Lindsey Seyler	:26.57	1991
10 Emily Dornbos	:26.73	1993
11 Christina Hutchens	:26.99	1995
12 Sue Rosely	:27.00	1978
13 Lindsay Burleson	:27.20	1993
14 Sarah Abbott	:27.37	1988
15 Kelli Schroeder	:27.40	1992
16 Amy Edson	27:15	1996
17 Katie Kilburg	:27.59	1983
18 Laura Fajardo	:27.67	1993
19 Leslie Davison	:27.90	1984
20 Libby Behm	:28.15	1989
21 Angie Beall	:28.21	1984
22 Monica Bullard	:28.29	1989
23 Chessa Schenk	:28.31	1992
24 Kat Rheem	:28.31	1992
25 Julie Riddle	:28.43	1992
STATE QUALIFING TIME	:25.69	1995

Diving		
1 Tonya Thompson	248.00	1990
2 Stephanie Watson	238.45	1982
3 Elizabeth Gaff	209.84	1984
4 Andrea Miller	206.25	1983
5 Karen Howe	205.75	1984
6 Rachel Dowdney	199.??	1996
7 Kristy Eldredge	198.??	1996
8 Leslie Paupore	192.50	1987
9 Willow Bartruff	189.40	1992
10 Jennifer Dunsmore	186.50	1987
11 Shelly Bates	185.75	1982
12 Christine Smith	177.80	1985
13 Renee Huckle	174.80	1989
14 Tasha Thompson	173.75	1990
15 Amanda Calipetro	169.25	1992
16 Tisha Thompson	166.45	1991
17 Wendy Schieber	165.20	1982
18 Lindsay Wills	155.??	1996
19 Stacie Brandt	153.22	1994
20 Melissa Risinger	152.25	1993
21 Lori Warmbold	145.65	1991
22 Gail Lehman	143.60	1978
23 Niqi Miessner	136.70	1994
24 Carrie Schimpke	????	1996
25 Tonya Rouse	132.10	1994
STATE QUALIFYING	TOP 12 AT	REGION

100 Butterfly		
1 Ashley Shaw	1:04.40	1994
2 Lindsey Seyler	1:04.72	1991
3 Tammy Baker	1:05.07	1993
4 Kelly Gest	1:06.34	1978
5 Sarah Abbott	1:06.47	1988
6 Lynn Brisson	1:07.40	1981
7 Jessica Ritchie	1:07.40	1995
8 Kim McTaggart	1:09.25	1985
9 Julie Stock	1:09.26	1995
10 Karen Brege	1:11.16	1992
11 Jennifer Ebinger	1:11.70	1983
12 Jodi Butzow	1:11.73	1990
13 Angie Beall	1:12.12	1987
14 Roberta Oishi	1:12.86	1994
15 Aimee McDonald	1:13.10	1988
16 Joni Sturgeon	1:13.48	1993
17 Stephanie Newman	1:13.59	1988
18 Courtney Padgett	1:13.84	1992
19 Laura Fajardo	1:14.68	1993
20 Julie Riddle	1:14.81	1992
21 Ellen Quirk	1:15.16	1992
22 Melanie Smith	1:15.75	1989
23 Jennifer Sachtleben	1:17.27	1993
24 Tricia Holmes	1:17.78	1985
25 Lisa Williams	1:19.78	1983
STATE QUALIFYING	1:02.59	1996

TROJAN BOYS MEET AND SEASON TEAM RECORDS (1978-PRESENT)

TRAVERSE CITY TROJANS Boy's Swimming TOP 25 1995-96 Page 3

100 Freestyle		
1 **BRIAN ADAMS**	**:48.93**	**1997**
2 Matt Medler	:50.87	1992
3 John Horton	:51.22	1989
4 **Chris Clark**	**:51.02**	**1997**
5 Kevin Fajardo	:51.56	1993
6 Jim Fields	:51.73	1989
7 Jeff Mead	:51.90	1981
8 **Jon Burian**	**:52.26**	**1997**
9 Shane McClure	:52.64	1996
10 Dave Aprea	:53.11	1985
11 **BEN COLLINS**	**:53.11**	**1997**
12 Chris Burian	:53.23	1994
13 Rob Harrington	:53.30	1981
14 Doug Seeley	:53.50	1989
15 Mike Hogue	:53.30	1992
16 **Ryan DeMarsh**	**:53.32**	**1997**
17 Travis Gray	:53.47	1996
18 Ryan Fajardo	:53.88	1992
19 Rick Anderson	:54.24	1982
20 Phil Collins	:54.65	1994
21 Mike Braden	:55.00	1990
22 Mark Kropf	:55.20	1994
23 Matt Isaacson	:55.31	1995
24 Wilson Elmer	:55.40	1993
25 **JEREMY CLARK**	**:56.25**	**1997**
STATE QUALIFYING	**:49.49**	1997

500 Freestyle		
1 **Brian Adams**	**5:07.72**	**1997**
2 Rob Harrington	5:17.99	1985
3 Marc Kropf	5:18.51	1995
4 Phil Collins	5:21.19	1994
5 Sergio Silvia	5:24.64	1990
6 Jim Fields	5:25.14	1989
7 Jon Burian	5:27.37	1996
8 Jeff Mead	5:30.00	1980
9 Ryan DeMarsh	5:31.61	1995
10 Wilson Elmer	5:31.76	1993
11 Jason Clark	5:34.82	1988
12 **JEFF VANDALSON**	**5:36.94**	**1997**
12 Tim Lyon	5:38.24	1993
13 Greg Million	5:39.69	1986
14 Chris Collins	5:41.56	1992
15 Ed Ackerman	5:41.80	1983
16 Matt Medler	5:44.80	1990
17 Dave Aprea	5:48.10	1983
18 Mike Hogue	5:48.71	1990
19 Mike Kurt	5:51.38	1989
21 **CHRIS DANIELS**	**5:54.88**	**1997**
20 Doug Seeley	5:56.18	1989
21 Brett Lyon	5:57.50	1991
22 Greg Seyler	5:58.37	1992
23 Jeremy Clark	5:59.27	1996
STATE QUALIFYING	**4:58.39**	1997

200 Freestyle Relay	
1 **B. Adams,M. Isaacson,J. Burian,C. Clark 1:30.14**	**1997**
2 **B. Adams,M. Isaacson,J. Burian,C. Clark 1:32.44**	**1997**
3 **C.Clark,B.Collins,K. Iverson,B. Adams 1:32.43**	**1997**
1 S. McClure, J. Burian, T. Gray, C. Clark 1:34.12	1996
2 B. Adams, T. Gray, J. Burian, C.Clark 1:34.74	1996
3 S. McClure, C. Burian, M. Isaacson B. Adams 1:35.00	1996
4 M. Isaacson, C. Clark, J. Burian S. McClure 1:35.23	1996
5 B. Adams, C. Burian, J. Burian, C. Clark 1:35.49	1996
6 Adams, Isaacson, Gray, C. Burian 1:36.20	1994
11 **C.Clark,J.Burian,M.Tubbs,M.Isaacson 1:36.32**	**1997**
7 Medler, Thompson, Hogue, Utter 1:36.33	1992
8 C. Clark, Isaacson,McClure, J.Burian 1:36.72	1996
9 C. Clark, Gray, DeMarsh, B. Adams 1:36.77	1996
10 Hogue, Medler, Utter, R. Fajardo 1:37.48	1992
11 Medler, R. Fajardo, Hogue, Burleson 1:37.49	1991
12 Adams, Isaacson, Kropf, C. Burian 1:37.39	1995
13 Isaacson, Gray, J. Burian, C. Burian 1:37.80	1995
14 Medler, K. Fajardo, R. Fajardo, Hogue 1:38.08	1992
15 **C. Clark,R.Demarsh,C. Burian, J. Burian 1:38.18**	**1996**
16 C. Clark, C. Burian, J. Burian, B.Adams 1:38.24	1996
17 R. DeMarsh, T. Gray, C. Burian, P. Collins 1:38.29	1996
18 M. Isaacson, T. Gray, S. McClure, R. DeMarsh 1:38.79	1996
19 Miller, Hogue, Burleson, R. Fajardo 1:39.31	1991
20 B. Adams, C. Burian, Gray, P. Collins 1:39.41	1995
25 **Isaacson,Woodward,J.Clark,DeMarsh 1:39.68**	**1997**
State Qualifing **1:31.99**	**`97**

TRAVERSE CITY TROJANS Girl's Swimming TOP 25 1995-96 Page 3

100 Freestyle		
1 **Jessica Ritchie**	**:55.11**	**1996**
2 Katie Cutler	:55.55	1994
3 Ashley Shaw	:56.17	1994
4 **Ann Townsend**	**:57.64**	**1995**
5 Kim McTaggart	:58.48	1986
6 Patty Clarke	:58.70	1980
7 Tammy Baker	:58.75	1992
8 Lindsey Seyler	:59.09	1991
9 Joni Sturgeon	:59.16	1992
10 Emily Dornbos	:59.18	1993
11 Sue Rosely	:59.20	1978
12 Sarah Abbott	:59.20	1988
13 **Jessie VanDalson**	**:59.71**	**1996**
14 Christina Hutchens	:59.91	1995
15 Katie Kilburg	1:00.24	1979
16 Heather Heffner	1:01.19	1990
17 Leslie Davison	1:01.24	1979
18 **Mandy Hitesman**	**1:01.51**	**1996**
19 Kelly Schroeder	1:01.69	1991
20 **Angela Kostrzewa**	**1:01.92**	**1996**
21 **Julie Stock**	**1:02.10**	**1996**
22 Laura Fajardo	1:02.21	1993
23 Trisha Samuelson	1:02.50	1981
24 Jennifer Ebinger	1:02.70	1983
25 Jennifer Sachtleben	1:02.72	1993
STATE QUALIFYING	56.09	1995

500 Freestyle		
1 Ashley Shaw	5:37.68	1994
2 Tammy Baker	5:43.40	1992
3 Kim McTaggart	5:47.83	1984
4 Lindsey Seyler	5:49.51	1991
6 **Jessie VanDalson**	**5:50.56**	**1996**
5 Stephanie Newman	5:53.95	1989
7 Amy Curry	5:59.66	1992
8 Sarah Abbott	6:01.88	1988
9 Heather Heffner	6:04.40	1990
10 Patty Clarke	6:06.04	1981
11 **Jennifer Edson**	**6:08.75**	**1995**
12 Kendra Lutes	6:11.52	1986
13 Chessa Schenk	6:11.52	1992
14 Julie Riddle	6:12.38	1990
15 Leya McVicker	6:13.80	1990
16 Laura Fajardo	6:15.03	1993
17 Angie Beall	6:17.20	1985
18 Trisha Samuelson	6:17.60	1982
19 Erica Hornby	6:19.49	1993
20 **Mandy Hitesman**	**6:20.38**	**1996**
21 Janis Mackkonen	6:21.22	1978
22 Tina Chapple	6:24.40	1988
23 Kirsten Beyer	6:30.30	1982
24 Emily Cutler	6:34.34	1994
25 Beth Douglas	6:36.69	1989
STATE QUALIFYING	5:28.39	1995

200 Freestyle Relay	
1 Baker, Dornbos, Shaw, K. Cutler 1:42.98	1994
2 Townsend, Shaw, K. Cutler, Ritchie 1:43.08	1995
3 **Townsend,Shaw,VanDalson,Ritchie 1:43.79**	**1996**
4 Baker, Stock, Shaw, K. Cutler 1:44.46	1994
5 **Hansen,Amy Edson,VanDalson,Ritchie 1:44.80**	**1996**
6 **Amy Edson, Townsend,Shaw,Ritchie 1:46.21**	**1996**
7 K. Cutler, Townsend, Shaw, Ritchie 1:46.27	1995
8 **Amy Edson,Townsend,Shaw,Ritchie 1:46:95**	**1996**
9 Sturgeon, Dornbos, Baker, Burleson 1:48.04	1993
10 K. Cutler, Baker, VanDalson, Shaw 1:48.20	1994
11 Schroeder, Sturgeon, Dornbos, Baker 1:48.26	1992
12 Townsend, K. Cutler, Hutchens, Shaw 1:48.45	1995
13 Townsend, Hutchens, K.Cutler, Ritchie 1:48.47	1995
14 Hutchens, Burleson, K. Cutler, Shaw 1:49.08	1995
15 **A.Edson,Townsend,VanDalson, Shaw 1:49.32**	**1996**
16 Sturgeon, Fajardo, Burleson, Baker 1:49.39	1993
17 Schenk, Sturgeon, Dornbos, Baker 1:49.57	1992
18 Sturgeon, Fajardo, Sachtleben, Baker 1:49.79	1993
19 **Townsend,A.Edson,Hansen,Shaw 1:49.80**	**1996**
20 Seyler, Abbott, Schroeder, Baker 1:49.93	1991
21 K. Cutler, Hutchens, VanDalson, Dornbos 1:50.06	1994
22 Shaw, Stock, Baker, Dornbos 1:50.41	1994
23 Townsend, Hutchens, VanDalson, K. Cutler 1:50.67	1995
24 Abbott, Seyler, Schroeder, Bartruff 1:50.89	1991
25 Fajardo, Burleson, Sachtleben, Baker 1:51.44	1993
STATE QUALIFYING TIME=1:44.49	1995

TROJAN BOYS MEET AND SEASON TEAM RECORDS (1978-PRESENT)

TRAVERSE CITY TROJANS Boys Swimming TOP 25 1995-96 Page 4

100 Backstroke

#	Name	Time	Year
1	Kevin Fajardo	:55.79	1993
2	Chris Clark	:59.42	1997
3	Sean Quinn	:59.50	1996
4	Brian Adams	:59.53	1995
5	Sergio Silva	:59.70	1990
6	Ken Iverson	1:00.90	1997
7	Paul Turner	1:02.17	1988
8	Tim Lyon	1:02.55	1994
9	Pat McManus	1:03.03	1997
10	Chris Collins	1:03.44	1992
11	Dan Kennedy	1:04.10	1997
12	Mike Hogue	1:04.24	1990
13	Ben Collins	1:05.07	1997
14	Dave Schlitt	1:05.19	1995
15	Sandy Rheem	1:05.29	1995
16	Todd Milarch	1:05.60	1984
17	Jeff Hughs	1:05.68	1980
18	John Waslawski	1:06.16	1987
19	Dave Aprea	1:06.80	1987
20	Scott Gest	1:06.84	1982
21	Doug Seeley	1:07.09	1989
22	Phil Krumm	1:07.80	1982
23	Rick Anderson	1:10.08	1982
24	Brett Lyon	1:10.19	1990
25	Marc Kropf	1:10.92	1993
	STATE QUALIFYING	:56.69	1996

100 Breaststroke

#	Name	Time	Year
1	Ed Ackerman	1:04.60	1985
2	Ben Collins	1:04.71	1997
3	Don Ackerman	1.05.56	1983
4	Ryan Fajardo	1:06.48	1992
5	Matt Isaacson	1:07.65	1997
6	Ken Iverson	1:08.12	1997
7	Aaron McDonald	1:08.29	1989
8	Scott Reichert	1:08.85	1997
9	Greg Seyler	1:09.78	1992
10	Andy Pierson	1:10.06	1994
11	Derek Skeen	1:11.49	1985
12	Greg Million	1:12.21	1987
13	Todd Milarch	1:12.40	1983
14	Marc Kropf	1:12.72	1994
15	Rick Utter	1:12.92	1992
16	Jon-Burleson	1:13.03	1990
17	Larry Thompson	1:13.07	1992
18	Mark Crossley	1:13.25	1982
19	Phil Krumm	1:13.25	1982
20	Jared Powell	1:13.60	1997
21	Billl Werthman	1:14.27	1988
22	Phil Collins	1:14.38	1994
23	Dean Murdick	1:14.80	1983
24	Brandon Marnett	1:15.55	1994
25	Pat McGarry	1:15.69	1997
	STATE QUALIFYING	1:03.19	1997

400 Freestyle Relay

#	Names	Time	Year
1	B.Adams,K. Iverson,B.Collins,C.Clark	3:23.29	1997
2	B.Adams,K.Iverson,J.Burian,C.Clark	3:23.69	1997
3	C. Clark, C. Burian, J. Burian,B. Adams	3:27.77	1996
4	Horton, Rields, Seeley, Hogue	3:31.90	1989
5	J.Burian,R.DeMarsh,B.Collins, K. Iverson	3:34.16	1997
6	J. Burian, P. Collins, Kropf, Adams	3:35.94	1995
7	B. Adams, J. Burian, R. DeMarsh, C. Clark	3:36.18	1996
8	Seeley, Hogue, Braden, Medler	3:37.17	1990
9	Hogue, Medler, Kropf, P. Collins	3:37.21	1992
10	Horton, Fields, Belovich, Seeley	3:37.23	1988
11	Medler, K.Fajardo, R. Fajardo, Hogue	3:37.27	1992
12	C. Burian, P. Collins, Kropf, Adams	3:37.64	1994
13	K. Fajardo, C. Burian, Kropf, Elmer	3:38.12	1993
14	Braden,Lyon, Medler, Seeley	3:38.30	1990
15	B. Adams, Gray, DeMarsh, C. Clark	3:39.42	1996
16	R. Fajardo, Hogue, Burleson,Quinn	3:39.78	1991
17	T. Gray, R. DeMarsh,P. Collins, J. Burian	3:39.85	1996
18	P. Collins, Kropf, C. Burian, Quinn	3:39.93	1994
19	Fields, Seeley, Kert, Braden	3:40.22	1988
20	Silva, Medler, Braden, Seeley	3:40.22	1990
21	J.Burian,R.DeMarsh,P.McGarry, S.Reichert	3:43.99	1997
22	C. Clark, DeMarsh, Quinn, B. Adams	3:44.30	1996
23	C.Burian,P.Collins,S.McClure,T.Gray	3:44.94	1996
24	R.Demarsh,P.McGarry,S.Reichert, B.Collins	3:45.36	1997
25	Gray, J. B urian, P. Collins, Adams	3:45.38	1995
	STATE QUALIFYING TIME=3:23.09		1997

TRAVERSE CITY TROJANS Girl's Swimming TOP 25 1995-96 Page 4

100 Backstroke

#	Name	Time	Year
1	Ann Townsend	1:02.99	1995
2	Patty Clark	1:03.82	1982
3	Jessica Ritchie	1:04.37	1996
4	Kelly Gest	1:05.34	1980
5	Jennifer Ebinger	1:06.60	1983
6	Sarah Abbott	1:08.27	1991
7	Julie Stock	1:08.97	1994
8	Julie Riddle	1:09.26	1992
9	Joni Sturgeon	1:09.85	1993
10	Courtney Padgett	1:10.58	1992
11	Lindsay Burleson	1:11.85	1995
12	Kate Kronk	1:11.93	1987
13	Barbara Glenn	1:12.06	1995
14	Kathy Szwalek	1:12.10	1991
15	Amy Johnson	1:13.46	1992
16	Amy Curry	1:14.57	1990
17	Kerri Otto	1:15.45	1994
18	Stephanie Newman	1:15.62	1988
19	Laura Fajardo	1:15.74	1993
20	Tara Mack	1;16.51	1996
21	Lena Nachmanson	1:16.60	1980
22	Alice Blackmore	1:16.97	1996
23	Roberta Oishi	1:16.90	1994
22	Katie Cutler	1:17.44	1995
23	Jodi Butzow	1:17.47	1991
	STATE QUALIFYING	1:03.49	1995

100 Breaststroke

#	Name	Time	Year
1	Joni Sturgeon	1:12.13	1993
2	Ashley Shaw	1:13.66	1995
3	Katie Kilburg	1:14.05	1985
4	Angela Kostrzewa	1:14:14	1996
5	Lindsey Seyler	1:14:67	1991
6	ANN TOWNSEND	1:17.03	1995
7	Kat Rheem	1:17.67	1992
8	Tricia Samuelson	1:18.60	1981
9	Monica Bullard	1:18.74	1989
10	Sarah Abbott	1:20.14	1989
11	Leya McVicker	1:21.13	1990
12	Heather Heffner	1:21.63	1988
13	Jeanne Kilburg	1:21.69	1981
14	Jennifer Ebinger	1:21.76	1983
15	Emily Newman	1:21.89	1996
16	Sara Ebinger	1:22.10	1984
17	Emily Newman	1:22.52	1995
18	Rachel Gloshen	1:22.94	1990
19	Jennifer Schmidt	1:23.48	1984
20	Willow Bartruff	1:23.80	1991
21	Kelli Woodrow	1:24.16	1989
22	Julie Kluzak	1:24.76	1984
23	Michelle Antaya	1:24.90	1993
24	Karen Brege	1:24.91	1992
25	Barb Bell	1:25.11	1978
	STATE QUALIFYING	1:11.59	1995

400 Freestyle Relay

#	Names	Time	Year
1	Ritchie, Townsend, VanDalson, Shaw	3:48.25	1995
2	Townsend,Shaw, VanDalson, Ritchie	3:48.39	1996
3	Shaw, Hutchens, Townsend, Ritchie	3:54.12	1995
4	Shaw, Baker, Stock, K. Cutler	3:55.97	1994
5	K. Cutler, Hutchens, VanDalson, Townsend	3:57.10	1995
6	Shaw,Stock,Townsend,Ritchie	3:58.73	1996
7	A. Edson,Shaw,VanDalson,Ritchie	3:58.84	1996
8	Shaw, Dornbos, Baker, K. Cutler	3:58.97	1994
9	Shaw, K. Cutler, Hutchens, Townsend	3:59.89	1995
10	A.Edson,Townsend,VanDalson, Ritchie	3:59.91	1996
11	Abbott, Seyler, Schroeder, Baker	4:01.10	1991
12	Hitesman,Ritchie,Shaw,VanDalson	4:02.21	1996
13	Schroeder, Dornbos, Baker, Sturgeon	4:02.54	1992
14	Baker, Dornbos, Fajardo, Sturgeon	4:03.17	1993
15	Baker, Fajardo, Burleson, Sturgeon	4:03.24	1993
16	Shaw, K. Cutler, VanDalson, Baker	4:03.59	1994
17	Hutchens, VanDalson, Townsend, Ritchie	4:03.60	1995
18	VanDalson, Hutchens, Townsend, Shaw	4:04.01	1995
19	Shaw, Hutchens, VanDalson, Townsend	4:04.92	1995
20	Kilburg, Beall, Davison, McTaggart	4:05.97	1986
21	Hutchens, VanDalson, Stock, Townsend	4:06.02	1995
22	Ritchie,Amy Edson,Shaw,Townsend	4:06.21	1996
23	Ritchie,Hitesman,VanDalson,Shaw	4:07.36	1996
24	K. Cutler, Shaw, Hutchens, Ritchie	4:07.84	1995
25	Baker,Dornbos,Stock,VanDalson	4:07.92	1991
	STATE TIME=3:51.95		

18

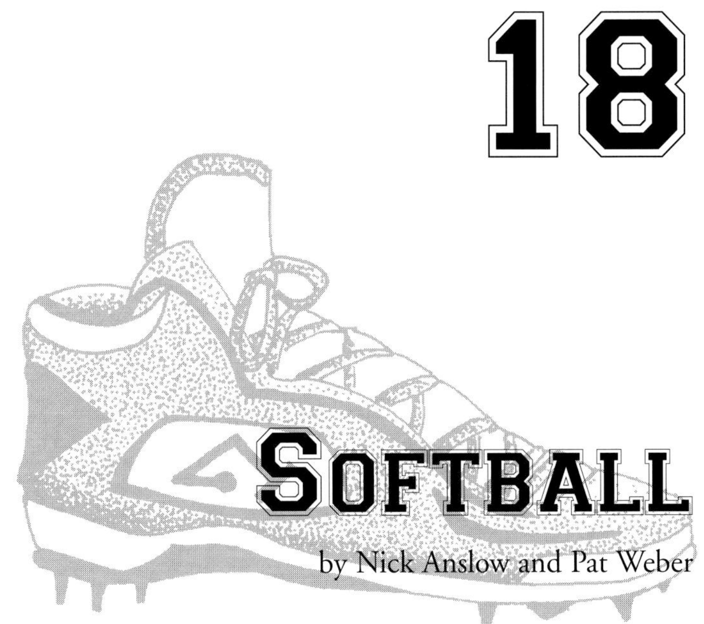

Softball

by Nick Anslow and Pat Weber

"Luck is a matter of preparation meeting opportunity."
- Oprah Winfrey

Softball has been a sport rising in popularity in many schools. Title IX certainly helped it along. In Traverse City, softball became a varsity sport in 1979. In their first season, the Lady Trojans posted a 3-13 record. Despite this disappointing start, the team had a positive season. "For a first-year team we had a lot of high points and improved tremendously throughout the season," said first-year coach Vicki Bush. The Trojans played undefeated Alpena and made them go seven full innings for the first time in their season.

The 1979 season was memorable for another reason, the weather. "Many games would begin in the sun and end in the cold; some began in cold rain and ended in snow," noted one player. Bad weather or not, nothing seemed to stop senior shortstop and pitcher, Jill Spencer. Spencer, who batted an even .500 with no strike-outs, was named the first softball Most Valuable Player.

The 1980 softball team sported an improved record at 9-14, including a victory against Alpena. The team had only two seniors, but earned some respect from the Lake Michigan Athletic Conference coaches despite their lack of experience. One LMAC coach praised the team for their "tremendous improvement and bright future." The MVP award that year went to junior Geri Nichols.

The 1981 softball season proved to be an eventful one. The girls posted a 14-11 record for the first winning season in the three years of the sport. This successful season put the team in second place in the LMAC. Their strong showing also clinched the conference All-Sports trophy for Traverse City. Three players were selected to the All-Conference team and four others earned honorable mention. Linda Blodgett, Diann Tomaszewski, Shelly Wright, Geri Nichols, Chris Mikowski, Julie Waldo and Jill Dooley headed this 1981 senior-led team.

Again in 1982, the Traverse City girls softball team finished second in the LMAC with an overall record of 7-15, 4-4 in league play. The season started out with a 1-12 record, but a line-up change combined with "hard work and dedication" turned the season around, finishing up 6-3. Stephanie Fraley led the team with a .556 league batting average, while Lisa Strang hit .500. Kelly Costigan held a .976 league defensive average and Debbie Anderson had a .952 LMAC fielding average. Jill Dooley and Amy Carmien were named All-Conference, with Costigan and Fraley Honorable Mention.

A most successful season occurred in 1985. In only their sixth season of softball at Traverse City, the Lady Trojans compiled a 24-11 record, winning first place in the LMAC. "The girls did a good job pulling together as a team, attitude- and skill-wise. There's always room for improvement, but I was pleased with the season," said second-year coach Ben Page.

"Unusual" can only describe the 1986 season from beginning to end. The season started out differently because first-year head coach Jack Clark didn't even know he had this coaching assignment until a month prior to the season's opening. With Traverse City no longer a part of the LMAC that year, the lack of a conference had a negative effect, especially since the girls had won the title outright the year before. But Coach Clark noted, "We have good speed in the legs of Angie Stone, Suzy Merchant, Natalie Gringras, and Laura Aylsworth. We have good pitching from senior Carrie Courtade, sophomores Carrie Groesser and Wendy Williams. And we have tremendous potential throughout."

Yet another coaching turnover took place in the 1987 season. Led by first-year coach, Tony Birch, the girls' 18-9 season landed them in the playoffs. The team got to the finals in the Grand Haven

1981 softball team, with the Trojans' first winning season. Front Row: Geri Nichols, Debbie Anderson, Julie Waldo, Diann Tomaszewski, Chris Mikowski, Kathy Spencer. Back Row: Lisa Strang, Linda Blodgett, Mgr. Joan Jerman, Coach Carolyn Keesor, Coach Vicki Bush, Stephanie Fraley, Jill Dooley, Shelley Wright, Audrey Grigsby, Amy Carmien, Joni Reed.

Invitational in late April without Coach Birch (who was at a prior commitment), and four of their starters (on spring break) before losing to Leland in the tournament championship. Pitching was the strong point for the entire season. Against Frankfort, Tricia Merchant threw six innings of one-hit ball, as the Lady Trojans won 1-0. "This year was fun. When you don't play in front of large crowds, there's much more personal satisfaction in winning," said first baseman Natalie Gingras.

In the district playoffs, the Trojans drew as their first-round opponent a solid Bay City Western team that had already won over 20 games. The outcome was a 5-1 loss.

Sue Jackson was one more new coach in the 1988 season and, as such, compiled a record-setting 25-5 season with her strong team, led by Tammy Trierweiler and Tricia Merchant. The Lady Trojans again qualified for the playoffs. Kelly Costigan, a former Trojan softball player, became the assistant coach under Jackson. This team was motivated by teamwork and friendship, not winning, so the team became winners. "We're just one big happy family of 16," said senior Tricia Merchant.

THE LATE 1980S AND EARLY 1990S had several outstanding players. Nikki Ritter and Misty Davidson were standouts, according to coach Kelly Costigan, who took over the Lady Trojans for the 1991 and 1992 seasons.

Doug Tornga came on board in 1993 and saw the need for a stronger tournament schedule. His 1993 squad had a 16-17 record, but worked very hard on defense and got better and better as the season went on. The season highlight was winning the Pizza Hut Invitational in Reed City with Cortney Smith as a strong force with a 10-5 pitching record.

First softball conference champions, the 1985 team. Back Row: Ass't Coach Jack Clark, Bobbie Courtade, Joni Williams, Carrie Courtade, Laura Holmes, Mimi Spaulding, Jill Warren, Natalie Gingras, Laura Aylsworth. Front Row: Shelly Taberski, Megan Brown, Suzy Merchant, Laura Tolene, Vicky Munn, Kim Howe, Angie Stone.

Treasa Gourlay, Traverse City's only softball All-Stater, at bat.

Katherine Brege had a two-week hitting streak where a .660 batting average resulted from switching from batting right-handed to batting left-handed. Lyle Zenner's expertise as the team's pitching coach also helped the girls out tremendously. Both men had played fast pitch softball for years and understood the need to get a tougher schedule to ready the team for state level competition.

The 1994 team was very young with nine underclassmen and just four seniors. Season highlights included Krista Gunderson hitting for the cycle at the Reed City Tournament. Treasa Gourlay as a freshman continued to lead the hitting with a pace of .347. Melissa Martin and Lisa Peoples were the two juniors who were the team leaders. The team record improved to 21-14 for this young team in a rebuilding season. Coach Tornga stated, "This is the year we looked for girls who really wanted to play softball and play it hard."

A stepped-up schedule in 1995 meant that the Lady Trojans played mostly Class A schools and had a tournament schedule that meant playing 3 to 4 games each Saturday. The team had strong finishes at each tournament and as a whole the team had a great attitude. The 25-12 record attests to the power of this fairly young team which won the Bellaire Classic Tournament. Sophomore Trisha Ansorge led the team in RBI's with 27. Treasa Gourlay continued leading the team with her batting average and Melissa Martin and Lisa Peoples had strong senior finishes. Junior pitchers Lyndsee Oien and Lindy Tornga had nearly identical records at 12-6 and 12-7 respectively. Lindy's ERA was an amazing 1.93, while Lyndsee's was 2.51.

LIKE MOST SPORTS, A GOOD FEEDER PROGRAM is at the core of a team's success. In softball, the VFW program has been replaced by TAGS (Traverse Area Girls Softball) and these athletes are just now hitting the high school level. The 1996 program saw the girls ranked in the honorable mention column in the state and moved as high as eighth in ranking during the season, which was a first for this program. The Grand Haven Big Buc Tournament and the Reed City Pizza Hut Tournament were both won by the Lady Trojans. Treasa Gourlay went on to break all school records both offensively and defensively. Lindy Tornga finished with a .438 batting average and broke the school record with an astonishing RBI total of 52. Amber Williams went to the lead-off spot and Treasa batted next for a powerful 1-2 punch. The season record was 23-15, with nine games being lost by just one run.

Treasa Gourlay ended her career All-District, All-Region and All-State, being Traverse City's first All-State softball player. Three other students made All-District: Lyndsee Oien, Lindy Tornga and Susan Riggs. Additionally, All State-Academic (3.5 GPA or better) honors went to Lindy Tornga, Stephanie Smith, Susan Riggs and Missy Ptak.

The 1997 squad has some big shoes to fill this season, but Coach Tornga knows the girls are ready for the challenge. "All the hard work since 1993 with hours of practice, with long Saturdays... are starting to show. This year we have an invitation to the Northview High School Invitational. This tournament is by invitation only and is based upon state ranking and tournament play. It has produced a state champion for the last 11 years. We are all looking forward to having fun."

CLASS A SOFTBALL ALL-STATE

1996 Treasa Gourlay

ACADEMIC ALL-STATE

1996 Missy Ptak
Susan Riggs
Stephanie Smith
Lindy Tornga

TROJAN SOFTBALL RECORDS

MANAGER RECORDS

Doug Tornga, Lyle Zenner	85-58
Vicki Bush	40-76
Ben Page	34-28

SINGLE GAME RECORDS – TEAM

Most at Bats	7	Vicki Munn	1985
Most Runs Scored	5	Vicki Munn	1985
	5	Carrie Courtade	1986
Most Walks	5	Suzy Merchant	1986
Most Stolen Bases	6	Jill Warren	1986
Most Hits	5	Natalie Gingras	1986
	5	Treasa Gourlay	1994

TEAM

Most Games	38	1996
At Bats	1030	1996
Runs	312	1996
Singles	320	1996
Doubles	37	1996
Triples	19	1996
Home Runs	6	1994
RBI's	249	1996
BB's	203	
Stolen Bases	182	
Wins	25	1995
Team BA	.357	1996

SEASON RECORDS

Best Won-Lost	25-12	1995
Games Played		
Stephanie Smith	38	1996
Treasa Gourlay	38	1996
Missy Ptak	38	1996
Amber Williams	38	1996

CAREER RECORDS

Most Games Played	Lisa Peoples	122
Most at Bats	Lisa Peoples	378
Most Runs	Lisa Peoples	126
	Natalie Gingras	98
	Treasa Gourlay	73
Most Singles	Lisa Peoples	134
	Treasa Gourlay	72
Most Doubles	Natalie Gingras	18
	Jeannine Hinds	17
Most Triples	Krista Gunderson	11
	Melissa Martin	5
Most Home Runs	Angie Stone	5
	Krista Gunderson	4
	Melissa Martin	3
Most Appearances by a Pitcher	Cortney Smith	48
	Lyndsee Oien	48
	Lindy Tornga	31
Complete Games	Lyndsee Oien	37
	Cortney Smith	33
	Lindy Tornga	21
Most Innings Pitched	Cortney Smith	245
	Lyndsee Oien	241
	Lindy Tornga	166
Most Strike-Outs	Lyndsee Oien	139
	Cortney Smith	124
	Lindy Tornga	117
Best ERA	Lyndsee Oien	2.27
	Lindy Tornga	2.41
	Cortney Smith	2.21
Career Pitching	Lyndsee Oien	27-13
	Lindy Tornga	24-16
	Cortney Smith	21-16
Most Stolen Bases	Lisa Peoples	98
Career Batting Average	Treasa Gourlay	.388
	Lindy Tornga	.360
	Lisa Peoples	.353
Most Hits	Lisa Peoples	146
	Treasa Gourlay	132
	Melissa Martin	78

TROJAN SOFTBALL COACHES

1979-1983	Vicki Bush
1984-1985	Ben Page
1986	Jack Clark
1987	Tony Birch
1988-1990	Sue Jackson
1991-1992	Kelly Costigan
1993 – present	Doug Tornga

19

Boys Soccer

By Aaron Dennis and Pat Weber

"It's not the speed toward the goal, but the direction ... forward."
– Unknown

When soccer became an interscholastic sport in 1981 (it was a club sport for the 1980 season), no one quite knew the popularity this field sport would eventually bring. Ironically, soccer is probably the oldest and most beloved sport world-wide, and a sport that makes quick converts. The new fields at the Coast Guard complex attract ample numbers of fans as this sport's popularity has surged both locally and throughout the United States in the 1990s.

Back in the late 1970s, however, success for Traverse City Senior High soccer was due in large part to the foresight and enthusiasm of some local men who spearheaded the drive to make soccer a sports option for the boys at Senior High. Chet Salisbury (a long-time TCAPS teacher), Dennis Brett, Hans Straub and Bruce Falberg were the men with the dream and the drive to make it happen. Salisbury continues today as the girls varsity coach and Falberg's record as boys varsity coach reads an impressive 225-82-20 after 16 years.

That very first season in 1981, the varsity pulled away with a 9-9-2 record, and the junior varsity with a 5-3 record. Salisbury coached varsity and Straub coached JV. The season opened in early September and finished with a 4-2 victory over Buckley in the Cherryland Conference on the first of November. John McHoskey was awarded Most Valuable Player during this first season. Scott Wagner set a team high of 23 goals followed by Gary Alexander's 21.

Bruce Falberg became assistant to Coach Salisbury in 1982. With Steve Brett and Tim Good in goal, the soccer season ended with an 8-4 record. Although the Trojans lost to Flint Carman-Ainsworth in the first round of the state playoffs, the record distinctly showed the direction in which the soccer program was headed. As stated by athletic director Dave Dye, "The sport also provided an opportunity for forty more students to be involved in the athletic program, represent the school, and possibly earn a varsity letter."

In 1983, the varsity soccer team had a dynamite 13-4-3 season. Coach Bruce Falberg took the team all the way through the districts to battle soccer titans Saginaw Eisenhower and Leland. Scott Archer was voted Most Valuable Player and made second team All-State along with Joe Finnegan, but Coach Falberg stated, "All the guys had a superior, banner year." It was just three years into the program when the team was ranked in the top eight in the state and two players were named to the All-State team.

The 1984 soccer season was the second straight outstanding one, ending with a 17-2 record. For the second year in a row they reached the state quarterfinals, but were defeated by Portage Northern in a very close game. The team ended up scoring a total of 171 goals with only 19 scored against them. To this day, this is believed to be a state record only Traverse City holds. Several varsity school records set that year by Tom Winowiecki, Dan Coats and Steve Keely still stand. In addition, Scott Archer set a defensive varsity record of 11 goals, while Scott Wickens and Kevin Kilburg posted a record 11 shut-outs. For the past two years, the Trojan soccer team had won all their home games. As Coach Falberg said, "It's not too often you find a team like this one." Matt Ligon and Kevin Kilburg shared goalie duties. Scott Archer, Joe Finnegan, Dan Coats and Scott Wickens made the All-State team.

AT THE BEGINNING OF THE 1985 SOCCER SEASON, coach Bruce Falberg was skeptical about the team. The previous year's team had consisted of all seniors, so there were no returning players. Falberg hoped for at least a winning season. Toward the beginning of the season, the team decided to have a meeting on their own and discuss their goals for the year. They decided they would work harder together as a team and their efforts definitely paid off. They ended the year with a 12-5-2 season and 51 goals total. For the third year in a row, the team made it to the final eight of the Class A teams in the state, losing a grueling 1-0 match to Okemos.

Being undefeated at home was already a habit when the 1986 season got under way. Continuing the four-year-old tradition of no home losses, this

1984 boys soccer team. Front Row: Tom Winowiecki, Greg Alexander, Dan Coats, Matt Ligon, Scott Wickens, Kevin Kilburg, Joe Finnegan, Steve Keely, Scott Archer. Back Row: Coach Bruce Falberg, Doug Casper, Pete Goudey, Jon Lund, Dave Sarya, Brady Schwert, Ed Ackerman, George Foerstner, Mike Whalen, Mgr. Stan Pitman. Not pictured: Dave Murdick.

team's 16-2-0 record indicated another impressive year. Nick Brown made the second team All-State as a junior and Jason Elsenheimer and Doug Baumgardner were the high goal-scorers. A 1-0 loss to Grand Haven in the regional finals only made the 1987 team more determined the following year.

The 1987 varsity soccer team had an outstanding season, led by top scorers Stu Salisbury (18 goals), Doug Baumgardner (15) and Nick Brown with 11 assists. Traverse City allowed only two goals in regulation time in their five playoff games. They came two games away from the state championship, winning districts and barely losing the regionals to East Lansing. After a game lasting for 110 minutes, the winner was determined in a shootout which ended in a 1-0 loss for the Trojans. This was a contest to try the endurance of any superior athlete. The boys played two 40-minute periods, went into two 10-minute overtimes, then two five-minute sudden death periods before the heartbreaking loss in the shoot-out. Despite the loss, the team had a great year, both on the field and off. The team's overall grade point average was a 3.4. Craig Archer, Clark Ardern (goalie) and Nick Brown were voted onto the All-State Class A team. Brown was then the second pick on the All-State Dream Team behind top choice Alexie Lalas that year. Brown continues to play semi-pro soccer in Hawaii. Falberg commented at the end of the season, "Out of all the years I've been coaching, I'm going to miss this team the most."

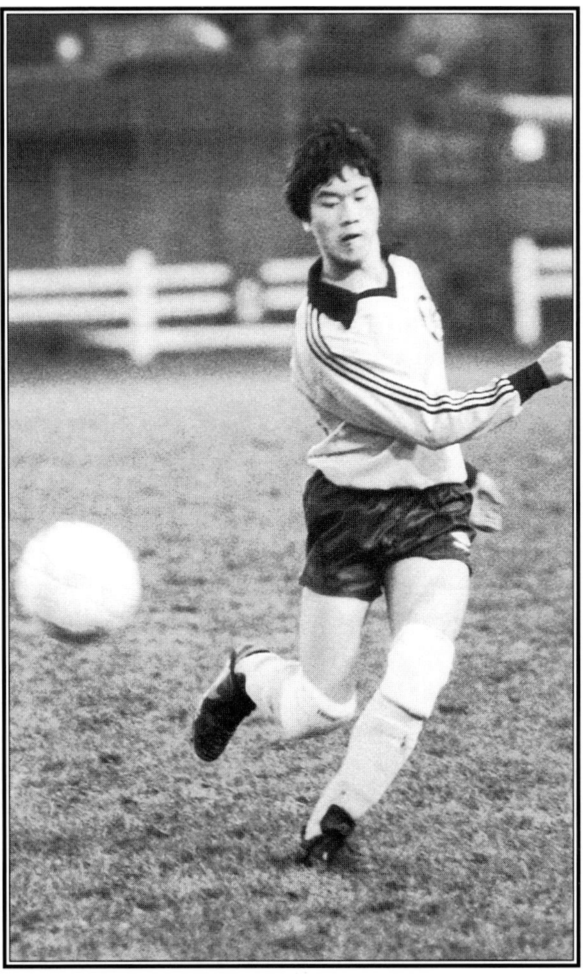

Nick Brown, first Trojan soccer Dream Team member, carefully eyes the ball.

SHUT-OUTS WERE BIG IN THE 1988 SEASON with goalies Tim Ford and Pat Murray having seven of them. With a 14-4-2 season, this was a rebuilding year with only three returning players from the 1987 team. However, winning their first eight games gave this group confidence. Jeremy Wells led a strong offensive attack with forceful defense from Trevor Klaasen, who was named All-State defender.

The 1989 team was supposed to be in another rebuilding year but ended up having a strong season. The varsity team had only a handful of returning players, yet still pulled away with a 17-4-1 season. "We had confidence in each other ... we were always in as good as, if not better shape, than our opponent," said Steve Million. Traverse City's top scorer was Dennis Richard with 30 goals. Richard, Scott Martin and Pat Murray were named All-State.

At the end of the 1990 regular season, the varsity team stood at 15-1-1. Beating all four teams in the district playoffs advanced them to the regionals where they defeated Grand Blanc 1-0. However, a loss in the semi-finals to Warren De LaSalle finished the season. Falberg noted proudly, "We set the record for the most shut-outs in a season (15)." The 1990 team also set new school records for the most wins (21) and the fewest season losses (2).

The Trojans also were able to advance to the state semifinals by winning their first regional. Jason Olman (21 goals), Andy Johnson (goalie), and Jason Carmien were named to the All-State team.

Some super sophomores emerged and stepped right into the starting lineup the next year: John Sirrine, Jason Buttleman and Scott Gloden would be the nucleus of the team for the next three years. The 1991 season totals were 11-4-3 with the Sirrine brothers, John and Rob, along with Jason Emerich as the leading goal scorers. John Sirrine made the All-State team as a sophomore mid-fielder.

One more win in the plus column headed the 1992 season which saw totals of 12-7-3. Five overtime games with a variety of ties, one win and one loss kept the fans on their feet. Chad Fournier and John Sirrine led in goal scoring and both were named to the All-State team.

Having a strong "feeder" program in place enables varsity sports to field experienced players and improve their games. Both the YMCA and TBAYS (Traverse Bay Area Youth Soccer Association) have been strong contributors to the success of the high school program. In 1993, the season totals reflected this at 20-3-0. Losing a heartbreaker to Lansing Waverly in the state playoffs did not diminish the accomplishments of this fine group of athletes. Bruce Falberg was named Coach of the Year in Region 5 and All-American Anders Kelto led the team with 17 goals and 21 assists. Five players made All-State: John Sirrine, Ben Warmbold (goalie), Anders Kelto, Scott Gloden and Jason Buttleman

With only five returning lettermen in the 1994 season, building a new team which understood each other and had faith and confidence in each other was a challenge. That challenge was met and the season totals of 14-5-1 reflect this. Junior National Team captain Anders Kelto led the way with 16 goals and 11 assists, was picked to the All-State Soccer Dream Team, and named All-American once again.

IN 1995, THE TROJAN SOCCER PROGRAM GOT A BOOST when it finally received a home. Earlier, a generous offer from the Traverse City Coast Guard Air Station to transfer 27 acres adjacent to their base near the airport to TCAPS for soccer fields had begun to pave the way for an entire soccer complex. Coast Guard Commander Tom Allard, TCAPS Board of Education member Tom

Another outstanding soccer team, the 1987 Trojans. Front Row: Dave Watts, Jon Carlson, Josh Block, Nick Brown, Jeremy Neihardt, Stu Salisbury, Craig Archer, Paul Manna, Jon Lint. Back Row: Mike Foley, Daryl DeYoung, Randy Brothers, Chad Allen, Frank Kullman, Clark Ardern, Audley Becker, John Rockwood, Matt Lambert, Doug Baumgardner, Coach Bruce Falberg.

The Trojans' Ben Warmbold stops a shot.

Alward and U.S. Representative Bart Stupak created a plan for this land transfer. Needing an act of Congress for approval, this process took almost two years to be finalized. By 1995, a ten-year lease had been arranged on ten of the acres which allowed for some work to begin on the property. Three regulation soccer fields were leveled, seeded and irrigated that summer and were ready for the beginning of the fall season when a new scoreboard was also installed.

The 1995 season record looked like the 1993 total, with one more win: 21-2-0. Coach Falberg summed up the year with, "A total team effort... unity, fun and the agony of defeat can all be found in this team." Shutouts totaled 11, as did one-goal games. Kelto and Matt Jacobs led in the goal-scoring department while Tom Littlefield and Mike Haley shared goaltending duties. In 13 years of coaching, Falberg said that this team had the best starting defense and subs he had ever seen. Weather and driving thousands of miles during the playoffs played key roles in the loss to Portage Northern in the Class A championship semifinals. Three inches of snow and a sometimes blinding snow storm made for less than ideal conditions on a non-regu-

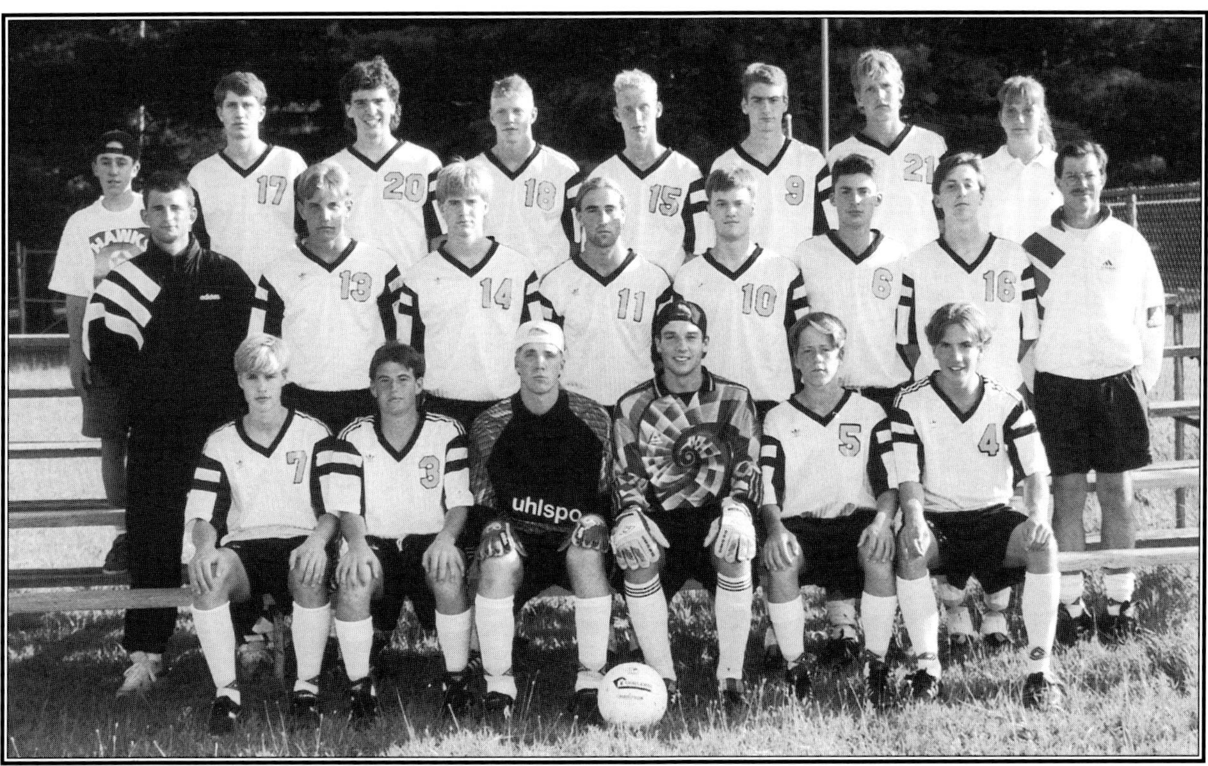

1993 Trojan soccer team which included five All-Staters. Back Row: Statistician Kyle Williams, Garren Moss, Scott Gloden, Ryan Senn, Jason Buttleman, Jim Palmer, Brian Lishawa, Trainer Sarah Valade. Middle Row: Ass't Coach Sander Scott, Eric Gray, Jason Plum, John Sirrine, Mike Abbott, Nate Richardson, Mike Lawson, Coach Falberg. Front Row: Anders Kelto, Ryan Johnson, Alan Plum, Ben Warmbold, Ryan Anderson, Mike Wares.

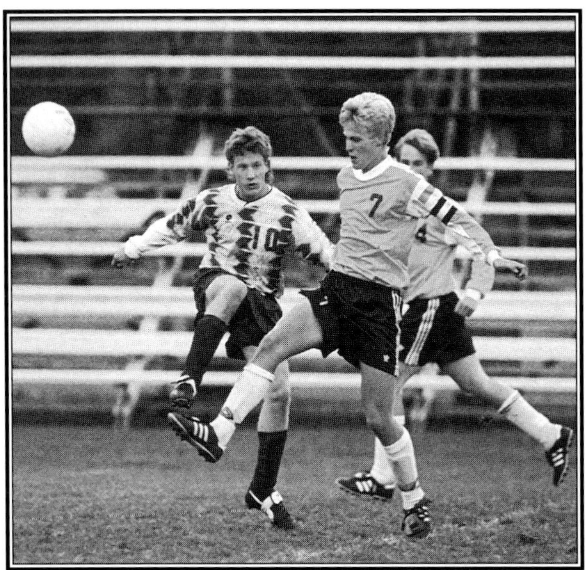

The Trojans' Anders Kelto (#7), 1995 Mr. Soccer and three-time All-American, beats his opponent to the ball.

lation field. Anders Kelto was honored as Mr. Soccer in Michigan and named to the All-American team for the third straight year. Garren Moss and Shane Lishawa joined Kelto on the All-State defense team.

In 1996, work continued at the Coast Guard Soccer Complex as lighting and bleacher seating were installed on the game field. In November, Congress finally approved the land transfer making the land officially the property of TCAPS. Remaining plans for that facility could now be finalized and constructed as the Between the Fences fundraising allowed.

A new year and a new team: the 1996 team had one tough act to follow. The season's record of 12-4-4 again illustrated the rebounding capacity of this soccer program after losing many key seniors to graduation the prior spring. Three of the losses were in overtime and the other one was a 1-0 loss. The 1996 season ended in an overtime district loss

1995 boys soccer team which played in the state semifinals. Front Row: Dave Joynt, Corey Mason, Mike Haley, Tom Littlefield, Matt Jacobs, Scott Chrenka. Middle Row: Neil Barkel, Patrik Johannson, Chris Call, Rodney Johnson, Ben Lane, Rob Keeley, Tom Haines, Trainer Amber Jewell. Back Row: Jon Rader, Ben Maier, Shane Lishawa, Coach Bruce Falberg, Garren Moss, Eric DeLonge, Nick Bates.

to Cadillac after two penalty kicks. Corey Mason led in points (25) and Matt Jacobs again led in goal scoring (13). Shane Lishawa was a repeat pick to the Class A All-State team.

And so it will continue to be a sport of endurance and patience and great expectations on the part of the players and fans. New fields at the Coast Guard base which Between the Fences helped develop and a complex in its final stages from TBAYS will add the necessary fields to accommodate thousands of area kids now playing soccer. There are huge shoes to fill here and the community is grateful to the soccer booster moms and dads, the coaches and the pioneers who put soccer on the map in Traverse City. The value and fun of this game called soccer is in the skills and teamwork developed, along with the camaraderie that each player experiences. Cheers to all who enjoy this game.

SOCCER ALL-STATE DREAM TEAM

1987	Nick Brown
1993	John Sirrine
1994	Anders Kelto
1995	Anders Kelto

CLASS A SOCCER ALL-STATE

1983	Scott Archer Joe Finnegan
1984	Scott Archer Dan Coats Joe Finnegan Scott Wickens
1986	Nick Brown
1987	Craig Archer Clark Ardern
1988	Trevor Klaasen
1989	Scott Martin Pat Murray Dennis Richard
1990	Jason Carmien Andy Johnson Jason Olman
1991	John Sirrine
1992	Chad Fournier John Sirrine
1993	Jason Buttleman Scott Gloden Anders Kelto
1995	Shane Lishawa Garren Moss
1996	Shane Lishawa

MR. SOCCER

1995	Anders Kelto

ALL-AMERICAN

1993	Anders Kelto
1994	Anders Kelto
1995	Anders Kelto

TROJAN BOYS SOCCER COACHES

1981-1982	Chet Salisbury
1983 - present	Bruce Falberg

TROJAN BOYS SOCCER RECORDS

Team Records

Fewest season losses, 2	1984, 1986, 1990, 1995
Most season shut-outs, 15	1990
Best season start, 9-0	1988, 1989
Most season wins, 21	1990. 1995
Most season goals, 171	1984
Most season goals against, 29	1994
Fewest season goals against, 15	1995
Most goals in a game, 21	1984, Northport
Most goals against in a game, 8	1990
District titles, 8	1983, 1984, 1987, 1989, 1990, 1992, 1993, 1995
Regional titles, 2	1990, 1995
Final four, 2	1990, 1995
Longest consecutive home streak, 38 wins, 2 ties	1983-1987

Individual Records

Most career goals, 68	1982-1984, Tom Winowiecki
Most season goals, 42	1984, Dan Coats
Most game goals, 7	1984, Steve Keely
Most season assists, 47	1984, Steve Keely
Best season goals against average, 47	1986, Clark Ardern

Coach Falberg Varsity Record 225 - 52 - 20

20

Cross-Country Skiing

By Jennie Stratton

"Cross-country skiing is a sport that's fun, but more importantly it has life benefits that can be continued for most of one's life. I think that makes this sport special, and for both the boys and girls to win the first state championship in this sport is something they'll never forget."

– Ivanka Baic-Berkshire

Although the Traverse City cross-country ski team is a relatively new program, our school has made a name for itself by dominating the sport for the past nine years. When the first state championship was held in 1987, Traverse City was there and set the precedent for the following years.

Started by a parent group led by Dr. Larry Skendzel and Dr. John Bruder, Traverse City had the first high school cross-country team in the state. In the first year of competition the only other school that actually had a team was Traverse City St. Francis.

This sport has more to offer than just a winning trophy. Coaches teach the athletes a personal work ethic and encourage them to strive to reach their maximum potential in both mental and physical conditioning. The year-round training regimen builds physical capacity and teaches a stick-to-it attitude that is necesssary for success in today's workplace. The tradition of winning the state championship has been passed down through the years as the team has never lost the state meet.

The original coaches were Ivanka Baic-Berkshire and Jerry Glenn. Glenn later left the position of coach, but he could usually be seen at the weekly races held at Hickory Hills or Jellystone. Vojin Baic, father of Ivanka, began helping with the team until Ivanka and Vojin left their posts as coaches after the 1994-1995 season. Replacing them in 1995 were Vicki Asmus as head coach and assistant coach Ron Ernsberger. In 1996, Vicki Asmus and John Kostrzewa served as co-coaches.

In the first state championship meet in 1987, Anne Mudgett won for the Traverse City girls, taking first place overall. Finishing the four kilometer race in 15 minutes and 29 seconds, she became the first Traverse City cross-country skier to receive a state medal, which is given to the top 20 overall finishers at the state meet. Christian Byar was the top male finisher for the Trojans, taking third with a time of 26 minutes and 38 seconds in the boys eight-and-a-half kilometer race. Coach Jerry Glenn said, "Byar wins every race he enters and has the potential to become a national skier." Traverse City won the meet with 123 points, 36 points ahead of second place.

In 1988, Anne Mudgett again won a state medal and was joined in that honor by Chad Weber. In 1989, Heidi Sherman had the best time of the team at the state meet, which the Trojans again won. Chad Weber was the top boys skier who, according to Coach Berkshire, was "the most consistent and probably the smoothest skier on the guys team."

MEMBERS OF THE 1990 TEAM were asked why they liked being on the cross-country ski team. Their reasons varied from Matt Bruder saying, "I like wearing flashy clothes," and Jenni Hunt, "I like to see the different ways people fall," to the more serious Clay Grueber stating, "It builds self-confidence." Heidi Sherman must have enjoyed the challenge since she earned a state medal that year.

Competition from other schools was still light in 1991, but it was continuing to grow. It has not been unusual for the teams to consist of many siblings. The Trojans have had twins Ann and

1988 Trojan cross country ski team at Hickory Hills, which included (not in order): Christian Byar, Dane Lueck, Aaron Prevo, Chad Weber, Anne Mudgett, Kim Glenn, Josh Block, Kris Bader, Jon Lint, Kelly Robson, Eric Shaw, Scott Howard, Steve Portenga, Bob Roe, Kelly Davis, Robin Gould, Peter Noverr, Kirsten Weise, Meg Jamieson, Dave Columbus, Steve Million, Julie Soloman, Ryan Halbert, Aaron Hullman, Jason Surratt, Mike Prevo, Aric Wood, Westley Sherman, Heidi Sherman, Matt Eister, John Waddington, Mindy Nye, Scott Casey.

Meghan Phillips, and their sister Katie; twins Heidi and Westley Sherman, Dave and Jeff Rundio; and a series of Plum family members, Ryan, Jason, Nathan and Trisha. The Rapid City team were mainly members of the Weir family.

One of the main challenges for the high school team deals with the lack of school competition in Michigan. Initially, the thought was that downstate schools would get involved, but because of their warm weather and little snow, the only people cross-country skiing seem to be from Cadillac north. St. Francis is the only other varsity team at the state meet; the other teams are all club teams. Trojan skiers do not just ski against other high school teams. For example, the Copper Country team includes skiers from the Ishpeming and Negaunee areas.

However, this does not indicate a lack of good individual competition. In a 1991 issue of *The Booster News*, coaches Ivanka Berkshire and Jerry Glenn stated, "They ski against some of the best midwest skiers as well as top Wisconsin and Minnesota high school racers." That year, Katie Tavener won the state girls championship, while Heidi Sherman placed third. Westley Sherman took second in the state for the boys team.

In 1992, there were no individual Trojan state champions, but the teams relied on their depth to pull out dual state titles as Tavener placed a strong second in the meet. Top Trojan finishers on the 1993 team were Andy Stevens and Molly Arnold, who both finished second in the state. Stevens had the best Trojan time again in 1994, repeating as second in the state. Close behind were Josh Timberlake, Dan Coles and Jason Plum. Libby Tomlinson led the girls that year with a seventh-place state finish; Holly Weber came in eighth.

"The first five years I was coaching, we had a big Winnebago in which the team traveled. The parents drove separately with the equipment," said Berkshire. Ski meet locations are Marquette, Tawas, Gaylord and Lewiston. The state tournaments have been held at a different location every year. The farthest from Traverse City it has been held was in Marquette.

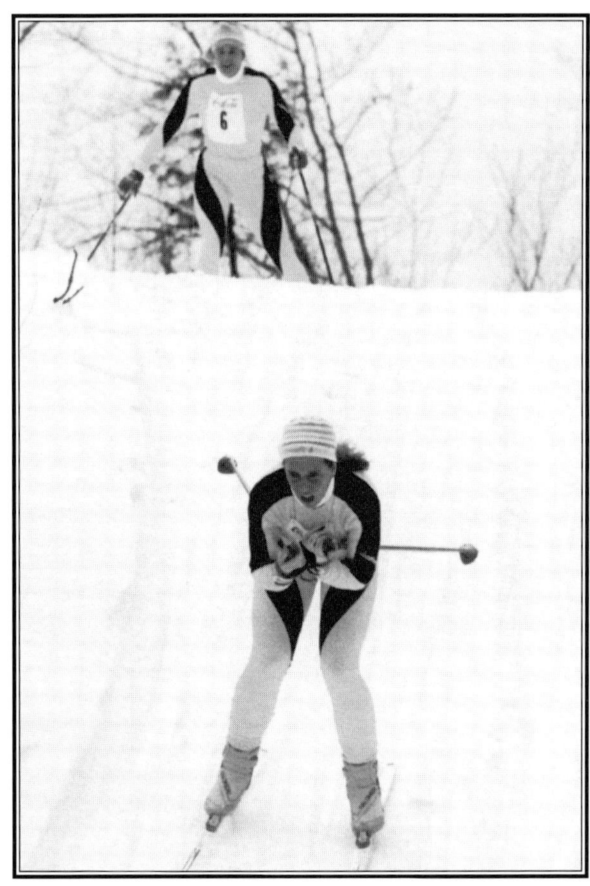

State champion Katie Tavener races down a hill with teammate Heidi Sherman ready to follow.

A new era for the cross-country team began when Vicki Asmus took over the job as head coach in the summer of 1995, with Ron Ernsberger as assistant. Leading the 1995 team were Clay Morrison with a third-place state finish and Angela Kostrzewa who placed fifth in the state. Other top ten finishers were Holly Weber (7th), Sarah Torbet (9th), Stephanie Barker (10th), Jason Gross (7th) and Melzar Coulter (9th).

In 1996, the format was changed from one freestyle (skating) meet to a combined meet with one freestyle and one classic (traditional) race. Changing the format was a better method to determine the best team and skiers in the state since now the racers must be proficient in both styles of nordic skiing. Even with the changes in place, Traverse

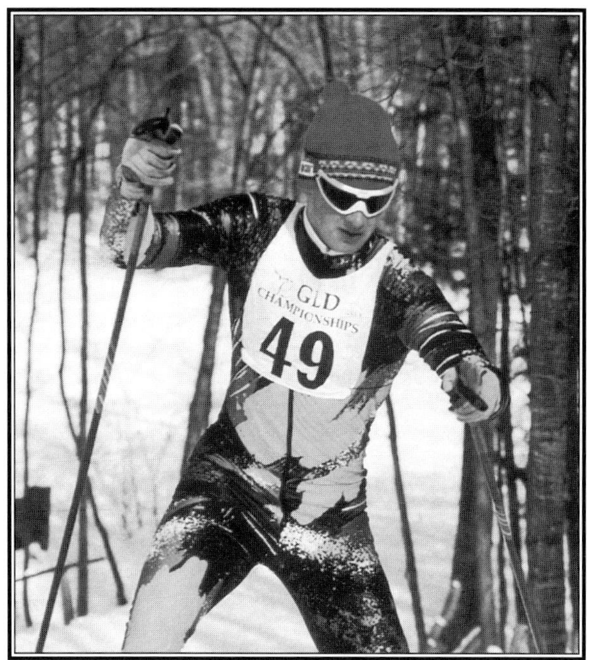

Andy Stevens, who twice placed second in the state.

City walked away the winner of the boys and girls championships for the tenth year in a row.

Top Traverse City racers who earned 1996 state medals were state champion Tricia Plum, Angela Kostrzewa, who placed second, Stephanie Barker, the third finisher, Sarah Torbet, Kevin Maki, who took third for the boys, Melzar Coulter, Jason Gross, Clay Morrison and Troy Kellogg. Several of these racers were also in the top group of finishers in 1997: Troy Kellogg, third in the state, Melzar Coulter, who repeated in fourth place, Mike Haley, Jr., Adam Granger, Ryan Lamott, and Tricia Plum, Angela Kostrzewa and Danielle Correll for the girls.

A "no-cuts" policy has been part of all the cross-country ski coaches' philosophies. Many students go out for cross-country skiing to stay in shape for other sports and end up loving this sport. Boys and girls practice together for about an hour and a half, five days a week, training both the skating and classic techniques. Coach Asmus is credited for bringing classical racing back to the team.

Besides competing for the school team, many Traverse City cross-country team members also ski in the United States Ski Association (USSA). These skiers race in a few extra meets a year and if they qualify, they can travel to the Junior Olympics. Members of the high school team who compete in the USSA circuit are usually the top finishers in any race, whether it is for the school or not.

Some former cross-country skiers who won the state meet and/or competed for the Trojans went to on to compete at the college varsity level. Westley Sherman skied for MIT; his sister Heidi raced at Bowdoin College. Dave Rundio skied at Middlebury; Jeff Rundio at University of Montana. Christian Byar and Katie Tavener continued their racing at Northern Michigan University, while Andy Stevens went on to race for Michigan Tech.

Much of the credit for the success of the relatively new cross-country ski program at Traverse City Senior High was due to the tremendous support of the parents throughout the years, explained former coach Ivanka Baic Berkshire. Cheers to all of them.

TROJAN CROSS-COUNTRY SKI COACHES

1987-1995 Ivanka Baic-Berkshire
1995-present Vicki Asmus

CROSS-COUNTRY SKI SCORING

The boys and girls cross-country teams practice and compete together but are scored separately. Each competitor is given a score based on his/her finishing place and the total score for a team determines the winner. Depending on the race, the top four or five finishers count. The state championship race is a Pursuit Race. There, the skiers do the freestyle on Saturday. On Sunday, they use classical skiing. On Sunday they start in the position in which they finished on Saturday. If a skier is beaten by five seconds on Saturday, they start five seconds behind that person on Sunday. Whoever crosses the finish line first on Sunday is the winner.

21

Girls Soccer

By Sarah Wahl

"The way I see it, if you want the rainbow, you gotta put up with the rain."

– Dolly Parton

On March 12, 1990, girls soccer became an official varsity sport at Traverse City Senior High. This was due to a group of parents led by Kathleen O'Connell who spent the time and energy researching girls soccer at other high schools in the state, surveying our own girls as to their interest and then presenting it all to the board of education where approval was made that same night. However, the new team needed a coach. Two weeks later they hired Harriet Grueber whose experience as both a coach and a referee made her an excellent choice.

For the first year the school board agreed to fund the coaching salary, but the newly-founded soccer boosters had to pay all other expenses such as uniforms, travel and equipment. Readily agreeing to this task was the first Soccer Booster Club headed by officers Kathleen O'Connell, president; Jim Swartz, vice-president; Sally Benner, secretary; Mike Gloden, treasurer. They realized the need for girls soccer after Kathleen O'Connell sent out questionnaires the previous fall and more than 100 came back with interest in this as a high school sport. O'Connell stated that "according to the Michigan High School Athletic Association, soccer is the fastest growing high school sport in the state." Including Traverse City, there were then 14 interscholastic girls soccer teams in the state.

However, the new team had a few problems. Kathleen O'Connell's daughter Erin, who had played on boys teams for many years, was not eligible by MHSAA rules because she had played soccer on the fall 1989 Traverse City boys team. She therefore became the girls team manager that first season. Having a field to play on was an additional headache, so in their first season they didn't have any home games. Another problem was that the girls were not in shape since most of them had not been planning to been planning to play soccer that spring. The final problem was the lack of experienced soccer players. No feeder program existed unless the girls had wanted to play boys soccer through the YMCA and then Traverse Bay Area Youth Soccer (TBAYS). "That year we basically had to tell the kids 'this is a soccer ball, this is the goal,'" said Grueber.

THE GIRLS SOCCER TEAM'S FIRST GAME was with Big Rapids on May 1, 1990. The team dedicated its first year to athletic trainer Anna Bosle, who had passed away earlier that year. The inaugural 1990 team finished with a 0-5 record. Players on this first Traverse City team were Sarah Abbott, Brittany Adams, Kelly Becker, Sara Benner, Amy Belovich, Kristin Bowman, Kami Carmien, Misha Corbin, Greta Dykstra, Beth Gaines, Michelle Gloden, Kari Grim, Amy Humfleet, Nicole Parasida, Jennifer Pelon, Meghan Phillips, Autumn Rademacher, Nicole Rousse, Katie Snell, Mindy Swartz, Sarah Teichman, Kelly T'Kindt, Sara Wares, Lori Warmbold and Meg Wilson.

In 1991, the girls were stronger and Coach Grueber started the season with optimism. Her team increased its schedule from five to 15 games that season, with four of them at home. In addition to senior Erin O'Connell, who was in goal that year, new players joining this team were seniors Amy Portenga, Kriss Cook and Heather Gillow, junior Steph Bowerman, and freshmen Emily Quinn, Stacey Emerich and Kara Ardern. O'Connell, Benner and Swartz served as tri-captains.

On the first home game played at Thirlby Field, the Trojans soundly defeated Big Rapids, 9-0, which was a real treat for the 1991 team. Grueber credited much of that year's improvement (the team ended with a 5-7-2 record) to student assistants Jason Carmien, Joe Osterling and Dennis Richard. The three were all members of the Trojan boys team which had advanced to the Class A semifinals the previous fall. "The boys have really helped the girls learn the game," said Grueber. "Their teaching of the game has really made the difference. Some girls didn't play soccer last year because of the uncertainty of the program. But now they can see that we're serious."

The third year of girls soccer in 1992 showed how much this sport had grown with the addition of a junior varsity team of 15 members and Dennis Richard and Matt Swartz, both former Trojan soccer players, as coaches. The varsity opened with a couple of losses, including a 1-6

1991 girls soccer team in their first full season. Back Row: Trainer Eric Neizgoda and Amy Machata, Assistant Coach Jason Carmien, Sara Benner, Kara Ardern, Beth Gaines, Molly Thompson, Kriss Cook, Mindy Swartz, Amy Portenga, Kami Carmien, Emily Quinn, Kelly T'Kindt, Brittany Adams, Assistant Coach Dennis Richard, Head Coach Harriet Grueber, Assistant Coach Amy Yee. Front Row: Stacey Emerich, Kate Snell, Lori Warmbold, Amy Belovich, Nicole Parasida, Erin O'Connell, Heather Gillow, Sara Canfield, Meghan Phillips, Stephanie Bowerman. Not pictured: Kelly Becker.

loss to Midland Dow. However, it was the first time that Traverse City had scored on Dow so the team was pleased with that success. Seniors this year were Steph Bowerman, Amy Belovich, Lori Warmbold and Meghan Phillips, with the core of the team still the same underclassmen as the previous year. It should be noted that Erin O'Connell went on to play Big Ten soccer as goalie at Michigan State for four years.

The 1993 season began with a new coach, Chet Salisbury, and his assistant, Bill Sirrine. Coach Salisbury decided that the best way to keep the Trojans improving was to have strong competition, so he expanded their schedule to include games with Mason, Lansing Waverly, Saginaw Heritage and Flint Carman-Ainsworth that year. Mike Gloden took over as junior varsity coach with 22 players. Home games were played at Thirlby Field. The Trojans ended the season 10-6-1, including a first-ever district win over Clio, "one of our goals at the start of the season," said Coach Salisbury. Stacey Emerich made a record-high 20 goals in her junior season. One interesting thing said by a player was that, "A team ritual was that at the beginning of home games we had a tape that had a mix

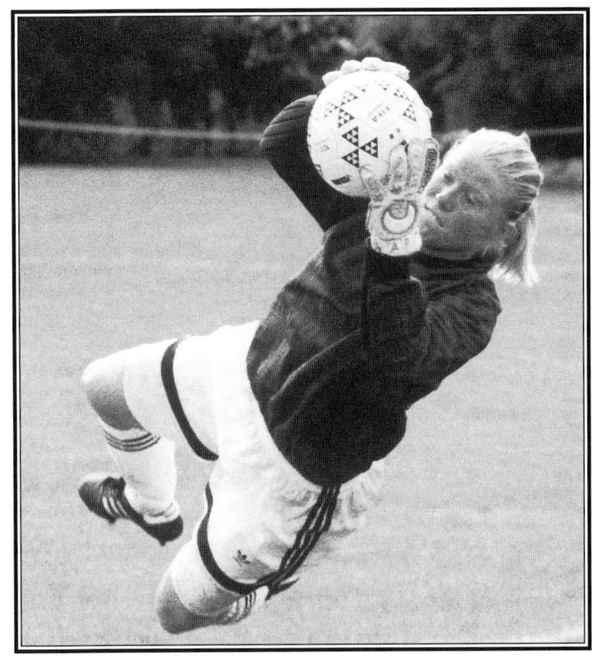

Goalie Erin O'Connell saves a shot on goal.

1993 girls soccer team. Back Row: Trainer Collin Murphy, Beth Gaines, Sara Benner, Kara Ardern, Molly Thompson. Middle Row: Coach Chet Salisbury, Kari Sloan, Mindy Swartz, Sara Wares, Emily Quinn, Stacey Portenga, Coach Bill Sirrine. Front Row: Stacey Emerich, Kelly T'Kindt, Anne Harrington, Brittany Adams, Sarah LaBelle, Kim Fournier, Sara Canfield.

All-time leading scorer Stacey Emerich (#7) battles a Dow player for possession of the ball.

of songs such as 'House of Pain' and we would play it to psych us up."

Coach Salisbury had made a firm commitment the previous year to build a strong girls soccer program at Traverse City. In 1994, he had to do some rebuilding. His team, which started out 0-4, had only five seniors on varsity: Kara Ardern, Stacey Emerich, Anne Harrington, Mary Beth Lewis and Jessica Hayes. Also returning were juniors Sarah LaBelle, Kim Fournier and Stacey Portenga, who had played varsity as sophmores, and junior varsity veterans Mindy Firebaugh (junior) and sophomore Wendy Boynton in goal. The team went the first part of its season 1-6, without even scoring a goal. However, this drought ended with a 12-0 win over Fruitport at the end of April. Later, a district game set a school record for the most goals scored in a game as Traverse City mercied Saginaw, 12-0.

The 1994 Trojans ended with a 6-12-1 season, but did "not let their losing record affect their attitude," according to LaBelle. Erin O'Connell spent the last part of the season back in town working with the team, teaching them "to play rough, yet fair," according to Coach Salisbury. MVP Stacey Emerich graduated this year, having set several school records which still stand today. In her four years on varsity, she had 51 goals plus 16 assists. She also started and played in all 65 games in her Trojan career.

In girls soccer's fifth season, they won 6 out of 18 games. The main task this year was to fill the void left by the graduation of leading scorer Stacey Emerich. In 1995, Coach Salisbury stated, "This wasn't the best year for several reasons. The schedule was among the hardest in history" as they played some of the top programs in the state. Also, they still had the problem of no field. Between the Fences had plans to begin work on the new soccer fields at the Coast Guard property, but they were not ready for the girls spring season. In the interim, a West Junior High field was used for games.

The only five seniors in 1995 were Kim Fournier, Stacey Portenga, Mindy Firebaugh, Sarah LaBelle and Erin Sullivan. Rounding out the team were juniors Wendy Boynton, Laura Blodgett, Kelly Blum, Alison Rice, Abbie Sirrine, Jill Mueller, Ellen Quirk, Amber Carlson, Annia Poulin, Jessica Spyhalski, and goalies Danielle Gore and Deidre O'Hare. Sophomore players were Alyssa Korhonen, Sarah Stilwill, Alane Schettler and Grace Ott. Although the majority of the 1995 team were underclassmen, they were not inexperienced. With only four of the 21 members not having seen varsity action the previous year, this group finished the season with a 5-11-3 record.

The 1996 team had a good combination of youth and experience. Returning from 1995 were senior goalies Deidra O'Hare and Danielle Gore, sweeper Allison Rice, fullbacks Sarah Stilwill and Jill Mueller, Kelly Blum and Wendy Boynton at midfield, and forwards Alyssa Korhonen and Laura Blodgett. Adding strength to this lineup were eight freshmen and four sophomores: Nicole Cook, Mary Richter, Natalie Plosky, Kinsley Robinson, Brooke Schulz, Tricia Plum, Emily Bowerman, Amanda Alward, Lauren Beers, Macare Kelly and Veleska Novorolsky.

Assisting Coach Salisbury with the 1996 team were Joe Osterling, Dan Tiesworth and goalkeeper coach John Hocking. This was the first girls team to play on their new home fields at the Coast

Guard Soccer Complex. One memorable out-of-town trip for the Trojans was their first district game against Saginaw. They ended up driving 300 miles for a free victory as only six Saginaw players showed up for the match. In their final game, Traverse City fell to Midland Dow in a close 1-0 contest to end the season at 9-9-1.

Traverse City girls soccer has improved a great deal, as Trojan teams now routinely play the best competition in the state. Most players prepare for the season by playing in the off-season on a TBAYS team in the summer and at indoor soccer in the winter. The feeder program for girls soccer is now beginning to have a positive effect. Since Erin O'Connell '91 went on to play soccer for Michigan State, four other former Trojan players have continued this sport on the college level. Jessica Hayes '94, Stacey Portenga '95 and Wendy Boynton '96 all are playing for Albion College, and Sarah LaBelle '95 has pursued soccer on Northern Michigan University's team. As the Traverse City soccer program continues to grow, there will most likely be many more Trojan grads playing college soccer in the future.

CLASS A SOCCER ALL-STATE

	First Team	Honorable Mention
1993		Mindy Swartz

ACADEMIC ALL-STATE

1991	Erin O'Connell	
1994		Stacey Emerich
1995	Stacey Portenga	

GIRLS SOCCER COACHES

Harriet Grueber	1990-1992
Chet Salisbury	1993-present

1996 girls soccer team, with best record to date. Front Row: Kinsley Robinson, Macare Kelly, Amanda Alward, Danielle Gore, Diedra O'Hare, Liz Tank, Lauren Beers, Nicole Cook. Second Row: Alyssa Korhonen, Emily Bowerman, Trisha Plum, Brooke Schulz, Sarah Stilwill, Natalie Ploskey, Mary Richter. Top Row: Assistant Coach Joe Osterling, Kelly Blum, Allison Rice, Wendy Boynton, Laura Blodgett, Jill Mueller, Erin Williams, Veleska Novorolsky, Coach Chet Salisbury.

22

Girls Golf

By Jennie Stratton

"Life is like the game of golf."

– Author Unknown

In 1587, the first woman golfer, Mary Queen of Scots, was executed, though not because her game went south. She popularized the term "caddie" by bringing young French cadets along to assist her. After Mary's execution for treason against Queen Elizabeth of England, the popularity of golf in Scotland declined for a couple hundred years.

Women's golf had a resurgence in the 1800s. The first women's tournament was played in 1810 by the Scottish fishwives at Musselburgh. The St. Andrews Ladies Golf Club was formed in 1867 and by 1886, five hundred women belonged to the club. National tournaments for women soon followed in Scotland, England and America.

Finally, 404 years after the death of the first woman player, girls golf was instituted into the Traverse City High School athletic program. In 1992, over 62 girls showed up for the first year's informational meeting, a turnout that overwhelmed coach Bob Lober. Not all of the girls who attended the meeting ended up trying out for the team, however. Of the original 62, 53 came to tryouts.

After a two-week trial, Coach Lober, along with assistant coaches Pat Walters and Ina Davis, selected the varsity squad of 12 to 16 players. The remainder of the girls were encouraged to join the intramural team so they could continue to improve their skills. Although it was officially a varsity sport, the 1991 girls golf team was funded by the Traverse City Junior Golf Association.

Overall, the 1991 season finished fairly well for a first-year team. The varsity ended with a record of two wins and five losses, while the junior varsity had three wins and two losses. In the six tournaments they attended, Traverse City took from fourth to tenth places.

On Friday, May 17, 1991, the Trojan girls finished sixth in their regional tournament. Coach

Lober responded to their finish by saying, "This was a great first year." He went on to comment, "The top three teams were all ranked in the top four in the state. If we were in another regional we might've qualified for the state meet." Low scorer on that first team was Missy Riggs, who achieved All-State Honorable Mention status for her first year on the team.

1992 brought about an outstanding season with the number of tournaments having increased to eight. In these eight, the Trojan girls golf team took five tournament titles. The varsity record improved to 16-0, and the junior varsity finished 2-0.

That year, the girls finished first at regionals, a vast improvement over the previous year's score. The team shot a 340, 27 strokes less than the second place finisher, Grandville. Missy Riggs led the Trojans with a 79. Her score broke the school record and equaled a personal best for Riggs. The regional win earned the team a trip to the state tournament.

East Lansing pulled away with an overall score of 347, leading them to a first-place finish. Left behind them, with a score of 376, were the Trojan girls. A disappointing finish like this one, however, did not seem as such to the team. "After playing so well in the regional we felt we had a good shot at winning, but the kids didn't play as well as they hoped. Still, I told them they have nothing to be ashamed of. Fifth in the state isn't bad for a team that's only been in existence for two seasons," said Coach Lober. Missy Riggs earned All-State for a successful season and Kathryn Kendall was All-State Honorable Mention.

PROMISING TO BE ANOTHER EXEMPLARY YEAR, the Traverse City girls entered the 1993 season strong. Expectations were high and the girls were going to try to live up to their potentials. Once again, they had perfect varsity records and near-perfect tournament records. The Gold varsity hailed 11-0, the Black varsity 5-0, and Gold won five tournaments.

On May 11, Traverse City competed in the Kalamazoo Golf Invitational. Upon first glance it appeared they had been edged by Ann Arbor Pioneer by two strokes. All of the officials saw it that way and no one questioned the final scores. Then Coach Lober received a phone call from a parent on Wednesday. The parent had just read the newspaper article on the previous day's tournament. Something about the scores did not ring true, so he recalculated the scores. Sure enough, Traverse City had won by two strokes. Coach Lober then called the officials who re-evaluated the scores, and it was true; Traverse City had won!

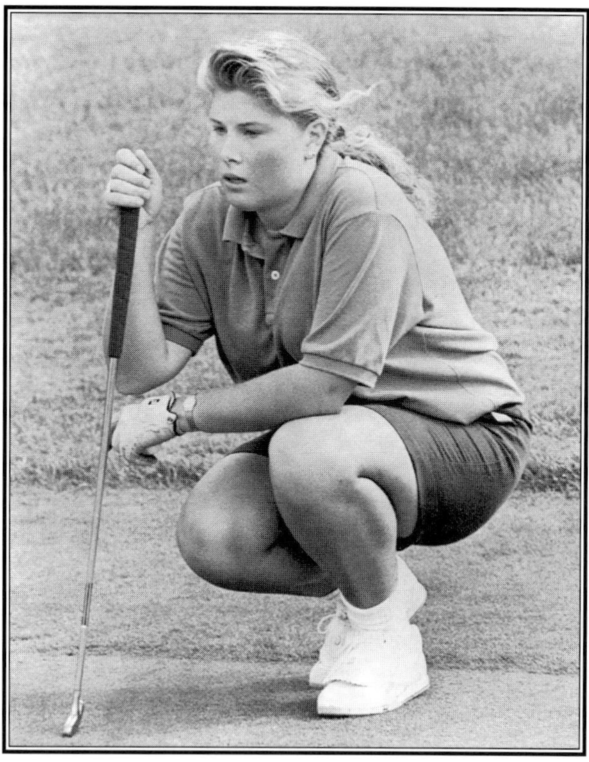

Missy Riggs studies the green before putting.

After being rated number one in the state for Class A, Traverse City entered the regional tournament ready. The team, however, could not top their previous year's score. This year at regionals the Trojans finished second to Grandville with a score of 366.

In 1993, the format for the golf finals was changed. Instead of one match that decided the top team in the state, there were now two matches on two separate days. On the first day of the tournament, the top 15 teams that qualified through regional play would compete. The top ten teams from that day's play then continue in the state finals the following day.

During the first day of play, Traverse City was in second place. They trailed Ann Arbor Pioneer by 20 strokes with a score of 358. Coach Lober was confident that they would have a comeback and defeat Pioneer. On the second day it appeared that Traverse City would maintain their second place finish. Then, in a twist of irony, senior Missy Riggs was disqualified. This unfortunate happening changed Missy's personal finish from the top ten and the team slipped from second to fourth.

Missy was disqualified because of a rules infraction. She was on the sixth hole and she was walking up to mark her ball on the green. As she was approaching the hole, another player's ball struck Missy as it was rolling up onto the green. After striking her, it rolled about five or six inches. Someone in the crowd reported it and thus Missy was no longer eligible for play. However, Missy was named to the All-State Super Team, while Gretchen Shaw was Class A All-State and Emilie Klohs Honorable Mention.

1994 was the fourth year of the girls varsity golf team at Traverse City High School. Three team members who had been on the team the inaugural year were now seniors. These girls, Jamie Haines, Carrie Hunt and Gretchen Shaw, led the team to further excellence. Coach Lober commented on how far these players had progressed in just four years, "I remember these ... seniors as freshmen learning the game.... I remember our first ever match.... Gretchen shot 103, Jamie shot 119 and Carrie shot 130.... Little did I know then that in four years these girls would be ... All-Staters on the golf courses throughout the state." By 1994, these golfers had made vast improvements as Shaw was then averaging 87.8 and both Haines and Hunt 90.2.

Once again in 1994, the Trojan girls team had perfect varsity records and respectable tournament finishes. Gold varsity had a five and zero finish and the Black, six and zero. In the ten tournaments that Gold competed in, they took three firsts and five seconds.

Before going into the regional match, Traverse City was ranked second in the state, following Kalamazoo Central. The Trojans proved their reputation yet again on May 21, 1994, cruising to a 23-stroke lead over their closest competitor. Coach Lober credited the regional victory to the depth of the team. Five of the top 12 finishers belonged to the Trojan team (Gretchen Shaw, 2nd; Carrie Hunt, 5th; Jamie Haines, 8th; Melody Orr, 11th; and Jill Kalat, 12th).

Keeping with the previous year's format, the state finals were again a two-day tournament played at Michigan State University's East and West Forest Akers Courses. After the first day Traverse City was ranked third. In between the Trojans and the state title were the teams that were ranked first and third in the state prior to the state tournament.

On the second day, Traverse City improved upon its previous day's score by eight strokes. However, this still was not enough to pull ahead of

Gretchen Shaw watches the flight of her shot.

Ann Arbor Pioneer or Bloomfield Hills Lahser. Overall, the Trojan girls finished third in the state with a score of 764. On the academic side, however, Traverse City was the state champion. Their average GPA was 3.72 which was higher than that of the other top ten finishing teams. Receiving All-State honors were Gretchen Shaw, Carrie Hunt and Jamie Haines.

With only two seniors on the team this year, and both competing at the junior varsity level, 1995 appeared to be a rebuilding year for the team. Their record, however, continued to be better than average. Gold varsity finished out the season with a record of 6-0 and the Black varsity was 6-1.

The 1995 regional tournament was the toughest that Traverse City had seen yet in their five years of regional play. Being a young team, other teams that had more experience would propose a specific challenge. Regional tournament play lived up to its name and Traverse City took the number four spot. Unfortunately, though, only the top three teams and top five individuals are allowed to advance to the state competition.

The team was not upset with this finish, however, because they had progressed through the season. There are advantages to being a young team. With the exception of two seniors, all of these girls on the team would be returning the following year. Looking forward to 1996, the future looked positive. Sophomore Jill Kalat was All-State Honorable Mention.

The 1996 season saw some of the most difficult weather conditions ever. It was the longest winter and toughest spring, so playing time on a golf course didn't come easily for the first six weeks of the season. Although the team won no tournament titles, the Gold varsity posted a 3-0 record and Black 4-1 in their shortened season. After the team's fourth place at regionals where Bridget Orr was fourth medalist and Jill Kalat took ninth place, both girls were nominated for All-State. Orr's finish qualified her for state competition as an individual.

Traverse City girls golf has progressed rapidly from the first team in 1991. The number of All-Staters is a tribute to how far the golf program has come and the quality of golf the Trojan girls now play.

1994 girls golf team, third in the state. Back Row: Coach Pat Walter, Susan Steves, Jill Kalat, Stacey Balchunas, Gretchen Shaw, Karen Turnquist, Jamie Haines, Carrie Hunt, Stephanie Truax, Coach Bob Lober. Front Row: Jenny Cook, Jenny Colman, Joey Doriot, Sarah Ott, Katie Jacobs, Cassy McQuaid, Bridget Orr, Melody Orr, Leeza Deal.

GIRLS GOLF ALL-STATE SUPER TEAM

1993 Missy Riggs

GIRLS GOLF CLASS A ALL-STATE

	First Team	Honorable Mention	Nominee
1991		Missy Riggs	
1992	Missy Riggs	Kathryn Kendall	
1993	Missy Riggs	Emilie Klohs	
	Gretchen Shaw		
1994	Gretchen Shaw		
	Jamie Haines		
	Carrie Hunt		
1995		Jill Kalat	
1996			Jill Kalat

TROJAN GIRLS GOLF COACH

1991-present Bob Lober

HALL OF FAME ATHLETICS

In 1952, photographer Bud Moyer established the Bo-Gi Hall of Fame to honor seniors from Traverse City and St. Francis who had excelled in particular areas. Because of the decline of senior high attendance at the Bo-Gi, the Bo-Gi Hall of Fame was renamed the Trojan Hall of Fame in 1970. Pictures of award recipients were then hung for one year at Traverse City Senior High instead of at the Bo-Gi.

For the early years of this award, some information could not be found. Listed below are names of the Athletic Award recipients which were available.

BO-GI HALL OF FAME – SPORTS

1952		
1953	Ned Kramer	Betty Lou Wolf
1954	Dave Bowers	
1955	Bob Pemberton	
1956		
1957	Dick Bezile	
1958		
1959		
1960		
1961	Jim Anderson	
1962		
1963	Glenn Merchant	
1964	Bill Alpers	
1965	Steve Lockman	
1966	Jerry Stanek	
1967	Paul Jacobs	
1968	John Naymick	
1969	Steve Wehr	
1970	Steve Rollo	

TROJAN HALL OF FAME - ATHLETICS

1971	James Demin	
1972	Dave Whiteford	
1973	Craig Gilmore	
1974	Thomas Chase	
1975	Paul Schneider	
1976	Mark Brammer	Julie Pulcipher
1977	Dave Mahn	Polly Prouty
1978	Mark Candey	Barb Becker
1979	Jeff Whiting	Lynne Richards
1980	Terry Goodell	Cynthia Newhouse
1981	Bill Core	Kristin Zimmerman
1982	Steve Majerle	Kelly Costigan
1983	Dan Majerle	Danielle Daniels
1984	Greg Bohn	Molly Piche'
1985	John Ansted	Biz Gaff
1986	Tim Lamie	Kimberly Hondorp
1987	Chris Bohn	Suzy Merchant
1988	Lance Morgan	Jennifer Dunsmore
1989	Greg Lobdell	Cara Sonnemann
1990	Brent Manthei	Meg Wilson
1991	Jason C. Smith	Amy Portenga
1992	Shawn Alpers	Libby Hoxsie
1993	Bryan Nykerk	Erika Schimik
1994	Samuel Sheffer	Gretchen Shaw
1995	Ryan Senn	Jillian Gregory
1996	Anders Kelto	Charla Holmes

The Dick Mattern Trojan Athlete-Scholar of the Year

The Trojan Athlete-Scholar of the Year Award is presented annually to the graduating male and female who best exemplify excellence in interscholastic athletics combined with high academic achievement. It is dedicated to the memory of Dick Mattern, a local businessman who through his life-style was an inspiration to all who knew him and who had a never-ending faith in the youth of Traverse City Senior High.

1973	Craig Gilmore	
1974	Tom Chase	
1975	Paul Schneider	
1976	Chris Buday	Jane Gilmore
1977	David Mahn	Carolyn Keesor
1978	Mark Spencer	Barbara Richards
1979	Brian Blevins	Barbara Bell
1980	Larry Czubak	Cindy Newhouse
1981	Jon Gauthier	Patty Cartwright
1982	Steve Majerle	Lori Peek
1983	Jonas Neihardt	Kathryn Skendzel
		Kristin Stehouwer
1984	John Wilson	Molly Piche'
1985	John Ansted	Karen Howe
1986	Chris Hathaway	Kim Hondorp
1987	Josh Fiebing	Mollie Schwarm
	Mark DeMeester	
1988	Nick Brown	Anne Mudgett
1989	Dave Rutkowski	Mary Kroupa
1990	Sean Murphy	Renee Huckle
1991	Geoff Moeke	Amy Portenga
1992	Jeff Gregory	Jennifer Hunt
1993	Bryan Nykerk	Karlene Kurtz
1994	Brian Lishawa	Rebecca Froehlich
1995	Matt Maitland	Stacey Portenga
1996	Kevin Sonnemann	Jill Orlikowski

The Trojan School & Fight Songs

The Trojan Fight Song, composed by Pete Clancy and John Davis in 1947, and the "Black and Gold" Alma Mater written by Karl Fisher in 1910, were both produced when these lyricists were Traverse City high school students. Pete Clancy explained that he and Davis, a high school band member, were part of a group who liked to put on pep assemblies before big games. Clancy and Davis talked about a pep song and produced it one night between breaks of Clancy's job as a part-time announcer at WTCM. Trojan Band Director Thad Hegerberg later re-scored it in 1966.

"The Black and Gold"
By Karl Fisher, Class of 1911

Every high school has its colors, of brown, red, white, or blue,
And every high school student to these colors should be true;
So we'll try to do our duty to the colors ne'er grown old,
And fight for good old Traverse and the dear old Black and Gold.

So we'll strive in all our studies, to prove to all the world,
That the Black and Gold of Traverse is the best flag yet unfurled;
On the gridiron, track and diamond; she leads the brave and bold,
So let us shout for gladness and the dear old Black and Gold.

When we leave the dear old high school, and face the world alone,
We'll think of days we've spent here as the best we've ever known;
And we hope in years to follow, that the story will be told,
How the flag that won the vict'ry was the dear old Black and Gold.

Trojan Fight Song
By Peter Clancy and John Davis, Class of 1947

Let's give a cheer for dear old Traverse
Come on and boost that score sky high,
And let the North woods ring with glory
For the tales of Central High.
And watch out you who stand against us
For we're out to win tonight.
We're gonna add to the glory of the
Black & Gold with the cry COME ON, FIGHT!!
And watch out you who stand against us
For we're out to win tonight.
We're gonna add to the glory of the
Black & Gold with the cry COME ON, FIGHT!!

Information on school songs taken from excerpts of *Booster News* article written by Ken Bell.

Appendix

The names listed below can be found in the following sections of Cheers:

Acknowledgements.............A
Appendix...........................AP
Baseball................................B
Book Jacket........................BJ
Boys Basketball..................BB
Boys Cross Country..........BC
Boys Golf..........................BG
Boys Soccer........................BS
Boys Track.........................BT
Cheerleading.......................C
Cross Country Skiing.....XCS
Downhill Skiing...........DHS
Football................................F
Foreward..........................FD
Girls Basketball................GB
Girls Cross Country......GCC
Girls Golf.........................GG
Girls Soccer......................GS
Girls Track........................GT
Gymnastics..........................G
Hockey...............................H
Introduction..........................I
Preface.................................P
Softball................................S
Swimming.......................SW
Tennis.................................T
Volleyball...........................V
Wrestling...........................W

Cell, Mike ....BT
Cerny, Ryan ....BG
Challender, Jack.......................F
Chamberlain, Allison..............V
Chambers, Liz...................DHS
Chambers, Sara ....DHS, T
Chandler, Jeff ....H
Chandler, Tom ....BG, H
Chapman, Dan ....F
Chapman, Dave ....BC
Chapman, Virginia C
Chappell, Gordon ....BB
Chapple, Tina ....S
Chase, Bob ....BT, F
Chase, Denny ....A, J
Chase, Thomas..................AP, F
Chervenka, G...........................B
Childs, Ross ....H
Chile, Scott ....W
Chirgwin, Chris ....DHS, T
Chirgwin, Erika ......DHS, GCC
Chrenka, Scott ....BS
Christopher, Brian.................BT
Christopher, Dale ....F
Christopher, Kathleen.............C
Chupp, Scott ....F
Cirtiss, Jean...........................BB
Cizek, Tom ....BG, F
Clancy, Peter ....AP
Clark, Chris ....S
Clark, Henry......................DHS
Clark, Jack ....S, W
Clark, Jeremy...........................S
Clark, Kelly ....F
Clark, Peter ....BG
Clark, Shawn ....W
Clark, Tom ....BB
Clarke, Al ....S
Clarke, Cathy........................GT
Clarke, James ....S
Clarke, Kevin ....BT
Clarke, Patty ....S
Cleland, Jeff.............................F
Cleveland..............................BB
Cleveland, Lloyd ....BT
Culp, Dan ....DHS
Coats, Dan ....BS
Cobb, Renee ....GCC
Cockrum, Alexa ....DHS
Cockrum, Lyra..................DHS
Coddington, Dan.................BT
Coesens, Kurt..........................H
Coffey, Jill V
Cogger, Ross ....S
Cole, Clark ....F
Cole, Morrell ....F
Cole, Vic ....F
Colenso, Mike ....H
Coles, Dan ....XCS
Colligan, Amy...................DHS
Collings, Toubo ....DHS
Collins, Ben ....S
Collins, Chris....................BT, S
Collins, John ....T
Collins, Matt ....F
Collins, Phil ....S
Collins, Ray.............................F
Colman, Jenny ....GG
Columbus, David...............XCS
Columbus, Jenny ....T
Comstock, Mike ....FD
Connell, John........................BG
Constant, Jon ....A, BB, T
Cook, Jennifer ......GCC, C, GG
Cook, Jon ....BT
Cook, Kriss...........................GS
Cook, Laurie.........................GT
Cook, Nicole ....GS
Cook, Randy ....F
Corbett, Barbara...................BT
Corbin, Misha ....GS
Core, Bill ....AP, B, F
Core, Jackie ....DHS
Core, Ken ....DHS, F
Core, Mike ....BB
Core, Rich.........................DHS
Cornwell, Gordon ....BC
Cornwell, Mollie...............GCC
Cornwell, Steve ....DHS
Correll, Adair ....T
Correll, Danielle.................XCS
Costigan, Kelly ....AP, S
Cottom, Cindy ....DHS
Coulter, Craig..........................F
Coulter, Melzar ....XCS
Courtade, Bobbie ....S
Courtade, Carrie......................S
Courtade, Matt ....BC
Cowell, Joey ....DHS
Cox, Jack ....BB, F
Cox, Mac.......................BB, BT
Cox, Mark ....F
Cox, Morgan.....................DHS
Coy, Marian ....GB
Cozzens, Bruce ....F, T
Cozzens, Jeff ....F
Cozzens, Matt ....T
Crain ....BT
Crain, Mike..........................BC
Cramer, Mike ....BC
Crammer, Kelly ....G
Crampton, Richard ....DHS, BC
Crandall, Drew ....BB
Crawford, Bill ....F
Crawford, Charles................BG
Crawford, Doug ....BB
Crewes, Christie ....G
Crewes, Dave ....S
Cross, Casey ....DHS, T
Crossley, Mark ....S
Crossley,Pat ....GB
Cullen, Joe ....J, BB
Culp, Dan ....DHS
Culp, Diane........BC, GCC, GT
Cummings, Jude ....H
Cummings, Larry.................BC
Cunningham, Dave.......BC, BT,
....DHS
Curry, Amy.............................S
Cutler, Katie ....S
Czubak, Larry ....AP, F
Dalrymple, Mike ....F
Dancer, Mark.....................DHS
Daniels, Chris ....S
Daniels, Chuck........................F
Daniels, Danielle ....AP, GB, GT
Daniels, Mark V
Davidson, Misty ....S
Davis, Corbin ....T
Davis, Ina ....GG
Davis, John ....AP
Davis, Kelly ....XCS
Davison, Laurie.......................T
Davison, Leslie..............DHS, S
Davison, Will ....S
Deacon, Debbie.......................V
Deal, Leeza ....GG

Dean, Garth ....B
Dean, Nancy............................C
Dear, Ryan ....BC
DeBruyn, Sara ....GCC, GT
Decker, Mike ....BC, BT
Decker, Scott.........................BC
Decker, Tias.............................F
Decker, Tobin...........................F
Deering, Jim..........................BC
Deikman, Coach......................F
Deir, Jim..................................F
DeKuiper, Jessica ....GCC
DeLonge, Eric........................BS
DeMarsh, Ryan ....S
DeMeester, Mark ....AP, F
Demin, James.....................AP, F
Denison, Doug.........................F
Dennis, Aaron ....A, J, BS, BT
Dennis, Courtney ....GB
Dennis, Eugene.....................BG
Dennis, Maurie ....F
Dennis, Sara..........................GB
DeNoyer, Jerry ....BC
Denton, Craig.......................BC
DePew, Brad...........................F
Derrick, Dave...........................F
Desmond, Hugh ....BT
DesPress, Harry.......................F
Detar, Dave ....H
Detar, John.............................H
Dettwiler, Jason ....BT, F
Dettwiler, Jeff........................BT
Devries, Karl ....T
DeWolfe, Jim ....BC
DeYoung, Daryl.....................BS
DeYoung, Dawn ....GB
DeYoung, Nick ....BG
DeYoung, Robert ....F
Diehl, Jim ....W
Diehl, Mike ....S
Diekman, Bill...........................F
Diller, Bob...............................F
Dincanson, A.J. ....F
Diola, Toni ....W
Ditta, Biz ....T
Dodge, Allison......................GT
Dodge, Rachel ....GCC
Dohm, Steve............................F
Dohm, Kathy ....GT

Domres, Sherry........................V
Don, Steve...............................F
Donahey, Tim ....BT
Donaldson, Jenny V
Donick, Bob............................F
Donner, Kelly V
Donoho, James.................BB, F
Donohoe, Cheryl......................C
Dooley, Jill ....S
Doriot, Joey..........................GG
Dorman, Francie...............DHS
Dornbos, Emily........................S
Doty, Matt............................BT
Dow, Jeff..............................BG
Dowden..................................F
Dowdney, Rachel ....G, S
Downer, Clyde ....F
Downer, Roger..................DHS
Downey, Lisa ....G
Drake, Bob ....BT
Drake, Dave ....F
Drake, Jo..............................GT
Draper, Mary Jane C
Dreves, Lori ....GCC
Drew, George.......................BG
Drilling, Mike ....H
Drulard, Robert....................BB
Drzweicki, Pat.........................C
Dunscombe, Amy ....T, V
Dunsmore, Don...........A, DHS
Dunsmore, Jennifer .AP, DHS, S
DuPries, Joe.............................F
Durocher, Jason ....BB
Durocher, Jeff..........................F
Dutmers, Chad ....F
Dwyer, Allys..............GCC, GT
Dye, Dave ....BS, S
Dyke, Tom ....BC
Dyksterhouse, Trevor............BB
Dykstra, Greta ....GS
Ealy, Larry ....F
Eash, T.J. ....BC
Easling, Marty ....F
Ebinger, Jennifer ....S
Ebinger, Lynn ....A, S
Eckhardt, Bruce ....T
Eckhold, Julie..........................T
Edginton, Jackie...................GT
Edson, Nick..........................P, A

Edwards, Joyce ....T
Egeler, Bob ....F
Ehrenberger, Darin..................F
Ehrenberger, Joe..................B, F
Ehrenberger, Scott ....F
Eikey, Carolyn......................GB
Eisner, Jim ....W
Eister, Matt ....XCS
Eldredge, Kristy..................S, G
Eley, Robin ....GT
Elkins, Ben........................DHS
Elkins, Nate ....DHS
Elliot, Robert........................BC
Elliott, Dan ....DHS
Elliott, Jon.........................DHS
Ellsworth, Noel........................S
Elsenheimer, Jason ....BS
Elsenheimer, John ....BC, BT
Elzinga, Al ....B
Elzinga, Craig..........................B
Elzinga, Steve........................W
Elzinga, Tim ....BB
Emerich, Jason ....BS
Emerich, Stacey ....GS
Emerson, Jack ....B, F
Enders, Doug..........................T
Enger ....B
English, Claudia C
Ensfield, Karl........................BT
Erb, Carl.................................F
Erde ....F
Erfourth, Dan ....F
Erickson, Justin ....F
Ernsberger, Ron ....XCS
Erway, Pat..............................H
Esman, Brian...........................F
Estes, Bill ....BB
Evans, Shane ....DHS
Evert, Rich ....BC
Exerby.....................................F
Exo, Bill ....S
Exo, Dan ....F
Fajardo, Kevin ....S
Fajardo, Laura..........................S
Fajardo, Ryan...........................S
Falberg, Bruce...................A, BS
Farley, Gary ....BC
Farrell, Jeff............................BG
Feiker, Jeanne....................DHS

Kroups, Mary ....AP
Krupilski, Scott ....BT
Kuemin, Rick ....F
Kulik, Nikki..........................GT
Kullman, Frank.....................BS
Kundrata, Fred ....BT
Kundrata, Rich ....W
Kurt, Mike...............................S
Kurtz, Karlene ....AP, GCC
Kurtz, Karlene......................GT
Kurtz, Mike ....BB
Kuschell, Andre ....W
Kyselka, Dottie C
Kyselka, Lottie ....GB
Kyselka, Luana..................DHS
Kyselka, Roberta ....DHS
Kysleka, Margaret ....DHS
LaBelle, Sarah ....GS
LaCharite, Darren ....BG, H
LaFranier, Myrtle ....C, GB
Lalas, Alexi ....BS
Lamb, John ....BC
Lambert, Matt............BS, DHS
Lamie, Tim ....AP, F, W
Lamott, Ryan ....XCS
Landis, Ross...........................W
Lane, Ben ....BS
Lane, Jack ....BT
Lang, Hunter ....BC
Langs, R.D. ....B
Lannin, Roy ....BT
Lantz, Pam ....DHS
Larcom, Ken............................F
Lardie, Stephen ....B, F
Lasich, Jeff.......................BT, W
Lather, Irene ....GB
Lather, Lori ....DHS
Laughter, Rosanna ....GCC
Lautner, Ben ....BC, BT
Lautner, Bernie ....F
Lautner, Dan.....................DHS
Lautner, Doug ....F
Lautner, Florabelle ....GB
Lautner, Michelle ....G
Lautner, Tammy................DHS
Lautner, Terry.......................BC
Lautner, Tod......................DHS
Lavalley, Dave.......................BC
Lawrence, George....................F
Lawson, Mike ....BS
Lawton, Betty ....GB
Leete, Jessica.........................GB
Leete, Lucas ....BB
Lehman, Gail............................S
Lehnhardt, JAn C
Lehouiller, Dan ....F, DHS
Leider, C.................................F
Leider, Kim V
Leighton, Curtis ....F
Leighton, Will ....B, F
Leismer, Bill.............................F
Lemcool, Carl.......................BT
LeMieux, Joe ....BC
Lendrum, Chuck ....A, S
Lenzini, John ....F
Leppek, Dave ....F
Lerew, Eric ....BC
Leuenberger, Cam.............DHS
Leuenberger, Justin..................F
Lewallen, Kristi.......................G
Lewis, Mary Beth ....GS
Lewy, David ....BC
Liggett, Eric ....F
Ligon, Chuck....................DHS
Ligon, Len.........................DHS
Ligon, Matt ....BS
Lilly, Margaret.........................T
Linder, Doug ....F
Lindquist, Donn ....F
Lindsay, Ken ....DHS
Lindsay, Tom.....................DHS
Linger, Jeff.................BC, BT, S
Linsell, Chris ....BC
Lint, Jon ....BS, XCS
Lint, Max...............................W
Lishawa, Brian ....AP, BS
Lishawa, Shane...............BB, BS
Littlefield, Tom ....BS
Livingston,Jeff ....H
Lobdell, Greg ....AP, BT, F
Lobdell, Jeff ....H
Lobdell, Marty....................F, H
Lober, Bob ....A, BG, GG
Lober, John ....A, BC, BT, FD
Lockman, Al ....B
Lockman, Jeff.......................GB
Lockman, Steve ....AP, F
Lockwood, Bruce..............DHS
Lockwood, Heather.......DHS, T
Lockwood, Karen..............DHS
Lockwood, Ted ....DHS
Loesel, Charlie......................BT
Loesel, John ....BT
Loesel, Mike............................T
Lombard, Janet ....T
Long, Tracey......................DHS
Longcore, Bob ....F
Look, Brandon ....H
Loomis, Bob.....................BT, T
Loomis, DIck ....B, T
Lorenz, Brandi C
Lorenz, Chad ....H
Lotan, Jim ....BT
Loveland, Terry........................F
Lovell, Joan ....DHS
Low, Andy..............................B
Ludka, Ben ....BT
Lueck, Dane.......................XCS
Lukens, Don ....BC
Lund, Joe ....BS
Lupiloff, Keith ....BB
Lutes, Kendra ....S
Luttinen, Russ..............A, DHS
Luzac, Dave ....H
Lynch, Jim ....F
Lynch, Ken........................DHS
Lynch, Pam............................G
Lyon, Brett..............................S
Lyon, Mike C
MacDonald, Gordon...........BB,
....................................BG, F, T
MacEachran, Bob............BC, T
Machata, Amy ....F, GS
MacInnis, Maxine...................C
MacIntosh, Emily...............T, V
MacIntosh, Harold..................F
MacIntosh, Julie.............A, T, V
Mack, Dean ....F
Mack, Sue C
Mackkonen, Janice ....S
MacPherson, R........................F
Madion, Cae ....DHS
Madion, Matt ....DHS
Madion, Megan ....DHS
Magoun, Andy ....S
Mahan, Abby ....GB
Mahn, David.....................AP, F

Miller, Gail ....G
Miller, Kathy ....T
Millien, Bill ....DHS
Milligan, Dave ....BG
Milliken, Bill ....BB, BT, T
Milliken, J.P. ....T
Milliken, Jim ....DHS, T
Milliken, Penny ....T
Million, Craig ....BC
Million, Greg ....BC
Million, Steve ....BS, XCS
Miner, Todd ....F
Mixer, Lynn C
Moeke, Geoff ....AP, F
Mohrhardt, Mike ....DHS
Molleman, John ....F
Monroe, Marion ....GB
Monson, Kurt ....F
Montague, Bert ....B
Monte, Caroline ....T
Monte, Judith ....T
Montez, Steve ....W
Montie, Emily ....GT
Montie, Marcus ....BT
Moon, Erika ....GT
Moore, Jenny ....T
Moore, Jon ....F
Moore, Tim ....T
Moore, William ....B
Moore. Jennifer ....T
Moorman, Chuck ....F
Moorman, Tom ....F
Morey, Kim ....GT
Morgan, Branbon ....BT
Morgan, Don ....F
Morgan, Jack ....BB
Morgan, Lance ....AP, F
Morrison, Clay ....XCS
Morrison, Doug ....T
Morrissey, Sean ....W
Morton, Derek ....F
Mosher, Jeff ....A, W
Moss, Garren ....BS
Moss, Gary ....FD
Moyer, Bob ....F
Mudgett, Anne .AP, XCS, GCC, GT
Mueller, Jill ....GS
Mullins, Dan ....BC
Munn, Vicki ....S
Munro, Dugald ....F
Murchie, Jack ....F
Murdick, Dave ....BS
Murner, Jim ....DHS
Murner, Rob ....H
Murphy, Collin ....GS
Murphy, Dick ....A, B, H
Murphy, Sean ....AP
Murray, Aaron ....T
Murray, Pat ....BS
Music, Mark ....DHS, F
Myer, Angie ....GCC
Myers, Bill ....BT
Nachazel, Meghan ....GB
Nadlicki, Mike ....W, F
Nadlilcki, Steve ....F
Nadolski, Chris ....GB
Nagy, Jim ....F
Nagy, Pat ....DHS
Nalcezak, Tony ....H
Namboothiri, Jay ....BC, BT
Naperalski, Jerry ....F
Naymick, John ....AP, BB, F
Neal, Ken ....BT
Neihardt, Coach ....BT
Neihardt, Jeremy ....BS
Neihardt, Joe ....BT
Neihardt, Jonas ....AP
Nelson, Dick ....B
Nelson, Jack DeWitt ....F
Nelson, John ....T
Nelson, Julie ....T
Nelson, Karen V
Nelson, Ken ....B
Nelson, Kevin ....BT, DHS
Nelson, Laura ....G
Nerbonne, Pat ....BB, F
Nerlinger, Amil ....F
Nesvacil, Kathy ....GCC
Neu, Kelly ....A, V
Neuman, Bob ....F
Neuman, Lance ....BG
Newhouse, Cindy ...AP, DHS, V
Newhouse, Cynthia ....AP
Newhouse, G.J. ....DHS
Newman, Scott ....BC
Newman, Steph ....S
Newmann, Miss ....GB
Newstead, Violet ....GB
Newton, Bud ....F
Newton, Germaine ....GB
Niblack, Matt ....BB
Nichols, Cathy V
Nichols, Geri ....S
Nickerson, Allene ....GB
Niehardt, Joe ....BC, F
Nielson, Steve ....BC
Nienhouse, Greg ....BT
Nienhouse, Todd ....F
Niezgoda, Eric ....GB, GS
Niswander, Bob ....BC
Nixon, Nick ....DHS
Noland, Jim ....F
Noland, Mike ....F
Noller, Kurt ....BT
Norcross, Pete ....DHS
Nordjford, Matt ....J
Northrup, Hubert ....F
Northway, Toby ....H
Norton, Dondi ....W
Norton, Jason ....W
Noteware, Thomas ....B
Nottke, Rick ....T
Novak, Bill ....T
Novak, Connie ....GB
Novak, Tom ....T
Noverr, Peter ....XCS
Novorolsky, Valeska ....GS
Novotny, Archie ....F
Novotny, Dorothy ....GB
Novotny, Frank ....B
Nutten, Katherine ....GB
Nuyens, Pat ....DHS
Nye, Mindy ....XCS
Nykerk, Bryan ....AP, T
Nykerk, Jill ....T
Nykerk, Larry ....A, T
Nykerk, Steve ....BB, T
Nyland, Sue ....G
O'Brien, Dan ....BC
O'Brien, Lloyd ....F
O'Connell, Erin ....GS
O'Connell, Kathleen ....A, GS
O'Hare, Deidre ....GS
O'Hearn, Charlie ....H
O'Hearn, Kevin ....H
O'Heren, Larry ....BC

Oberling, Bill.................BC, BT
Oberling, Jim........................BC
Ockert, John...........................W
Ogden, Jerry..........................BT
Ohrenberger, John...................F
Oien, Lyndsee..........................S
Olman, George........................F
Olman, Jason.........................BS
Olson, Jim.........................DHS
Olson, John.............................F
Olson, Larl............................BC
Olson, Tony............................F
Ooley, Jim........BT, DHS, F, FD
Oom, Kristi..........................GB
Oosse, Chris...........................F
Oosse, Steve..........................BT
Opper, Vince..........................H
Orchard, Ken................BC, BT
Orlikowski, Jill..........AP, GT, G
Orr, Bridget.........................GG
Orr, Les.....................BB, BT, F
Orr, Melody.........................GG
Oster, Andrew.......................BB
Osterling, Joe........................GS
Ostlund, Roy....................BB, F
Ott, Cindy...........................GB
Ott, Grace............................GS
Ott, Johnny........................B, F
Ott, Sarah............................GG
Otten, Doug..........................BS
Overholt, Jerry......................BG
Overholt, Robert...................BG
Owen, Dan...........................BT
Owens, Jeff........................DHS
Owens, Jim.......................DHS
Owens, Steve.....................DHS
Padgett, Courtney....................S
Paffi, Jim..............................BT
Page, Ben...............................S
Pahl, Marcie.........................GT
Palmer, Jim............B, BS, DHS
Pampu, John............................F
Panatella, Joe........................BC
Parasida, Nicole....................GS
Park, Bob......................BC, BT
Park, Tom.............................BC
Parker, Tim...........................BC
Parks, Jason............................S
Parr, Edith.......................C, GB
Parshall, Doug.........................F
Parsons, Meredith.............DHS
Pascoe, Lindsay.................GCC
Paulos, Cathy....................DHS
Paupore, Joe....................BT, W
Paupore, Leslie....................G, S
Pawloski, Rob........................W
Payne, Jenny.............GCC, GT
Payne, Patti.......................GCC
Peavler, Ken..........................BT
Peck, Chris............................BB
Peek, Kim...............................V
Peek, Lori.......................AP, GT
Peet, C.H. Coach....................B
Pelon, Jennifer..............GS, GB
Pelto, Julie.........................DHS
Pelto, Mauri.........................BC
Pelto, Tom............................BC
Pemberton, Bob.........BB, BT, F
Penney, Lonny.........................F
Pennington, Bill......................F
Pennington, Ike.......................F
Pennington, Levi.....................F
Pennington, Rance................W
Peoples, Aaron.................BT, F
Peoples, Lisa............................S
Perdue, Kevin.........................H
Perdue, Mike..........................H
Perkett, Beth.....................DHS
Perry, George..........................F
Perry, Hank............................F
Perry, John..............................F
Peters, Jenny.............GCC, GT
Peters, Keith.........................BT
Peters, Mike..........................BC
Peterson, Craig........................F
Peterson, Dave........................H
Petertyl, Ruth........................GB
Petroskey, Troy.......................W
Petty, Chip.........................DHS
Petty, Lisa..........................DHS
Pfannenschmidt, Irene.........GB
Phelps, Dave.....................DHS
Phillips, Ann......................XCS
Phillips, Katy......................XCS
Phillips, Mark..........................F
Phillips, Meghan.........XCS, GS
Picard, John..........................BT
Piche', Don....................BG, H
Piche', Molly......AP, GB, GT, V
Piche', Pete...............................S
Pickard, Vickie.....................GB
Piedmonte, Jason....................F
Pierce, Rollie,..........................F
Pierson, Fred.........................BT
Pike, Mary Ellen.....................C
Pillow, Wanda...................GCC
Pilon, Mike..............................F
Pind, Dave...............................F
Pitkaabo, Satu......................GT
Pitman, Stan.........................BS
Pitylak, Alex............................B
Ploskey, Natalie.....................GS
Plosky, Dave..........................BS
Plough, John...........................F
Plum, Jason...........................BS
Plum, Jason........................XCS
Plum, Ryan.........................XCS
Plum, Trisha................XCS, GS
Plummer, Jon................BB, BT
Plummer, Tara......................GB
Podleski, Richard.....................F
Poehlman, Mike...................BT
Portenga, Amy...........AP, DHS,
....GS, T
Portenga, Diane...........A, F, FD
Portenga, Stacey.........AP, GS, T
Portenga, Steve...................XCS
Porter.....................................H
Potter, Cammy..........GCC, GT
Poulin, Annia.......................GS
Powell, Jared............................S
Power, Jeff...............................T
Powers, Lyle............................S
Preston, Jon.............................T
Preston, Steve..........................T
Preston, Tim.........................BC
Prevo, Aaron...............BC, XCS
Prevo, Mike........................XCS
Price, John............................BB
Pritchard, Pete.........................F
Prouty, Polly..................AP, GT
Provins, Dennis.......................F
Provins, Gary..........................F
Prusick, Vince......................FD
Pryor, Jason..........................BB
Ptak, Missy..............................S
Puffer, Nicole..........................F

Pugliese, Vince..........................F
Pulcipher, Gina.........GB, GT, V
Pulcipher, Julie.......................AP
Purvis, Frank ....F
Quick, Gary ....BC
Quinn, Emily........................GS
Quinn, Sean ....S
Quirk, Ellen...............DHS, GS
Rabinski, Norma..................GB
Rademacher, Autumn....GB, GS
Rademacher, Jeff....................BB
Rader, Jon ....BS
Raehl, Alisha ....DHS
Raff, George ....F
Raftshol, Meredith............DHS
Raftshol, Sharon................DHS
Raftshol, Warren ....T
Rahm, Cathy ....T
Rakin, Gary..............................F
Rakin, Greg..............................F
Raven, Terry.......................DHS
Ray, Rocky ....BC
Raymond, Jim.......................BG
Read, Pete ....T
Reamer, Stacie...........................S
Reed, Don ....BT
Reed, Joni ....S
Reed, Sheryl ....GB
Reed,Stefi................................G
Regan, Chris ....BG
Regenmorter, Jane ....S
Reichert, Scott ....S
Reimer, Bert ....F
Reimer, Hubert ....F
Remillard, Lynn...................GT
Renehan, Jack........................BT
Renfer, Bethany ....S
Rennie, Jim ....DHS
Reynolds, Nate ....W
Reynolds, Vern ....F
Rheem, Kat ....S
Ribel, Ryan ....BB
Rice, Allison ....GS
Richard, Dennis.............BS, GS
Richards, Barbara ....AP, GT
Richards, Lynne ..AP, GCC, GT, G
Richards, Tim ....BT, F
Richardson, Nate ....BS
Richardson, Tracy...................G
Richter, Art............................BT
Richter, Mary ....GS
Richter, Richard ....F
Rickard, Sue.............................V
Riddle, Julie.............................S
Rife, Steve.............................BB
Riggs, Brian ....F, H
Riggs, Missy ....GG
Riggs, Susan.........................C, S
Riley, Gail ....T
Ringsmuth, Blake ....T
Ripper, Mike ....H
Risinger, Melissa ....S
Ritchie, Jessica ....S
Ritter, Nicki ....GB, S
Rittman, Jerry ....T
Rixon, Kyle..............................S
Rizer, Jeff..............................BC
Robb, Amy........................DHS
Robb, Matt ....DHS
Robbins, Leroy ....BB
Robbins, Stan ....BT
Robbins, Steve..........................B
Robinson, Kelly ....BG
Robinson, Kinsley ....GS
Robson, Kelly.....................XCS
Rockwood, John..........BS, DHS
Rode, Debbie............GCC, GT
Rodiguez, Pedro ....F
Roebke, Paul..........................W
Rogers, Joe............................BT
Rogers, Sally..........................GT
Rohwetter, Eric ....DHS
Rokos, Frank...........................B
Rokos, Jack..............................F
Rollo, Francis.........................BB
Rollo, Steve ....AP, F
Rombouts, Paul....................BC
Rompola, Ryan ....F
Roney, Stacey..........................G
Roos, Tom ....S
Root, Dale ....BT
Rose, Carson.....................BT, F
Rose, Chris ....T, V
Rosely, Sue...............................S
Rosendale, Dave ....W
Roser, Jenny.......................GCC
Rosetti, Bill..............................F
Rothermel, Bob.....................BC
Round, Dick..........................BB
Round, Michael ....F
Rourke, Carol ....GCC
Roush, Patty ....GT
Rousse, Nicole.......................GS
Rowe, Bob...................BT, XCS
Ruggles, Coach......................BB
Rumanes, Louis........................B
Rumanes, Pete ....F
Rundio, Dave......................XCS
Rundio, Jeff.........................XCS
Runyon, Ken...........................H
Rushlow, Amber C
Russell, Frank ....BT
Rutkowski, Dave.......AP, BG, H
Ruttkofsky, Josh ....F
Sabo, Marena...........................G
Safronoff, Joel........................BC
Salathiel, Kristen ....DHS
Salathiel, Lyndon......A, DHS, T
Salisbury, Chet ....A, BS, GS
Salisbury, Collin ....DHS
Sammons, Paula...................GB
Sampson, William....................B
Samuelson, Dayna...................G
Samuelson, Mandy ....A, G
Samuelson, Trisha ....S
Sanborn, Terry......................F, T
Sander, Amy ....GCC
Sanderson, Joel ....S
Sanford, Dave........................BT
Sarris, George ....F
Sarya, Arne.............................H
Sarya, Dan...............................F
Sarya, Dave.......................BS, H
Savage, Bud..........................B, F
Sbonek, Jim.............................B
Scala, Bim.............................BT
Scala, Ta..................................G
Schafer, Becky ....GB
Schafer, Mark........................BG
Schaub, Brian ....BT
Scheiber, Ty ....BC
Schenk, Francesca.....................S
Schettler, Alane......................GS
Schichtel, Dennis ....F
Schichtel, Mickey C
Schieber, Wendy ....S

Schimik, Erika.....AP, GCC, GT
Schlosser, John ....BC
Schmalenberg, Jeff.................BB
Schmidt, Dave ....T
Schmidt, Ken ....F
Schmidt, Mike ....F
Schneider, Jay ....BC
Schneider, Paul ....AP, DHS
Schnurr, Ben ....H
School, Krisit ....G
Schopieray, Chris.....................G
Schramm, Lisa ....GT
Schreiner, Jerry ....BB
Schroeder, Kelli.........................S
Schroeder, Larry ....BG
Schroeder, Nole ....BC
Schrotenboer, Chum ....BC
Schrotenboer, Sue ....DHS
Schubert, Art......................DHS
Schubert, Kathy.......................G
Schuknecht, Ed ....BG, F
Schuler, Ron ....BB
Schultz, Brad ....H
Schultz, Karl ....BT, F
Schultz, Kim ....T
Schultz, Mike ....BG
Schulz, Brooke ....DHS, GS
Schulz, Marin............DHS, GT
Schwarm, Brad...................DHS
Schwarm, Mollie..AP, DHS, GT
Schwarm, Scott ....DHS
Schwenter, Scott ....BC, BT
Schwert, Brady ....BS
Scott Krupilski ....BT
Scott, Sander ....BS
Scott, Wendi ....GT
Scrubb, Sarah ....T
Scussel, Randy ....W
Scussel, Rick ....F
Sebright, John....................BT, F
Sebright, Ted ....F
Seekins, Sean ....BC
Seeley, Doug ....S
Seeley, Randy ....W
Seipke, Brian ....BG
Selkirk, Larry ....F
Sellers, Larry ....FD
Senn, Ryan.......................AP, BS
Seyler, Greg..............................S
Seyler, Lindsey ....S
Sharp, Rob........................BT, F
Shaw, Ashley ....S
Shaw, Bill ....F
Shaw, Cam ....DHS
Shaw, Eric ....XCS
Shaw, Gretchen..........AP, GG, T
Shaw, John ....BC
Shaw, Jon ....BG
Shawbitz, Tammy C
Sheffer, Judy ....GB
Sheffer, Samuel................AP, BT
Shelby, Justin......................DHS
Sherberneau, Barbara ....DHS
Sherman, Harold ....B, BB
Sherman, Heidi ....XCS
Sherman, Westley................XCS
Shield, Betty.......................DHS
Shield, Sandy ....DHS
Shield, Tom ....DHS
Shields, Tom ....DHS
Shrader, Hugh ....S
Shugart, Greg ....F
Shumsky, Amy........................G
Siderman, Dan ....BC
Sievers, Dan..........................BT
Silva, Sergio ....S
Simmerman, Kain ....F
Simmerman, Myria ....GCC
Simmons, Aaron......................F
Simmons, Steve....................B, F
Simon, Sonja ....GCC
Simone, John...........................F
Simpson, Lester ....BT
Simpson, Megan .....DHS, GCC
Simpson, Mike...................DHS
Sirrine, Abby ....GS
Sirrine, Bill ....GS
Sirrine, John ....BS
Sirrine, Rob ....BS
Sivek, Bob ....F
Sivits, Dave ....F, W
Skeen, Wayne..........................T
Skendzel, Dan ....XCS
Skendzel, Kathryn........AP, DHS
Skendzel, Larry...................XCS
Skendzel, Marybeth ....DHS
Skrubb, Sara ....T, V
Slack, Tim..........................F, BT
Slater, Jack ....F
Slater, Leon...........................BT
Sleder, Dewey ....F
Sleder, Erich......................BT, F
Sleder, Jason.............................F
Sleder, Julius ....BT, F
Sloan, Kari ....GS
Sloan, Tom ....FD
Slocum, Dale...........................B
Smart, Don..............................S
Smedley, John ....B
Smidt, Dave..........................BB
Smith, Jason ....BC, BT
Smith, A.J. ....BT, F
Smith, Amanda.........GCC, GT
Smith, Bill ....W
Smith, Bob..............................T
Smith, Chad ....W
Smith, Cortney ....S
Smith, Dan.............................H
Smith, Darren ....BT, W
Smith, Dudley......................BG
Smith, Ed ....W
Smith, Ethan ....W
Smith, Gramps ....F
Smith, Jason................AP, BT, S
Smith, Jim ....BC
Smith, Justin ....DHS
Smith, Kyle ....H
Smith, Laurie ....T
Smith, Mark..........................BC
Smith, Mike ....BG
Smith, Nate.......................DHS
Smith, Pat...............................H
Smith, Ralph ....B
Smith, Raquel ....GCC
Smith, Scott.............................F
Smith, Stephanie ....S
Smith, Tammy ....GT
Smith, Teya ....GT
Smith, Tim ....BC
Smith, Tim ....F
Smith, Tim ....W
Smits, Jan ....BG
Snell, Brian ....BT
Snell, Kate ....GS
Snow, Martha ....GT
Snushall, Bill............................F
Snyder, Christina ....G

Thirlby, Mary....................DHS
Thirlby, Rick.....................DHS
Thomas ....F
Thomas, Dan ....BB
Thomas, Joe..................BT, F, S
Thomas, Ken........................BB
Thomas, Verlin........................F
Thompson, Cary ....DHS
Thompson, Jeff.......................F
Thompson, Josh.....................H
Thompson, Justin ....H
Thompson, Molly ....GS
Thompson, Pam ....DHS
Thompson, Robert ....FD
Thompson, Scott ....BG, DHS
Thompson, Tonya ....S
Thompson, Ty.........................F
Thompson, Walter ....F
Thoreson, Eric ....T
Thorpe, Tony........................BB
Tibaldi, Joe..............................J
Tiberg, Mike..........................W
Tiesworth, Dan ....GS
Timberlake, Jill ....G
Timberlake, Josh ....XCS
Timmins, Gordon ....F
Titus, Harold........................BT
Toerper, Judy C
Tokie, Dave ....W
Tolene, Laura...........................S
Tomaszewski,Diann.................S
Tomlinson, Libby...............XCS
Tompkins, Budd ....F
Tompkins, Doug ....F
Tompkins, Paul ....F
Topping..................................B
Torbet, Sara.............GCC, XCS
Tornga, Doug ....A, S
Tornga, Lindy..........................S
Tousain, Kyle...................BG, T
Townsend, Ann ....S
Trahan, Erin............................T
Trepte, Hugo........................BG
Trierweiler, Tammy..................S
Truax, Stephanie..................GG
Truelove, Larry ....FD
Trussell, Tim ....S
Tubbs, Mike ....S
Turner, Paul ....S
Turner, Steve...........................H
Turnquist, Karen ....GG
Tway, Jenny ....T
Tylor, Gerald................B, BB, F
Ubl, Jake...............................W
Ufer, Holly...........................GT
Umlor, George......................BB
Underwood, Dan ....BT
Underwood, Sara..................BT
Unger, Bill ....F
Unkefer, Nate ....BT
Upton, Sam ....F
Urban, Emily ....GB
Valade, Sarah ....BS, H
Valerio, Chris...........................F
Van Der Molen, Hilbert ....B
Van Epps, Bill..........................F
Van Peenan, Chuck ....S
VanAlstine, Tom ....BT
VanAntwerp, Joe ....H
VanAntwerp, Tom..................H
VanBrocklin, Jim ....T
Vance, Blake ....S
VanDalson, Jeff........................S
VanDalson, Jessica ....S
VandenBerge, Jill ....T
Vanderley, Ed ....BT
Vanderley, Ralph ....BT
Vanderlinde, Justin ....W
Vandervort, Frank..............F, W
VanderWall, Marge ....DHS
Vann, Kevin ....BC
VanStratt, Jim..........................F
VanWezel, John....................BG
VanWingerden, Erin...BT, GCC
Village Press ....A
Visser, Konrad ....F
Vogelsong ....F
Voelker, Mr...........................BT
Volk, Bryan ....BB, F
Vranich, Chris ....BC
Vrondran, Amy.................GCC
Waddington, John..............XCS
Wadkins, Chance..........BC, BT
Wadsworth, Allison C
Wagaman, Mary C
Wagener, Jim.....................DHS
Wagner, Mandy ....S
Wagner, Scott........................BS
Wagoner, Mike.......................H
Wahl, Sarah..................J, GS, G
Wahl, Vondal ....BB
Wait, Harry ....BT
Waldo, Jill................................S
Waldo, Julie ....S
Wales, Terin ....T
Walker, Polly ....A, GT
Walker, Robert ....BT
Waller, Mike ....F
Walsh, Chas. ....B
Walter, Josh ....F
Walter, Robert ....F
Walters, Bob ....F
Walters, Pat..........................GG
Walton, Stephanie ....GCC
Walton, Stephanie................GT
Wanageshik, Fran..........BB, BT
Wangen, Bruce ....T
Wangen, Norm ....F
Wares, Dale ....BB, F, T
Wares, Mike ....BS
Wares, Sara ....GS
Warmbold, Ben.....................BS
Warmbold, Lori................GS, S
Warner, Jason ....F
Warner, Jim ....H
Warren, Adam.....................BG
Warren, Brad ....F
Warren, Jill ....S
Washburn, Loren ....BG
Waslawski, John.......................S
Waters, Rick ....F
Watkins, Doug.....................BC
Watson, Bob...........................F
Watson, Steffie........................G
Watson, Stephanie ....S
Watts, Dave...........................BS
Weaver, "Buck".......................F
Weaver, Bob ....BG
Weaver, Jim.............................T
Weber, Al ....F, W
Weber, Chad ....XCS
Weber, Dennis.........................F
Weber, Frank ....W
Weber, Holly..............XCS, GT
Weber, Kelly ....GT
Weber, Pat ....J, BS, C, S
Weber, Randy ....W

Weber, Ted....W
Webster, Dave....DHS
Webster, Lisa....T
Weede, Bud....F
Wehr, Chuck....F
Wehr, Steve....AP, F
Wehr, Ward....F
Weir Family....XCS
Weise, Kirsten....XCS
Weitz, Elliott....T
Wells, Craig....BT
Wells, Jeremy....BS
Wells, Mike....DHS
Wenzel, Wey....B
Werner, Bob....DHS
Werner, Jessica....GCC
Werthman, Bill....S
Wetter, Chris....BT
Whalen, Mike....BS
Wharton, Peter....FD
Wheat, Ryan....BC
Wheddock, Stacey....T
Wheeler, Adam....BC, BT
Wheelock, Chet....F
White, Barb....C
Whiteford, Dave....AP, BB,
....BT, F, FD
Whiting, George....BB, BT
Whiting, Jeff....AP, BT, F
Whittaker, Jason....BC, BT
Wickens, Scott....BS
Wiens, Pete....BC
Wightman, Mildred....GB
Wilbur, Laura....DHS
Wilcox, Willard....T
Wildman, Nate....J, T
Wildman, Nathan....S
Wiley, Paul....DHS
Wiley, Tim....DHS
Wiley, Tom....DHS
Wilhelm, Amy....GCC
Wilhelm, H.....F
Wilhelm, Tom....B, F
Wilkes, Kurt....BC
Willard, Randy....T
Willard, Stephanie....T
Williams, Amber....S
Williams, Erin....GS
Williams, Jenny....C
Williams, Joni....S
Williams, Karen....GS
Williams, Kyle....BS
Williams, Libby....T
Williams, Lisa....S
Williams, Mary Jo....DHS
Williams, Michele....GCC, GT
Williams, Mike....BC
Williams, Wendy....S
Willis, Katie....GT
Willman, Shawna....T
Willson, Heather ...DHS, GT, T
Wilson, Bud....F
Wilson, Dean....BT, F
Wilson, Holly....T
Wilson, John....AP, BB
Wilson, Kay....C
Wilson, Kellie....GCC
Wilson, Ken....T
Wilson, Kris....GCC
Wilson, Meg....AP, GS, GT, T
Wilson, Mike....DHS
Wilson, Robert....F
Wilson, Shelley....DHS
Winninger, Beth....GT
Winowiecki, Tom....BS
Wise, Jim....BC, BT
Wisniewski, Tony....BC
Witkop, Becky....GCC
Witt, Ron....BB
Wolf, Angel....GT
Wolf, Betty Lou....AP
Wolf, Charlie....BC, BT
Wolf, Don....F
Wolff, B.J.....W
Wolff, Rob....F
Wolfgram, Laverne....W
Wollam, Kick....BC
Wood, Aric....XCS
Wood, James....B
Wood, Kelly....S
Wood, Mark....H
Wood, Mike....H
Wood, Roger....F, FD
Woodburne, Jim....DHS
Woodburne, Tim....DHS
Woodrow, Kelli....S
Woods, Mike....S
Woodward, Ben....BC, S
Wooters, Ron....BG
Worth, Mark....BB, C
Wright, Andy....F
Wright, Ben....F
Wright, Lynn....DHS
Wright, Patrick....F
Wright, Shelley....S, V
Wuerfel, Josh....F
Wuerful, Rondi....DHS
Wyatt, Paul....BG
Wyckoff, Charlie....BT
Wylie, Aaron....BC
Wysong, Peter....DHS
Wysong, Trini....T
Yankee, Gary....F
Yankee, Larry....F
Yee, Amy....GS
York, Anna May....C
Youker, Roy....F
Young, Adam....BC
Young, Dan....BC, BG, BT,
....GCC, GT
Yunker, Harold....F
Zacks, Connie....T
Zager, Scott....BT
Zagers, Bert....S
Zakusylo, Alex....W
Zehner, Knute....DHS, F
Zeits, Ben....W
Zenner, Kyle....F
Zenner, Lyle....S
Ziantek, Diane....C
Zientak, Bob....BC
Zimba, Sandy....G
Zimmerman, KristinAP, GB, GT
Zimmerman, Richard....F
Zimmerman, Scott....DHS, F
Zimmerman, Tom....F
Zook, Sally....GT
Zoutendyk, Paul....DHS
Zoutendyke, Chris....DHS
Zue, Bud....DHS
Zue, Richard....DHS